Mockito Cookbook

Over 65 recipes to get you up and running with unit testing using Mockito

Marcin Grzejszczak

BIRMINGHAM - MUMBAI

Mockito Cookbook

First published: June 2014

Production reference: 1170614

Published by Packt Publishing Ltd.
Livery Place
35 Livery Street
Birmingham B3 2PB, UK.

ISBN 978-1-78398-274-5

www.packtpub.com

Cover image by Poonam Nayak (pooh.graphics@gmail.com)

Credits

About the Author

Marcin Grzejszczak is an experienced Java programmer. He is enthusiastic about clean coding and good design. He has contributed to several open source projects (Drools, Moco, Mockito, Spock, and so on) and to Groovy core. He is the co-organizer of the Warsaw Groovy User Group. He is a member of the Most Valuable Blogger program at DZone and Java Code Geeks.

Marcin is the author of *Instant Mockito*, *Packt Publishing*, and *Drools Refcard* at DZone. You can visit his blog, `http://toomuchcoding.blogspot.com`, or his home page, `http://www.marcin.grzejszczak.pl`. Or, you can follow him on Twitter at `http://twitter.com/MGrzejszczak`.

I would like to thank my beloved Marta for showing extreme support, understanding, and encouragement during the creation of this book. I would also like to thank Tomasz Kaczanowski for the indispensable guidelines that allowed me to put the book on the right track. All the discussions with Brice Dutheil helped to deepen my understanding of the philosophy behind Mockito and testing as such. I would like to thank Jakub Nabrdalik, Maciej Zieliński, Kamil Trepczyński, and Michal Pasiński for the brainstorming sessions and reviews. Last but not least, I would like to express my gratitude to all of the official reviewers who helped to increase the quality of this book.

About the Reviewers

Esfandiar Amirrahimi, born in 1984, started programming while he was still in high school, when his father bought him his first computer. He attended Glasgow Caledonian University in Scotland and graduated with a BSc in Computer Science in 2004. He pursued graduate studies at Concordia University in Montreal and completed his Masters of Applied Computer Science. He is currently a software developer at Hybris, an SAP company. He mainly works on enterprise systems in the JVM world. He has a taste for functional programming and a passion to further dive into the functional world by learning, using, and promoting Scala.

Brice Dutheil is a Java and technology enthusiast. He is an independent contractor who has worked with several clients on projects where it was critical to the application to handle heavy load while ensuring that business development goes on. More recently, he got involved in Devoxx France as the Java Track Lead of the program committee.

He has been a regular committer on the Mockito project for several years, as he believes that the TDD approach is enabling the industry to build better software and that Mockito is a good fit in the development approach.

Ivan Hristov has been working in the software industry since 2003. His experience covers multiple projects in different branches and industries, such as telecommunications, banking, research and development, and social networks. At present, he is a technical lead at Hortis—a consulting and software service provider based in Geneva, Switzerland. In his free time, he is an open source committer, blogger (`http://ingini.org`), and Geneva MongoDB User Group leader (`http://genevamug.ch`).

Carlo Micieli has been working as a software engineer for over 10 years now. His choice of programming languages are Java and C#. His main area of interest is application life cycle management with a strong focus on topics such as software design and testing.

Tim Perry is a technical lead and the open source champion at Softwire (`softwire.com`), a bespoke software development company in North London. He guides teams, builds a variety of great software at every scale for his clients, and pushes Softwire to engage with and give back to the wider software development community. He daily works with a huge range of tools, from Java, Spring, and JUnit to JavaScript web components to SQL analytics engines.

He's a frequent technical speaker and a prolific open source contributor on a wide variety of projects, including JUnit, Mockito, Knockout, and Lodash, and some of his own, such as loglevel and grunt-coveralls. He is feverishly keen on all things related to automated testing, polyglot persistence, and good old-fashioned, high-quality software development.

I'd like to thank my wonderful girlfriend, Rachel, for her endless patience and support and for genuinely appearing delighted when I signed up for yet another side project.

www.PacktPub.com

Support files, eBooks, discount offers and more

You might want to visit www.PacktPub.com for support files and downloads related to your book.

Did you know that Packt offers eBook versions of every book published, with PDF and ePub files available? You can upgrade to the eBook version at www.PacktPub.com and as a print book customer, you are entitled to a discount on the eBook copy. Get in touch with us at service@packtpub.com for more details.

At www.PacktPub.com, you can also read a collection of free technical articles, sign up for a range of free newsletters and receive exclusive discounts and offers on Packt books and eBooks.

http://PacktLib.PacktPub.com

Do you need instant solutions to your IT questions? PacktLib is Packt's online digital book library. Here, you can access, read and search across Packt's entire library of books.

Why Subscribe?

- ▶ Fully searchable across every book published by Packt
- ▶ Copy and paste, print and bookmark content
- ▶ On demand and accessible via web browser

Free Access for Packt account holders

If you have an account with Packt at www.PacktPub.com, you can use this to access PacktLib today and view nine entirely free books. Simply use your login credentials for immediate access.

Table of Contents

Preface

According to Google Trends, Mockito, compared to its main Java mocking framework competitors, EasyMock and jMock, has been the most widely used since 2011 and this trend has been upward ever since. Given its extremely simple and elegant API, Mockito gives you the possibility to test your application in a readable manner. Furthermore, it's syntax is so intuitive that you'll learn it in no time at all.

The very concept behind this book is to give the reader the possibility to use Mockito in order to write beautiful and comprehensive tests. The Mockito documentation as such is of very high quality, so you should always, regardless of the tool you are using, refer to it when in doubt. This book is an extension to this documentation since it covers its content but puts it in a real-life example. Where the Mockito documentation proves that the library, as such, is doing what it is supposed to do, you can come to a point where you don't actually know how to use it versus your production code. Worry not! *Mockito Cookbook* comes to the rescue. This book contains solutions to more than 60 problems that you may encounter throughout your Mockito testing endeavor. You will learn how to write tests that become the living documentation of your code. You will become A Mockito expert. (Since the book also explains some Mockito internals you might even be tempted to become its contributor!) And hopefully, your tests will become an example to be followed by your colleagues.

What this book covers

Chapter 1, Getting Started with Mockito, covers the Mockito configuration for JUnit and TestNG and some of its experimental features.

Chapter 2, Creating Mocks, presents numerous ways to create mocks.

Chapter 3, Creating Spies and Partial Mocks, covers the process of instantiating spy objects and partial mocks.

Chapter 4, Stubbing Behavior of Mocks, shows how to stub the method executions of mock objects.

Chapter 5, Stubbing Behavior of Spies, presents ways to stub the method executions of spies.

Chapter 6, Verifying Test Doubles, covers the process of behavior verification of test doubles.

Chapter 7, Verifying Behavior with Object Matchers, shows how to confirm that your application works as it should using Hamcrest or AssertJ.

Chapter 8, Refactoring with Mockito, covers the process of easily refactoring your production and test code, thanks to Mockito.

Chapter 9, Integration Testing with Mockito and DI Frameworks, presents ways to inject mocks into your Spring- or Guice-based applications.

Chapter 10, Mocking Libraries Comparison, shows the differences and similarities between several mocking libraries and Mockito.

What you need for this book

In order to run the code presented in this book, you will need Java Development Kit 1.6 or newer, Mockito Version 1.9.5 appended to your classpath, and in the majority of the presented tests, AssertJ Version 1.6.0. The GitHub repository that contains the code has a configuration ready for use with Gradle and Maven, so you need either of these installed on your machine to run the tests.

Who this book is for

If you are a developer who either has never used Mockito or want to extend your knowledge about this framework, this the book for you. This book not only shows you how to solve issues with Mockito, but also dives into the internals of Mockito in order to help you understand the tool better. The book can also be addressed by test enthusiasts who want to see another approach to the tests that are behavior-driven.

Conventions

In this book, you will find a number of styles of text that distinguish between different kinds of information. Here are some examples of these styles and an explanation of their meaning.

Code words in text, database table names, folder names, filenames, file extensions, pathnames, dummy URLs, user input, and Twitter handles are shown as follows: "Where `NewIdentityCreator` contains the logic for generating new identity."

A block of code is set as follows:

```
<dependency>
  <groupId>junit</groupId>
  <artifactId>junit</artifactId>
  <version>4.11</version>
  <scope>test</scope>
</dependency>
```

 Warnings or important notes appear in a box like this.

 Tips and tricks appear like this.

Reader feedback

Feedback from our readers is always welcome. Let us know what you think about this book—what you liked or may have disliked. Reader feedback is important for us to develop titles that you really get the most out of.

To send us general feedback, simply send an e-mail to `feedback@packtpub.com`, and mention the book title via the subject of your message.

If there is a topic that you have expertise in and you are interested in either writing or contributing to a book, see our author guide on `www.packtpub.com/authors`.

Customer support

Now that you are the proud owner of a Packt book, we have a number of things to help you to get the most from your purchase.

Downloading the example code

You can download the example code files for all Packt books you have purchased from your account at `http://www.packtpub.com`. If you purchased this book elsewhere, you can visit `http://www.packtpub.com/support` and register to have the files e-mailed directly to you. The project setup for usage with Maven or Gradle with all of the code from the book and some additional tests and use cases is also present on GitHub at `https://github.com/marcingrzejszczak/mockito-cookbook`.

Errata

Although we have taken every care to ensure the accuracy of our content, mistakes do happen. If you find a mistake in one of our books—maybe a mistake in the text or the code—we would be grateful if you would report this to us. By doing so, you can save other readers from frustration and help us improve subsequent versions of this book. If you find any errata, please report them by visiting `http://www.packtpub.com/submit-errata`, selecting your book, clicking on the **errata submission form** link, and entering the details of your errata. Once your errata are verified, your submission will be accepted and the errata will be uploaded on our website, or added to any list of existing errata, under the Errata section of that title. Any existing errata can be viewed by selecting your title from `http://www.packtpub.com/support`.

Piracy

Piracy of copyright material on the Internet is an ongoing problem across all media. At Packt, we take the protection of our copyright and licenses very seriously. If you come across any illegal copies of our works, in any form, on the Internet, please provide us with the location address or website name immediately so that we can pursue a remedy.

Please contact us at `copyright@packtpub.com` with a link to the suspected pirated material.

We appreciate your help in protecting our authors, and our ability to bring you valuable content.

Questions

You can contact us at `questions@packtpub.com` if you are having a problem with any aspect of the book, and we will do our best to address it.

1
Getting Started with Mockito

In this chapter, we will cover the following recipes:

- ▸ Adding Mockito to a project's classpath
- ▸ Getting started with Mockito for JUnit
- ▸ Getting started with Mockito for TestNG
- ▸ Mockito best practices - test behavior, not implementation
- ▸ Adding Mockito hints to exception messages in JUnit (Experimental)
- ▸ Adding additional Mockito warnings to your tests in JUnit (Experimental)

Introduction

For those who don't know Mockito at all, I'd like to write a really short introduction about it.

Mockito is an open source framework for Java that allows you to easily create test doubles (mocks). What makes Mockito so special is that it eliminates the common expect-run-verify pattern (which was present, for example, in EasyMock—please refer to `http://monkeyisland.pl/2008/02/24/can-i-test-what-i-want-please` for more details) that in effect leads to a lower coupling of the test code to the production code as such. In other words, one does not have to define the expectations of how the mock should behave in order to verify its behavior. That way, the code is clearer and more readable for the user.

On one hand, Mockito has a very active group of contributors and is actively maintained; on the other hand, unfortunately, by the time this book is written, the last Mockito release (Version 1.9.5) have been in October 2012.

You may ask yourself the question, "Why should I even bother to use Mockito in the first place?" Out of many choices, Mockito offers the following key features:

- There is no expectation phase for Mockito—you can either stub or verify the mock's behavior
- You are able to mock both interfaces and classes
- You can produce little boilerplate code while working with Mockito by means of annotations
- You can easily verify or stub with intuitive argument matchers

Before diving into Mockito as such, one has to understand the concept behind **System Under Test** (**SUT**) and test doubles. We will base our work on what Gerard Meszaros has defined in the xUnit Patterns (`http://xunitpatterns.com/Mocks,%20Fakes,%20Stubs%20 and%20Dummies.html`).

SUT (`http://xunitpatterns.com/SUT.html`) describes the system that we are testing. It doesn't have to necessarily signify a class or any part of the application that we are testing or even the whole application as such.

As for test doubles (`http://www.martinfowler.com/bliki/TestDouble.html`), it's an object that is used only for testing purposes, instead of a real object. Let's take a look at different types of test doubles:

- **Dummy**: This is an object that is used only for the code to compile—it doesn't have any business logic (for example, an object passed as a parameter to a method)
- **Fake**: This is an object that has an implementation but it's not production ready (for example, using an in-memory database instead of communicating with a standalone one)
- **Stub**: This is an object that has predefined answers to method executions made during the test
- **Mock**: This is an object that has predefined answers to method executions made during the test and has recorded expectations of these executions
- **Spy**: These are objects that are similar to stubs, but they additionally record how they were executed (for example, a service that holds a record of the number of sent messages)

An additional remark is also related to testing the output of our application. Throughout the book, you will see that the tests (in general, all of them apart from the chapter related to verification) are based on the assertion of behavior instead of the checking of implementation. The more decoupled your test code is from your production code, the better, since you will have to spend less time (or even none) on modifying your tests after you change the implementation of the code.

Coming back to the chapter's content—this chapter is all about getting started with Mockito. We will begin with how to add Mockito to your classpath. Then, we'll see a simple setup of tests for both JUnit and TestNG test frameworks. Next, we will check why it is crucial to assert the behavior of the system under test instead of verifying its implementation details. Finally, we will check out some of Mockito's experimental features, adding hints and warnings to the exception messages. The very idea of the following recipes is to prepare your test classes to work with Mockito and to show you how to do this with as little boilerplate code as possible.

Due to my fondness for the behavior driven development (`http://dannorth.net/introducing-bdd/` first introduced by Dan North), I'm using Mockito's `BDDMockito` and AssertJ's `BDDAssertions` static methods to make the code even more readable and intuitive in all the test cases. Also, please read Szczepan Faber's blog (author of Mockito) about the given, when, then separation in your test methods—`http://monkeyisland.pl/2009/12/07/given-when-then-forever/`—since these are omnipresent throughout the book.

Even though some of the previous methods might sound not too clear to you or the test code looks complicated—don't worry, it will all be explained throughout the book. I don't want the book to become a duplication of the Mockito documentation, which is of high quality—I would like you to take a look at good tests and get acquainted with Mockito syntax from the beginning. What's more, I've used static imports in the code to make it even more readable, so if you get confused with any of the pieces of code, it would be best to consult the repository and the code as such.

Adding Mockito to a project's classpath

Adding Mockito to a project's classpath is as simple as adding one of the two jars to your project's classpath:

- ▶ `mockito-all`: This is a single jar with all dependencies (with the `hamcrest` and `objenesis` libraries—as of June 2011).
- ▶ `mockito-core`: This is only Mockito core (without `hamcrest` or `objenesis`). Use this if you want to control which version of `hamcrest` or `objenesis` is used.

How to do it...

If you are using a dependency manager that connects to the Maven Central Repository, then you can get your dependencies as follows (examples of how to add `mockito-all` to your classpath for Maven and Gradle):

For Maven, use the following code:

```
<dependency>
    <groupId>org.mockito</groupId>
    <artifactId>mockito-all</artifactId>
    <version>1.9.5</version>
    <scope>test</scope>
</dependency>
```

For Gradle, use the following code:

```
testCompile "org.mockito:mockito-all:1.9.5"
```

Downloading the example code

You can download the example code files for all Packt books you have purchased from your account at `http://www.packtpub.com`. If you purchased this book elsewhere, you can visit `http://www.packtpub.com/support` and register to have the files e-mailed directly to you.

If you are not using any of the dependency managers, you have to either download `mockito-all.jar` or `mockito-core.jar` and add it to your classpath manually (you can download the jars from `https://code.google.com/p/mockito/downloads/list`). To see more examples of adding Mockito to your classpath, please check the book, *Instant Mockito, Marcin Grzejszczak, Packt Publishing*, for more examples of adding Mockito to your classpath (it includes Ant, Buildr, Sbt, Ivy, Gradle, and Maven).

See also

▶ Refer to *Instant Mockito, Marcin Grzejszczak, Packt Publishing* for an introduction to Mockito together with examples of Mockito configuration in several build tools at `http://www.packtpub.com/how-to-create-stubs-mocks-spies-using-mockito/book`

Getting started with Mockito for JUnit

Before going into details regarding Mockito and JUnit integration, it is worth mentioning a few words about JUnit.

JUnit is a testing framework (an implementation of the xUnit framework) that allows you to create repeatable tests in a very readable manner. In fact, JUnit is a port of Smalltalk's SUnit (both the frameworks were originally implemented by Kent Beck). What is important in terms of JUnit and Mockito integration is that under the hood, JUnit uses a test runner to run its tests (from xUnit—test runner is a program that executes the test logic and reports the test results).

Mockito has its own test runner implementation that allows you to reduce boilerplate in order to create test doubles (mocks and spies) and to inject them (either via constructors, setters, or reflection) into the defined object. What's more, you can easily create argument captors. All of this is feasible by means of proper annotations as follows:

- ▶ @Mock: This is used for mock creation
- ▶ @Spy: This is used to create a spy instance
- ▶ @InjectMocks: This is used to instantiate the @InjectMock annotated field and inject all the @Mock or @Spy annotated fields into it (if applicable)
- ▶ @Captor: This is used to create an argument captor

By default, you should profit from Mockito's annotations to make your code look neat and to reduce the boilerplate code in your application.

Getting ready

In order to add JUnit to your classpath, if you are using a dependency manager that connects to the Maven Central Repository, then you can get your dependencies as follows (examples for Maven and Gradle):

To add JUnit in Maven, use the following code:

```
<dependency>
  <groupId>junit</groupId>
  <artifactId>junit</artifactId>
  <version>4.11</version>
  <scope>test</scope>
</dependency>
```

To add JUnit in Gradle, use the following code:

```
testCompile('junit:junit:4.11')
```

If you are not using any of the dependency managers, you have to download the following jars:

- `junit.jar`
- `hamcrest-core.jar`

Add the downloaded files to your classpath manually (you can download the jars from `https://github.com/junit-team/junit/wiki/Download-and-Install`).

For this recipe, our system under test will be a `MeanTaxFactorCalculator` class that will call an external service, `TaxService`, to get the current tax factor for the current user. It's a tax factor and not tax as such, since for simplicity, we will not be using `BigDecimals` but `doubles`, and I'd never suggest using `doubles` to anything related to money, as follows:

```java
public class MeanTaxFactorCalculator {

    private final TaxService taxService;

    public MeanTaxFactorCalculator(TaxService taxService) {
        this.taxService = taxService;
    }

    public double calculateMeanTaxFactorFor(Person person) {
        double currentTaxFactor = taxService.
getCurrentTaxFactorFor(person);
        double anotherTaxFactor = taxService.
getCurrentTaxFactorFor(person);
        return (currentTaxFactor + anotherTaxFactor) / 2;
    }

}
```

How to do it...

To use Mockito's annotations, you have to perform the following steps:

1. Annotate your test with the `@RunWith(MockitoJUnitRunner.class)`.
2. Annotate the test fields with the `@Mock` or `@Spy` annotation to have either a mock or spy object instantiated.

3. Annotate the test fields with the @InjectMocks annotation to first instantiate the @InjectMock annotated field and then inject all the @Mock or @Spy annotated fields into it (if applicable).

4. Annotate the test fields with the @Captor annotation to make Mockito instantiate an argument captor (refer to *Chapter 6, Verifying Test Doubles*, for more details).

The following snippet shows the JUnit and Mockito integration in a test class that verifies the SUT's behavior (remember that I'm using BDDMockito.given(...) and AssertJ's BDDAssertions.then(...) static methods; refer to *Chapter 7, Verifying Behavior with Object Matchers*, for how to work with AssertJ or how to do the same with Hamcrest's assertThat(...) method):

```
@RunWith(MockitoJUnitRunner.class)
public class MeanTaxFactorCalculatorTest {

    static final double TAX_FACTOR = 10;

    @Mock TaxService taxService;

    @InjectMocks MeanTaxFactorCalculator systemUnderTest;

    @Test
    public void should_calculate_mean_tax_factor() {
        // given
        given(taxService.getCurrentTaxFactorFor(any(Person.class)))
.willReturn(TAX_FACTOR);

        // when
        double meanTaxFactor = systemUnderTest.
calculateMeanTaxFactorFor(new Person());

        // then
        then(meanTaxFactor).isEqualTo(TAX_FACTOR);
    }

}
```

To profit from Mockito's annotations using JUnit, you just have to annotate your test class with @RunWith(MockitoJUnitRunner.class).

How it works...

The Mockito test runner will adapt its strategy depending on the version of JUnit. If there exists a `org.junit.runners.BlockJUnit4ClassRunner` class, it means that the codebase is using at least JUnit in Version 4.5. What eventually happens is that the `MockitoAnnotations.initMocks(...)` method is executed for the given test, which initializes all the Mockito annotations (for more information, check the subsequent *There's more...* section).

There's more...

You may have a situation where your test class has already been annotated with a `@RunWith` annotation and, seemingly, you may not profit from Mockito's annotations. In order to achieve this, you have to call the `MockitoAnnotations.initMocks` method manually in the `@Before` annotated method of your test, as shown in the following code:

```java
public class MeanTaxFactorCalculatorTest {

    static final double TAX_FACTOR = 10;

    @Mock TaxService taxService;

    @InjectMocks MeanTaxFactorCalculator systemUnderTest;

    @Before
    public void setup() {
        MockitoAnnotations.initMocks(this);
    }

    @Test
    public void should_calculate_mean_tax_factor() {
        // given
        given(taxService.getCurrentTaxFactorFor
(Mockito.any(Person.class))).willReturn(TAX_FACTOR);

        // when
        double meanTaxFactor = systemUnderTest.
calculateMeanTaxFactorFor(new Person());

        // then
        then(meanTaxFactor).isEqualTo(TAX_FACTOR);
    }

}
```

> To use Mockito's annotations without a JUnit test runner, you have to call the `MockitoAnnotations.initMocks` method and pass the test class as its parameter.

Mockito checks whether the user has overridden the global configuration of `AnnotationEngine` and, if this is not the case, the `InjectingAnnotationEngine` implementation is used to process annotations in tests. What is done internally is that the test class fields are scanned for annotations and proper test doubles are initialized and injected into the `@InjectMocks` annotated object (either by a constructor, property setter, or field injection, in that precise order).

> You have to remember several factors related to the automatic injection of test doubles as follows:
>
> - If Mockito is not able to inject test doubles into the `@InjectMocks` annotated fields through either of the strategies, it won't report failure—the test will continue as if nothing happened (and most likely, you will get `NullPointerException`).
> - For constructor injection, if arguments cannot be found, then null is passed
> - For constructor injection, if nonmockable types are required in the constructor, then the constructor injection won't take place.
> - For other injection strategies, if you have properties with the same type (or same erasure) and if Mockito matches mock names with a field/property name, it will inject that mock properly. Otherwise, the injection won't take place.
> - For other injection strategies, if the `@InjectMocks` annotated object wasn't previously initialized, then Mockito will instantiate the aforementioned object using a no-arg constructor if applicable.

See also

- JUnit documentation at `https://github.com/junit-team/junit/wiki`
- Martin Fowler's article on xUnit at `http://www.martinfowler.com/bliki/Xunit.html`
- Gerard Meszaros's *xUnit Test Patterns* at `http://xunitpatterns.com/`
- `@InjectMocks` Mockito documentation (with description of injection strategies) at `http://docs.mockito.googlecode.com/hg/1.9.5/org/mockito/InjectMocks.html`

Getting started with Mockito for TestNG

Before going into details regarding Mockito and TestNG integration, it is worth mentioning a few words about TestNG.

TestNG is a unit testing framework for Java that was created, as the author defines it on the tool's website (refer to the *See also* section for the link), out of frustration for some JUnit deficiencies. TestNG was inspired by both JUnit and TestNG and aims at covering the whole scope of testing—from unit, through functional, integration, end-to-end tests, and so on. However, the JUnit library was initially created for unit testing only.

The main differences between JUnit and TestNG are as follows:

▸ The TestNG author disliked JUnit's approach of having to define some methods as static to be executed before the test class logic gets executed (for example, the @ BeforeClass annotated methods)—that's why in TestNG you don't have to define these methods as static

▸ TestNG has more annotations related to method execution before single tests, suites, and test groups

▸ TestNG annotations are more descriptive in terms of what they do, for example, the JUnit's @Before versus TestNG's @BeforeMethod

Mockito in Version 1.9.5 doesn't provide any out-of-the-box solution to integrate with TestNG in a simple way, but there is a special Mockito subproject for TestNG (refer to the *See also* section for the URL) that should be part one of the subsequent Mockito releases. In the following recipe, we will take a look at how to profit from that code and that very elegant solution.

Getting ready

When you take a look at Mockito's TestNG subproject on the Mockito GitHub repository, you will find that there are three classes in the org.mockito.testng package, as follows:

▸ MockitoAfterTestNGMethod

▸ MockitoBeforeTestNGMethod

▸ MockitoTestNGListener

Unfortunately, until this project eventually gets released, you have to just copy and paste those classes to your codebase.

How to do it...

To integrate TestNG and Mockito, perform the following steps:

1. Copy the `MockitoAfterTestNGMethod`, `MockitoBeforeTestNGMethod`, and `MockitoTestNGListener` classes to your codebase from Mockito's TestNG subproject.

2. Annotate your test class with `@Listeners(MockitoTestNGListener.class)`.

3. Annotate the test fields with the `@Mock` or `@Spy` annotation to have either a mock or spy object instantiated.

4. Annotate the test fields with the `@InjectMocks` annotation to first instantiate the `@InjectMock` annotated field and inject all the `@Mock` or `@Spy` annotated fields into it (if applicable).

5. Annotate the test fields with the `@Captor` annotation to make Mockito instantiate an argument captor (check *Chapter 6, Verifying Test Doubles*, for more details).

Now let's take a look at this snippet that, using TestNG, checks whether the mean tax factor value has been calculated properly (remember that I'm using the `BDDMockito.given(...)` and AssertJ's `BDDAssertions.then(...)` static methods—refer to *Chapter 7, Verifying Behavior with Object Matchers*, on how to work with Hamcrest `assertThat(...)` method):

```
@Listeners(MockitoTestNGListener.class)
public class MeanTaxFactorCalculatorTestNgTest {

    static final double TAX_FACTOR = 10;

    @Mock TaxService taxService;

    @InjectMocks MeanTaxFactorCalculator systemUnderTest;

    @Test
    public void should_calculate_mean_tax_factor() {
        // given
        given(taxService.getCurrentTaxFactorFor(any(Person.class)))
.willReturn(TAX_FACTOR);

        // when
        double meanTaxFactor = systemUnderTest.
calculateMeanTaxFactorFor(new Person());

        // then
        then(meanTaxFactor).isEqualTo(TAX_FACTOR);
    }

}
```

How it works...

TestNG allows you to register custom listeners (your listener class has to implement the `IInvokedMethodListener` interface). Once you do this, the logic inside the implemented methods will be executed before and after every configuration, and test methods get called. Mockito provides you with a listener whose responsibilities are as follows:

- ▶ Initialize mocks annotated with the `@Mock` annotation (it is done only once)
- ▶ Validate the usage of Mockito after each test method

 Remember that with TestNG all mocks are reset (or initialized if it hasn't already been done) before any TestNG method!

See also

- ▶ The TestNG homepage at `http://testng.org/doc/index.html`
- ▶ The Mockito TestNG subproject at `https://github.com/mockito/mockito/tree/master/subprojects/testng`
- ▶ The *Getting started with Mockito for JUnit* recipe on the `@InjectMocks` analysis

Mockito best practices – test behavior not implementation

Once you start testing with Mockito you might be tempted to start mocking everything that gets in your way. What is more, you may have heard that you have to mock all of the collaborators of the class and then verify whether those test doubles executed the desired methods. Of course, you can code like that, but since it is best to be a pragmatic programmer, you should ask yourself the question whether you would be interested in changing the test code each time someone changes the production code, even though the application does the same things.

It's worth going back to distinguishing stubs from mocks. Remember that, if you create a mock, it's for the sake of the verification of its method execution. If you are only interested in the behavior of your test double—if it behaves as you tell it to—then you have a stub. In the vast majority of cases, you shouldn't be interested in whether your test double has executed a particular method; you should be more interested in whether your application does what it is supposed to do. Also, remember that there are cases where it makes no sense to create a stub of an external dependency—it all depends on how you define the system under test.

It might sound a little confusing but, hopefully, the following recipe will clear things up. We will take a look at the simple example of a tax factor summing class that changes in time (whereas its tests should not change much).

Getting ready

Let's assume that we have the following tax factor calculator that calculates a sum of two tax factors:

```
public class TaxFactorCalculator {

    public double calculateSum
(double taxFactorOne, double taxFactorTwo) {
        return taxFactorOne + taxFactorTwo;
    }

}
```

After some time, it turned out that we read about a library that allows you to hide the implementation details of summing and you decided to rewrite your calculator to use this library. Now your code looks as follows:

```
public class TaxFactorCalculator {

    private final Calculator calculator;

    public TaxFactorCalculator(Calculator calculator) {
        this.calculator = calculator;
    }

    public double calculateSum
(double taxFactorOne, double taxFactorTwo) {
        return calculator.add(taxFactorOne, taxFactorTwo);
    }

}
```

How to do it...

Since you want to test whether your system under test works fine, you should focus on the following points:

 ▶ Start by writing a test—not with an implementation. That way, you will constantly ask yourself the question of what you want to do and only then will you think about how to do it.

 ▶ Focus on asserting the result—what you want to verify in most cases is whether your system under test works as it is supposed to. You shouldn't care much how exactly it is done.

Let's take a look at a test of the first version of the class (I'm using the `BDDMockito.given(...)` and AssertJ's `BDDAssertions.then(...)` static methods—refer to *Chapter 7, Verifying Behavior with Object Matchers,* for how to work with AssertJ or how to do the same with Hamcrest's `assertThat(...)` method):

```
    @Test
    public void should_calculate_sum_of_factors() {
        // given
        TaxFactorCalculator systemUnderTest =
new TaxFactorCalculator();
        double taxFactorOne = 1;
        double taxFactorTwo = 2;
        double expectedSum = 3;

        // when
        double sumOfFactors = systemUnderTest.
calculateSum(taxFactorOne, taxFactorTwo);

        // then
        then(sumOfFactors).isEqualTo(expectedSum);
    }
```

As you can see, we are testing a class that should add two numbers and produce a result. We are not interested in how it is done—we want to check that the result is satisfactory. Now, assuming that our implementation changed—having a good test would require only to comply to the new way that our system under test is being initialized and the rest of the code remains untouched. In other words, change `TaxFactorCalculator systemUnderTest = new TaxFactorCalculator()` to `TaxFactorCalculator systemUnderTest = new TaxFactorCalculator(new Calculator())`. Moreover, since we are checking behavior and not the implementation, we don't have to refactor the test code at all.

See also

- ▶ Martin Fowler on TDD at `http://martinfowler.com/bliki/TestDrivenDevelopment.html`
- ▶ Kent Beck's Test Driven Development on Amazon at `http://www.amazon.com/Test-Driven-Development-By-Example/dp/0321146530`
- ▶ Mockito's wiki page concerning how to write good tests at `https://github.com/mockito/mockito/wiki/How-to-write-good-tests`

Adding Mockito hints to exception messages (JUnit) (Experimental)

When a JUnit test fails, an exception is thrown and a message is presented. Sometimes, it is enough to find a reason for this mistake and to find the solution. Mockito, however, goes a step further and tries to help the developer by giving him additional hints regarding the state of the stubbed methods.

 Remember that this feature is experimental and the API, name, or anything related to it may change in time. What is more, the whole feature may get deleted in time!

Getting ready

For this recipe, let's assume that our system is the `MeanTaxFactorCalculator` class that calculates tax through `TaxService`, which has two methods— `performAdditionalCalculation()` and `getCurrentTaxFactorFor(...)`. For the sake of this example, let's assume that only the latter is used to calculate the mean value:

```
public class MeanTaxFactorCalculator {

    private final TaxService taxService;

    public MeanTaxFactorCalculator(TaxService taxService) {
        this.taxService = taxService;
    }

    public double calculateMeanTaxFactorFor(Person person) {
        double currentTaxFactor = taxService.
getCurrentTaxFactorFor(person);
        double anotherTaxFactor = taxService.
getCurrentTaxFactorFor(person);
        return (currentTaxFactor + anotherTaxFactor) / 2;
    }

}
```

We wanted to check whether our system under test is calculating the proper result, so we wrote the following test but made a mistake and stubbed a wrong method (I'm using the `BDDMockito.given(...)` and AssertJ's `BDDAssertions.then(...)` static methods—refer *Chapter 7, Verifying Behavior with Object Matchers*, for how to work with AssertJ or how to do the same with Hamcrest's `assertThat(...)` method):

```
@RunWith(MockitoJUnitRunner.class)
public class MeanTaxFactorCalculatorTest {

    static final double UNUSED_VALUE = 10;

    @Test
    public void should_calculate_mean_tax_factor() {
        // given
        TaxService taxService = given(Mockito.mock(TaxService.class).
performAdditionalCalculation()).willReturn(UNUSED_VALUE)
.getMock();
        MeanTaxFactorCalculator systemUnderTest =
 new MeanTaxFactorCalculator(taxService);

        // when
        double meanTaxFactor = systemUnderTest.
calculateMeanTaxFactorFor(new Person());

        // then
        then(meanTaxFactor).isEqualTo(UNUSED_VALUE);
    }

}
```

The test fails and what we can see is the standard JUnit comparison failure being thrown (presenting only the most important part of the stack trace) as follows:

```
org.junit.ComparisonFailure:
Expected :10.0
Actual   :0.0
```

Now let's take a look at how to use Mockito's experimental features to get more Mockito related information appended to the error message.

How to do it...

If you want to have more information presented in your error message, you have to perform the following steps:

1. Annotate your JUnit test with `@RunWith(VerboseMockitoJUnitRunner.class)`.

2. Define your mocks and perform stubbing inside the test method (unfortunately, you can't use annotations or initialize fields outside test methods).

What happens next is that additional exception messages can be seen in the exception that is thrown as follows:

```
org.mockito.internal.exceptions.
ExceptionIncludingMockitoWarnings:
 contains both: actual test failure *and* Mockito warnings.
This stubbing was never used   -> at ...MeanTaxFactorCalculatorTest.
should_calculate_mean_tax_factor
(MeanTaxFactorCalculatorTest.java:30)

 *** The actual failure is because of: ***

Expected :10.0
Actual   :0.0
```

How it works...

When the test is run, `VerboseMockitoJUnitRunner` appends a listener. When the test is started, this listener finds all the stubs through `WarningsCollector`, including the unused stubs for given mocks.

As the Mockito developers state it in the code, they are indeed using a very hacky way to append a message to the thrown exception after the test fails. The `JUnitFailureHacker` class is instantiated and, by means of the `Whitebox` class, the internal state of a private field of the JUnit's `Failure` object is modified with additional Mockito messages.

Adding additional Mockito warnings to your tests (JUnit) (Experimental)

If you would like Mockito to append some additional warning messages to the console, which would help you when your test fails, then this recipe is perfect for you. It's very much related to the previous one so, in order to understand the background, please refer to the introductory part of the previous recipe.

 Remember that this feature is experimental and the API, name, or anything related to it may change in time. What's more, the whole feature may get deleted in time!

How to do it...

If you want to have more information presented in your error message, you have to perform the following steps:

1. Annotate your JUnit test with `@RunWith(ConsoleSpammingMockitoJUnitRunner.class)`.

2. Define your mocks and perform stubbing inside the test method (unfortunately, you can't use annotations or initialize fields outside test methods).

What happens then is that additional exception messages gets printed on the console after the exception that is thrown:

```
This stubbing was never used  -> at ....MeanTaxFactorCalculatorTest
.should_calculate_mean_tax_factor
(MeanTaxFactorCalculatorTest.java:25)
```

How it works...

When the test is run, `ConsoleSpammingMockitoJUnitRunner` appends a listener that finds all the stubs through `WarningsCollector`, including the unused stubs for given mocks. When all of the warnings get collected, the `ConsoleMockitoLogger` class prints them to the console after the test has failed.

2
Creating Mocks

In this chapter, we will cover the following recipes:

- ► Creating mocks in code
- ► Creating mocks with annotations
- ► Creating mocks with a different default answer
- ► Creating mocks with different default answers with annotations
- ► Creating mocks with custom configuration
- ► Creating mocks of final classes with PowerMock
- ► Creating mocks of enums with PowerMock

Introduction

Mockito, as the name suggests, is all about working with mocks. It is worth mentioning that before you go and start mocking every class that is in your codebase, it's good to really understand the idea behind mocking and when to mock an object.

While performing unit testing, you will want to test your system in isolation. You're doing it because you want to test a part of the system as a unit and control any external interactions. Remember that in new, well-designed code, your system should follow the **SOLID** principles (for more details, check out Uncle Bob's blog at `http://butunclebob.com/ArticleS.UncleBob.PrinciplesOfOod` and read *Agile Software Development, Principles, Patterns, and Practices, Robert C. Martin*, which is available at `http://www.amazon.com/Software-Development-Principles-Patterns-Practices/dp/0135974445`). The complete description about what SOLID stands for is given as follows:

- ▸ **(S) Single responsibility principle**: A class should have only a single responsibility. In other words, your class should be dedicated to doing only one thing and should have only one reason to change.

- ▸ **(O) Open/closed principle**: Your code should be open for extension but closed for modification. If you want it to be possible to change the behavior of your code, don't force other developers into changing the source code; instead, give them a chance to extend it.

- ▸ **(L) Liskov substitution principle**: Let's assume that you have a class B that extends a class A. When treated like class A, class B is expected to behave in the same way as an instance of class A would.

- ▸ **(I) Interface segregation principle**: You don't want your classes to be forced to be dependent on methods they don't need to use. In other words, the ISP suggests that you should split large interfaces into smaller ones that are highly specific (these interfaces are called **role interfaces**)

- ▸ **(D) Dependency inversion**: The concept behind this rule is to decouple your classes from one another. To put it simply, try to depend on abstractions rather than concrete implementations. (In other words, once you change the implementation, for example, some third-party library to another, you will have to change the whole code of your application instead of its single part.)

Assuming that we follow the SOLID principles, we have a class that is dependent on some other components where each component is responsible for a single functionality. When testing that class (if it makes sense, of course), we can create test doubles (to check out the differences between different types of test doubles (refer to *Chapter 1, Getting Started with Mockito*) for the components that are passed as collaborators (most probably through constructors). Here, Mockito comes to the rescue and helps you easily create mocks for those components.

The next chapter focuses on showing tests created to test some real-life examples of production code simplified for the sake of readability). We will focus on numerous ways of creating mocks (in the majority of cases, you should be using only the default annotation-based approach).

A standard reminder that you will see throughout the book is as follows:

Because I am very fond of behavior-driven development (http://dannorth.net/introducing-bdd/ first introduced by Dan North), I'm using Mockito's BDDMockito and AssertJ's BDDAssertions static methods in all the test cases to make the code even more readable and intuitive. Also, please read Szczepan Faber's blog (author of Mockito) about the given, when, then separation in your test methods, from http://monkeyisland.pl/2009/12/07/given-when-then-forever/, since these separation methods are omnipresent throughout the book.

Even though some of the mentioned methods might sound not too clear to you, or the test code will look complicated, don't worry, it will all be explained through the course of this book. I don't want the book to become a duplication of the Mockito documentation. I would like you to take a look at nice tests and get acquainted with Mockito syntax from the very beginning. I have used static imports in the code to make it even more readable, so if you get confused with any of the pieces of code, it would be best to refer to the repository and the code as such.

Creating mocks in code

Before a mock is interacted with, it needs to be created. Mockito gives you several overloaded versions of the `Mockito.mock` method. Let's take a look at a few of them:

- `mock(Class<T> classToMock)`: This method creates a mock of a given class with a default answer set to returning default values (if not overriden by a custom Mockito configuration). When creating mocks in code, you will most likely be using this method.

- `mock(Class<T> classToMock, String name)`: This method creates a mock of a given class with a default answer set to returning default values. It also sets a name to the mock. This name is present in all verification messages. That's very useful in debugging, since it allows you to distinguish the mocks.

- `mock(Class<T> classToMock, Answer defaultAnswer)`: This method creates a mock of a given class with a default answer set to the one passed as the method's argument. In other words, all of the nonstubbed mock's method will act as defined in the passed answer.

- `mock(Class<T> classToMock, MockSettings mockSettings)`: This method creates a mock of a given class with customizable mock settings. You should hardly ever need to use that feature.

Getting ready

In the following code, our system under test is a class that calculates a mean value of tax factors retrieved through a web service:

```
public class MeanTaxFactorCalculator {

    private final TaxService taxService;

    public MeanTaxFactorCalculator(TaxService taxService) {
        this.taxService = taxService;
    }
```

```
      public double calculateMeanTaxFactorFor(Person person) {
          double currentTaxFactor = taxService.
   getCurrentTaxFactorFor(person);
          double anotherTaxFactor = taxService.
   getCurrentTaxFactorFor(person);
          return (currentTaxFactor + anotherTaxFactor) / 2;
      }

   }
```

Let's now write a test for the system that will check whether it can properly calculate the mean value of the tax factor. We have to create a stub of `TaxService` and stub its behavior (we don't want it to send any real requests).

How to do it...

To create a mock of a given class using the `Mockito` static method, you have to call the static `Mockito.mock(Class<T> classToMock)` method with the type of class to mock.

The following test is written for JUnit. For the TestNG configuration, refer to *Chapter 1, Getting Started with Mockito* (I'm using the `BDDMockito.given(...)` and AssertJ's `BDDAssertions.then(...)` static methods. Refer to *Chapter 7, Verifying Behavior with Object Matchers*, on how to work with AssertJ or how to do the same with Hamcrest's `assertThat(...)`).

```
   public class MeanTaxFactorCalculatorTest {

     static final double TAX_FACTOR = 10;

     TaxService taxService = mock(TaxService.class);

     MeanTaxFactorCalculator systemUnderTest = new MeanTaxFactorCalculato
   r(taxService);

     @Test
     public void should_calculate_mean_tax_factor() {
       // given
       given(taxService.getCurrentTaxFactorFor(any(Person.class))).
   willReturn(TAX_FACTOR);

       // when
       double meanTaxFactor = systemUnderTest.
   calculateMeanTaxFactorFor(new Person());
```

```
    // then
    then(meanTaxFactor).isEqualTo(TAX_FACTOR);
  }


}
```

 You can statically import the method to increase readability, as presented in the following example:

```
import static org.mockito.Mockito.mock;
TaxService taxService = mock(TaxService.class);
```

How it works...

Internally, Mockito calls the overloaded `mock` method that takes the `MockSettings` argument and executes it with a default answer set to the `RETURNS_DEFAULT` value (in other words, returns zeroes, empty collections, null values, and so on.) Next, by means of the `MockitoCore` class, a custom CGLIB proxy is created and returned to the user.

See also

▶ Refer to Martin Fowler's article on mocks and stubs from `http://martinfowler.com/articles/mocksArentStubs.html`

▶ Refer to the xUnit pattern's comparison of test doubles from `http://xunitpatterns.com/Mocks,%20Fakes,%20Stubs%20and%20Dummies.html`

Creating mocks with annotations

In the previous recipe, we saw how to create a mock by means of the `Mockito.mock` static method. It's much better, however, to use Mockito's annotations to make your tests look even nicer. Before going into the details of how to do it, let's take a closer look at the system under test (it's the same as in the previous recipe, but in order for you not to jump around pages, let's take a look at it here).

Getting ready

In this recipe, our system under test is a class that calculates a mean value of tax factors retrieved through a web service, as shown in the following code:

```
public class MeanTaxFactorCalculator {

    private final TaxService taxService;

    public MeanTaxFactorCalculator(TaxService taxService) {
        this.taxService = taxService;
    }

    public double calculateMeanTaxFactorFor(Person person) {
        double currentTaxFactor = taxService.
getCurrentTaxFactorFor(person);
        double anotherTaxFactor = taxService.
getCurrentTaxFactorFor(person);
        return (currentTaxFactor + anotherTaxFactor) / 2;
    }

}
```

Let's now write a test for the system that will check whether it can properly calculate the mean value of the tax factor. We have to create a stub of `TaxService` and stub its behavior (we don't want it to send any real requests).

How to do it...

Since Mockito integrates very nicely with JUnit (refer to *Chapter 1, Getting Started with Mockito*, for more details regarding both JUnit and TestNG configuration), let's remove the unnecessary code and make the test more readable. To do that, you have to perform the following steps:

1. Annotate your test with `@RunWith(MockitoJUnitRunner.class)`.
2. Define the collaborators that you would like to mock.
3. Annotate those dependencies with `@Mock` annotation.

Of course, this JUnit approach will work only if you haven't already annotated your test class with another `@RunWith` annotation.

Now, let's take a look at the test written for JUnit (remember that I'm using the `BDDMockito.given(...)` and AssertJ's `BDDAssertions.then(...)` static methods. Refer to *Chapter 7, Verifying Behavior with Object Matchers,* to learn how to work with AssertJ or how to do the same with Hamcrest's `assertThat(...)`). Have a look at the following code:

```
@RunWith(MockitoJUnitRunner.class)
public class MeanTaxFactorCalculatorTest {

    static final double TAX_FACTOR = 10;

    @Mock TaxService taxService;

    @InjectMocks MeanTaxFactorCalculator systemUnderTest;

    @Test
    public void should_calculate_mean_tax_factor() {
        // given
        given(taxService.getCurrentTaxFactorFor(any(Person.class))).
willReturn(TAX_FACTOR);

        // when
        double meanTaxFactor = systemUnderTest.
calculateMeanTaxFactorFor(new Person());

        // then
        then(meanTaxFactor).isEqualTo(TAX_FACTOR);
    }

}
```

How it works...

A more precise description of how `MockitoJUnitRunner` works and how it creates mocks is provided in *Chapter 1, Getting Started with Mockito.* So please refer to it for more details.

See also

▸ Refer to Martin Fowler's article on mocks and stubs from `http://martinfowler.com/articles/mocksArentStubs.html`

▸ Refer to the xUnit pattern's comparison of test doubles from `http://xunitpatterns.com/Mocks,%20Fakes,%20Stubs%20and%20Dummies.html`

Creating mocks with a different default answer

If not changed by the custom configuration, Mockito sets the mock `ReturnsEmptyValues` answer by default (for details on that answer, please check the subsequent *There's more...* section). Note that in *Chapter 4, Stubbing Behavior of Mocks*, where we deal with stubbing of particular methods, you can learn how to stub particular methods with a custom answer.

In the following recipe, we will see how to change the default answer to a custom or a predefined one.

Getting ready

It is more than probable that you will not ever need to create a custom answer for Mockito—there are plenty of them already bundled in Mockito and there is no need to reinvent the wheel. Why would you want to create a custom answer anyway? Let's take a look at a couple of possible answers to that question:

  ▸ It is possible that for debugging purposes, you would like to log the arguments that were passed to the stubbed method

  ▸ You could also want to perform some more complex logic on the passed argument rather than just return some fixed value

  ▸ You want to stub asynchronous methods that have callbacks (you provide those callbacks in the custom `Answer` implementation)

  ▸ Believe me, you don't want to capture the arguments and check them! Check *Chapter 6, Verifying Test Doubles*, for more information

If you thought it over and still want to create a custom answer, please check if there isn't one already existing in Mockito.

In the provided Mockito API, you can find the following answers in the `AdditionalAnswers` class (check the Javadoc of that class for examples):

  ▸ `returnsFirstArg`: This answer will return the first argument of the invocation

  ▸ `returnsSecondArg`: This answer returns the second argument of the invocation

  ▸ `returnsLastArg`: This answer returns the last argument of the invocation

  ▸ `returnsArgAt`: This answer returns the argument of the invocation provided at the given index

  ▸ `delegatesTo`: This answer delegates all methods to the delegate (you will in fact call the delegate's method if the method hasn't already been stubbed)

  ▸ `returnsElementsOf`: This answer returns the elements of the provided collection

There is also the Mockito class itself that contains some `Answer` interface implementations (they are static final fields, thus their names are in uppercase). These are `RETURNS_ DEFAULT`, `RETURNS_SMART_NULLS`, `RETURNS_MOCKS`, `RETURNS_DEEP_STUBS`, and `CALLS_REAL_METHODS`; they all delegate to answers described in more depth in the *There's more...* section.

If you feel that none of these answers satisfy your requirements, you have to create your own implementation of the `Answer` interface. The next part of this recipe will show how to pass the answer to the created mock. Our system under test is a class that calculates a mean value of tax factors retrieved through a web service. Have a look at the following code:

```
public class MeanTaxFactorCalculator {

    private final TaxService taxService;

    public MeanTaxFactorCalculator(TaxService taxService) {
        this.taxService = taxService;
    }

    public double calculateMeanTaxFactorFor(Person person) {
        double currentTaxFactor = taxService.
getCurrentTaxFactorFor(person);
        double anotherTaxFactor = taxService.
getCurrentTaxFactorFor(person);
        return (currentTaxFactor + anotherTaxFactor) / 2;
    }

}
```

How to do it...

To set a different default answer without annotations, you have to use the overloaded `Mockito.mock(Class<T> classToMock, Answer defaultAnswer)` static method.

The following snippet shows an example of a test that uses the `ThrowsExceptionClass` answer set on a mock as its default answer:

```
public class MeanTaxFactorCalculatorTest {

    TaxService taxService = mock(TaxService.class, new ThrowsExceptionCl
ass(IllegalStateException.class));

    MeanTaxFactorCalculator systemUnderTest = new MeanTaxFactorCalculato
r(taxService);
```

```
@Test
public void should_throw_exception_when_calculating_mean_tax_
factor() {
    // expect
    try {
        systemUnderTest.calculateMeanTaxFactorFor(new Person());
        fail("Should throw exception");
    } catch (IllegalStateException exception) {}
}

}
```

How it works...

Mockito takes the passed answer type argument and creates `MockitoSettings` from it as follows:

```
public static <T> T mock(Class<T> classToMock, Answer defaultAnswer) {
        return mock(classToMock, withSettings().
                                defaultAnswer(defaultAnswer));
    }
```

In this way, the default mock's answer is changed to the custom one. In this way, if not previously stubbed, all of the mock's methods will, by default, execute the logic from the passed `Answer` implementation.

There's more...

Here is the list of additional, interesting Mockito `Answer` implementations together with a short description (mind you, they are part of the Mockito internals, so I'm presenting them for you to understand what happens under the hood while using Mockito. Be cautious when using them):

▶ `Returns`: It always returns the object passed in the constructor of this `Answer` implementation.

▶ `ReturnsEmptyValues`: When creating a mock, all of its methods are stubbed as follows based on the method's return type:

- ❏ For primitives: It returns default Java-appropriate primitive values (0 for integer, false for boolean, and so on)

- ❏ For primitive wrappers: It returns the same values as for primitives

- ❏ For most commonly used collection types: It returns an empty collection

- ❏ For the `toString()` method: It returns the mock's name

- ❏ For `Comparable.compareTo(T other)`: It returns 1 (meaning that the objects are not equal to each other)
- ❏ For anything else: It returns null

- ▶ `ReturnsMoreEmptyValues`: This implementation extends the `ReturnsEmptyValues` functionality with the following additional default return types:
  - ❏ For arrays: It returns an empty array
  - ❏ For strings: It returns an empty string ("")
  - ❏ Returns an empty array for methods that return arrays
  - ❏ Returns an empty string ("") for methods returning strings

- ▶ `ReturnsSmartNulls`: If a `NullPointerException` gets thrown on mock, Mockito catches it and rethrows `SmartNullPointerException` with additional helpful messages. Additionally, it acts like `ReturnsMoreEmptyValues`.

- ▶ `DoesNothing`: This method always returns null for objects (non-primitive types) and default values for primitives.

- ▶ `CallsRealMethods`: This method creates a partial mock by default, unstubbed methods delegate to real implementations.

- ▶ `ReturnsArgumentAt`: This method returns an argument at a specified position of an array (for -1, it returns its last element).

- ▶ `ReturnsElementsOf`: This method keeps returning subsequent elements of the collection that is passed in the constructor. Once it arrives at the tail of the collection, it will always return that value.

- ▶ `ReturnsDeepStubs`: This method allows easy nested mock creation and method chain stubbing. Check *Chapter 8, Refactoring with Mockito*, for usage examples and suggestions why you should not use it.

- ▶ `ThrowsExceptionClass`: This method throws the exception passed as the argument to the constructor of `Answer` for each method. Mockito will instantiate the exception for you.

- ▶ `ThrowsException`: This method throws an instantiated exception passed to the constructor of `Answer`.

- ▶ `ReturnsMocks`: First, this method tries to return values such as the ones defined in `ReturnsMoreEmptyValues` and, if that fails, it tries to return a mock. Eventually, if this attempt fails at either of them, `ReturnsMocks` returns null. Please think twice before using this answer (or use it only to refactor some legacy code), since it clearly means that something is wrong with your design.

Another interesting feature is that if you create a class called `MockitoConfiguration` that implements `IMockitoConfiguration` or extends the `DefaultMockitoConfiguration` class in the `org.mockito.configuration` package. You can then set a global answer for all your mocks. The following snippet shows what a Mockito configuration class should look like in order to change the default answer of any mock to `ReturnsSmartNulls`:

```
public class MockitoConfiguration extends
DefaultMockitoConfiguration {

    public Answer<Object> getDefaultAnswer() {
        return new ReturnsSmartNulls();
    }

}
```

See also

▸ Refer to the Mockito AdditonalAnswers API from `http://docs.mockito.googlecode.com/hg/1.9.5/org/mockito/AdditionalAnswers.html`

▸ Refer to the Google testing blog on when and how to use Mockito Answer from `http://googletesting.blogspot.com/2014/03/whenhow-to-use-mockito-answer.html`

Creating mocks with different default answers with annotations

In the previous recipe, you have seen how to pass an implementation of the `Answer` interface to your mock to change its default behavior. In this recipe, we will focus on doing the same when creating mocks using annotations.

All versions of Mockito up until version 1.9.5 allow you to pass only elements of the `Answers` enum that delegate to answers present in the public Mockito API, as the arguments of the annotation. In the next Mockito release, there should be a possibility of passing a custom answer too, but until then it's not possible to do that.

Getting ready

In the following code, our system is a class that, based on the person's country, collects his **Internal Revenue Service** (**IRS**) address and formats it properly:

```
public class TaxFactorInformationProvider {

    private final TaxService taxService;

    public TaxFactorInformationProvider(TaxService taxService) {
        this.taxService = taxService;
    }

    public String formatIrsAddress(Person person) {
        String irsAddress = taxService.getInternalRevenueServiceAddres
s(person.getCountryName());
        return "IRS:[" + irsAddress + "]";
    }

}
```

Let's now write a test for the system that will check whether the address will be properly formatted if the IRS address is an empty string. We will create a stub of `TaxService` and stub its behavior (we don't want it to send any real requests).

How to do it...

If you want to pass a nondefault answer to the `@Mock` annotated field you have to set the `answer` property with a proper value of the `Answers` enum on the `@Mock` annotation.

Now, let's take a look at the test written for JUnit. For the TestNG configuration, please refer to *Chapter 1, Getting Started with Mockito* (I'm using the `BDDMockito.given(...)` and AssertJ's `BDDAssertions.then(...)` static methods. Check out *Chapter 7, Verifying Behavior with Object Matchers*, on how to work with AssertJ or how to do the same with Hamcrest's `assertThat(...)`).

```
@RunWith(MockitoJUnitRunner.class)
public class TaxFactorInformationProviderTest {

    @Mock(answer = Answers.RETURNS_SMART_NULLS) TaxService taxService;
```

```
        @InjectMocks TaxFactorInformationProvider systemUnderTest;

        @Test
        public void should_calculate_mean_tax_factor() {
            // when
            String parsedIrsAddress = systemUnderTest.formatIrsAddress(new
Person());

            // then
            then(parsedIrsAddress).isEqualTo("IRS:[]");
        }

    }
```

By passing `Answers.RETURNS_SMART_NULLS`, we've managed to define that if an unstubbed method returns a string, then from now on it will return an empty string by default. In that way, at the end, we get an empty value of the address.

How it works...

When the Mockito's `MockitoJUnitRunner` runner logic is executed at the end of the day, it calls the `MockitoAnnotations.initMocks` method. That is where the default `AnnotationEngine` is used, which, if not overriden in the global Mockito configuration, is `InjectingAnnotationEngine`. This engine delegates the processing of annotated elements to the `DefaultAnnotationEngine` that has different `FieldAnnotationProcessors` for different types of Mockito-related annotations. In this case, the `MockAnnotationProcessor` is called, which instantiates a `MockSettings` object on which the code calls methods matching the annotation parameters, such as `extraInterfaces(...)`, `name(...)`, and `defaultAnswer(...)`. In the previous example, the `ReturnsSmartNulls` answer coming from the passed `Answers.RETURNS_SMART_NULLS` was passed to the aforementioned `defaultAnswer(...)` method of `MockSettings`. That is why the code eventually behaves as we expected it to.

See also

▶ Refer to *Chapter 1, Getting Started with Mockito*, for additional information on the annotation-based Mockito configuration for both TestNG and JUnit

▶ Refer to *Chapter 4, Stubbing Behavior of Mocks*, to see how to stub the mock's method so that they return custom answers

Creating mocks with custom configuration

Even though in the majority of cases you will not need the feature discussed in the preceding recipe, sometimes you may want your mock to satisfy some additional prerequisites. Thanks to Mockito's `Mockito.withSettings` fluent interface, you can easily set up your custom `MockitoSettings` object that you can pass to the `Mockito.mock` method that will create your mock. When you check out the Javadoc of `MockitoSettings`, you will see a note that you shouldn't use that class too often. That's good advice, because you should make it a practice to write your code and tests in such a way that it is either of high quality or low complexity. In other words, in real life, you shouldn't need to configure your mocks in such a complex way.

Getting ready

Let's take a look at the following `MockitoSettings` interface methods:

- `extraInterfaces(...)`: This method specifies which additional interfaces the mock should implement. It can be quite useful when dealing with legacy code. Check out *Chapter 8*, *Refactoring with Mockito* (you shouldn't need to ever have to use it in well-written code).

- `name(...)`: By calling this method, you define a custom mock name. It can be useful when debugging your test since the provided name will be omnipresent in the verification errors.

- `spiedInstance(...)`: This method specifies the instance to spy on (refer to *Chapter 3*, *Creating Spies and Partial Mocks*, for more details on spies).

- `defaultAnswer(...)`: This method is used by the mock if not defined otherwise by explicit method stubbing (in other words, if you don't stub a method here, you define what should happen when you execute it).

- `serializable()`: This method makes the mock serializable; however, generally speaking, you shouldn't have the need to call this method in well-designed code.

- `verboseLogging()`: This method logs method invocations on the mock; it might be useful for debugging to verify which interaction was unnecessary on the mock.

- `invocationListeners(...)`: If you want to perform some additional debugging actions on your mocks each time a method gets executed on it, you have to implement your own listener and register it on the mock via this method.

In the following code, our system under test is a class that collects a person's IRS address and formats it properly based on his or her country:

```
public class TaxFactorInformationProvider {

    private final TaxService taxService;

    public TaxFactorInformationProvider(TaxService taxService) {
        this.taxService = taxService;
    }

    public String formatIrsAddress(Person person) {
        String irsAddress = taxService.getInternalRevenueServiceAddres
s(person.getCountryName());
        return "IRS:[" + irsAddress + "]";
    }

}
```

Let's now write a test for the system under test that will check whether the address will be properly formatted if the IRS address would be an empty string. We have to create a stub of `TaxService` and stub it's behavior (we don't want it to send any real requests).

How to do it...

To customize your mock's configuration via the `MockitoSettings` interface, you have to perform the following steps:

1. Create the `mock(Class<T> classToMock, MockSettings mockSettings)` method.
2. Pass the `MockSettings` object via the static `withSettings()` method as the second method's parameter.

Now let's take a look at the test written for JUnit. For the TestNG configuration, refer to *Chapter 1, Getting Started with Mockito* (I'm using the `BDDMockito.given(...)` and AssertJ's `BDDAssertions.then(...)` static methods. Check out *Chapter 7, Verifying Behavior with Object Matchers*, on how to work with AssertJ or how to do the same with Hamcrest's `assertThat(...)`).

```
public class MeanTaxFactorCalculatorTest {

    static final double TAX_FACTOR = 10;

    TaxService taxService = mock(TaxService.class, withSettings().
serializable());
```

```
    MeanTaxFactorCalculator systemUnderTest = new MeanTaxFactorCalculato
r(taxService);

    @Test
    public void should_calculate_mean_tax_factor() {
      // given
      given(taxService.getCurrentTaxFactorFor(any(Person.class))).
willReturn(TAX_FACTOR);

      // when
      double meanTaxFactor = systemUnderTest.
calculateMeanTaxFactorFor(new Person());

      // then
      then(meanTaxFactor).isEqualTo(TAX_FACTOR);
      then(taxService).isInstanceOf(Serializable.class);
    }

}
```

How it works...

What Mockito does internally is that it calls the `MockitoCore` class that is the point of entry for creating mocks. Then, a mock is created using the provided `MockitoSettings` object.

There's more...

If you are using annotations to create your mock, you also have some possibilities of customization. Take a look at the following `@Mock` annotation's additional parameters:

- ▶ answer: This parameter is one of the predefined answers present in the Answers enum
- ▶ name: This parameter is the name of the mock
- ▶ extraInterfaces: This parameter specifies which additional interfaces the mock should implement

The following is an example of a `@Mock` annotated field containing all of the previously mentioned parameters (the probability that you will use more than one parameter, if any, is very small):

```
@Mock(answer = Answers.RETURNS_SMART_NULLS, extraInterfaces =
{Iterable.class, Serializable.class}, name = "Custom tax service
mock")
    TaxService taxService;
```

▸   Refer to the Mockito documentation on MockitoSettings class from `http://docs.`
    `mockito.googlecode.com/hg/1.9.5/org/mockito/MockSettings.html`

Creating mocks of final classes with PowerMock

Although these situations should not take place in a well-written and test-driven system, there are cases in which it is necessary to mock some legacy code or third-party libraries that are impossible to be mocked only by means of Mockito. In this recipe, we will see how to deal with those abnormal situations using the `PowerMock` library. Remember, however, that this tool is extremely powerful and the very need to use it suggests that something may really be wrong with your code. The best outcome of using this library would be to use it as means to refactor the bad code and, at the end of the day, remove the PowerMock dependency from the system since it is no longer needed.

Getting ready

In order to use PowerMock with Mockito, you need to include the following library in your classpath. If you are using a dependency management system such as Gradle or Maven, you can add it to the code as follows:

The dependency definition for Gradle is as follows:

```
testCompile 'org.powermock:powermock-api-mockito:1.5.2'
```

The dependency definition for Maven is as follows:

```
<dependency>
      <groupId>org.powermock</groupId>
      <artifactId>powermock-api-mockito</artifactId>
      <version>1.5.2</version>
      <scope>test</scope>
</dependency>
```

Now, depending on the integration with JUnit or TestNG, there is an additional JAR file needed.

If you are using JUnit, then provide either of the following dependencies:

The dependency definition for Gradle is as follows:

```
testCompile 'org.powermock:powermock-module-junit4:1.5.2'
```

The dependency definition for Maven is as follows:

```
<dependency>
      <groupId>org.powermock</groupId>
      <artifactId>powermock-module-junit4</artifactId>
      <version>1.5.2</version>
      <scope>test</scope>
</dependency>
```

Assuming that you are using TestNG, configure your dependencies as follows:

The dependency definition for Gradle is as follows:

```
testCompile 'org.powermock:powermock-module-testng:1.5.2'
```

The dependency definition for Maven is as follows:

```
<dependency>
      <groupId>org.powermock</groupId>
      <artifactId>powermock-module-testng</artifactId>
      <version>1.5.2</version>
      <scope>test</scope>
</dependency>
```

You can also download the JAR files from PowerMock's website at `https://code.google.com/p/powermock/wiki/Downloads?tm=2`.

Our system under test will be a class whose responsibility it is to calculate the tax factor for the current person. It interacts with `TaxService`, which happens to be a final class (we'll omit its implementation since it's irrelevant for this recipe; what's important to remember is that it's a final class). Have a look at the following code:

```
public class TaxFactorCalculator {

    public static final double INVALID_TAX_FACTOR = -1;

    private final TaxService taxService;

    public TaxFactorCalculator(TaxService taxService) {
        this.taxService = taxService;
    }

    public double calculateTaxFactorFor(Person person) {
        try {
```

```
            return taxService.calculateTaxFactorFor(person);
        } catch (Exception e) {
            System.err.printf("Exception [%s] occurred while trying to
calculate tax for person [%s]%n", e, person.getName());
            return INVALID_TAX_FACTOR;
        }
    }

}
```

How to do it...

To use PowerMock with JUnit, you have to perform the following steps:

1. Annotate your test class with @RunWith(PowerMockRunner.class).

2. Provide all the classes that need to be prepared for testing (most likely bytecode manipulated) in the @PrepareForTest annotation (in the case of our scenario, it would be @PrepareForTest(TaxService.class) since TaxService is a final class). In general, classes that need to be prepared for testing will include classes with final, private, static or native methods; classes that are final and that should be mocked; and also classes that should be returned as mocks on instantiation.

Let's take a look at the JUnit test that will verify whether the tax factor is properly calculated (I'm using the BDDMockito.given(...) and AssertJ's BDDAssertions.then(...) static methods. Check out *Chapter 7, Verifying Behavior with Object Matchers*, on how to work with AssertJ or how to do the same with Hamcrest's assertThat(...)). Have a look at the following code:

```
@RunWith(PowerMockRunner.class)
@PrepareForTest(TaxService.class)
public class TaxFactorCalculatorTest {

    static final double TAX_FACTOR = 10000;

    @Mock TaxService taxService;

    @InjectMocks TaxFactorCalculator systemUnderTest;

    @Test
    public void should_calculate_tax_factor() {
        // given
        given(taxService.calculateTaxFactorFor(Mockito.any(Person.
class))).willReturn(TAX_FACTOR);
```

```
        // when
        double taxFactorForPerson = systemUnderTest.
calculateTaxFactorFor(new Person());

        // then
        then(taxFactorForPerson).isEqualTo(TAX_FACTOR);
    }

}
```

To use PowerMock with TestNG, you have to perform the following steps:

1. Make your class extend the `PowerMockTestCase` class.

2. Implement a method annotated with the `@ObjectFactory` annotation that returns an instance of the `PowerMockObjectFactory` class (this object factory will be used for the creation of all object instances in the test).

3. Provide all the classes that need to be prepared for testing (most likely bytecode manipulated) in the `@PrepareForTest` annotation (in the case of our scenario, it would be `@PrepareForTest(TaxService.class)` since `TaxService` is a final class). This includes classes with final, private, static, or native methods; classes that are final and that should be mocked; and also classes that should be returned a mock on object instantiation.

Let's take a look at the following JUnit test that will verify whether the tax factor is properly calculated (consult the introduction to the analogous JUnit example discussed earlier in terms of `BDDMockito` and `BDDAssertions` usage):

```
@PrepareForTest(TaxService.class)
public class TaxFactorCalculatorTestNgTest extends PowerMockTestCase {

    static final double TAX_FACTOR = 10000;

    @Mock TaxService taxService;

    @InjectMocks TaxFactorCalculator systemUnderTest;

    @Test
    public void should_calculate_tax_factor() {
        // given
        given(taxService.calculateTaxFactorFor(any(Person.class))).
willReturn(TAX_FACTOR);
```

```
        // when
        double taxFactorForPerson = systemUnderTest.
calculateTaxFactorFor(new Person());

        // then
        then(taxFactorForPerson).isEqualTo(TAX_FACTOR);
    }

    @ObjectFactory
    public IObjectFactory getObjectFactory() {
        return new PowerMockObjectFactory();
    }

}
```

How it works...

The internals of PowerMock go far beyond the scope of this recipe but the overall concept is that part of the logic of `PowerMockRunner` is to create a custom classloader and bytecode manipulation for the classes defined using the `@PrepareForTest` annotation in order to mock them and to use these mocks with the standard Mockito API. Due to bytecode manipulations, PowerMock can ignore a series of constraints of the Java language, such as extending final classes.

See also

- ▶ Refer to the PowerMock website at `https://code.google.com/p/powermock/`
- ▶ Refer to *Chapter 8, Refactoring with Mockito*, to see how to use PowerMock to refactor bad code

Creating mocks of enums with PowerMock

Believe it or not, in some legacy systems you can find solutions where the business logic is implemented inside an enum. What we will discuss here is how to mock and stub (you will learn about stubbing more in *Chapter 4, Stubbing Behavior of Mocks*) an enum using PowerMock (since it's impossible to do it in Mockito). The PowerMock library setup has been described in the previous recipe, so we'll skip it. I will, however, repeat that the best outcome of using the PowerMock library would be to use it as a means to refactor the code, and, at the end of the day, remove the PowerMock dependency from the system since it is no longer needed.

Getting ready

Let's assume that we have the following enum containing business logic:

```
public enum Country implements TaxRateCalculator {
    POLAND {
        @Override
        public double calculateTaxFactorFor(Person person) {
            return new PolishWebService().doLongOperation(person);
        }
    },
    OTHER {
        @Override
        public double calculateTaxFactorFor(Person person) {
            return new OtherWebService().doLongOperation(person);
        }
    };

    public static Country fromCountryName(String countryName){
        if(POLAND.name().equalsIgnoreCase(countryName)){
            return POLAND;
        }
        return OTHER;
    }
}
```

The system under test changes in a way that it can use the enum to perform computations. The enum is chosen based on the person's country name via the execution of the enum's `fromCountry(...)` static method. Have a look at the following code:

```
public class TaxFactorCalculator {

    public static final double INVALID_TAX_FACTOR = -1;

    public double calculateTaxFactorFor(Person person) {
        Country country = Country.fromCountryName(person.
getCountryName());
        try {
            return country.calculateTaxFactorFor(person);
        } catch (Exception e) {
            System.err.printf("Exception [%s] occurred while trying to
calculate tax for person [%s]%n", e, person.getName());
            return INVALID_TAX_FACTOR;
        }
    }

}
```

How to do it...

To mock an enum using PowerMock, you have to perform the following steps:

1. Set up PowerMock for your test runner (please refer to the *How to do it...* section of the previous recipe for JUnit and TestNG).

2. Mock it like any other final class, since enum is a type of a final class (please refer to the previous recipe on how to mock a final class).

The following code shows a JUnit test (for a TestNG setup, please refer to the previous recipe, *Creating mocks of final classes with PowerMock*) that verifies whether the system under test properly calculates the tax factor. The `mockStatic(...)` method is statically imported from PowerMockito and is used for stubbing static methods. Don't worry if you don't entirely understand the concept of stubbing, because you can learn more about it in *Chapter 4, Stubbing Behavior of Mocks*.

As for the test itself, please remember that I'm using the `BDDMockito.given(...)` and AssertJ's `BDDAssertions.then(...)` static methods. Check out *Chapter 7, Verifying Behavior with Object Matchers*, on how to work with AssertJ or how to do the same with Hamcrest's `assertThat(...)`. Have a look at the following code:

```
@RunWith(PowerMockRunner.class)
@PrepareForTest(Country.class)
public class TaxFactorCalculatorTest {

    static final double TAX_FACTOR = 10000;

    @Mock Country country;

    @InjectMocks TaxFactorCalculator systemUnderTest;

    @Test
    public void should_calculate_tax_factor() {
        // given
        mockStatic(Country.class);
        given(Country.fromCountryName(anyString())).
willReturn(country);
        given(country.calculateTaxFactorFor(any(Person.class))).
willReturn(TAX_FACTOR);

        // when
        double taxFactorForPerson = systemUnderTest.
calculateTaxFactorFor(new Person());

        // then
        then(taxFactorForPerson).isEqualTo(TAX_FACTOR);
    }

}
```

How it works...

As seen in the previous example, the internals of PowerMock go far beyond the scope of this recipe, but the overall concept is such that part of the `PowerMockRunner` logic is to create a custom classloader and bytecode manipulation for the classes defined using the `@PrepareForTest` annotation in order to mock them and to use these mocks with the standard Mockito API. Due to bytecode manipulations, PowerMock can ignore a series of constraints of the Java language, such as extending final classes.

See also

- ▶ Refer to the PowerMock website at `https://code.google.com/p/powermock/`
- ▶ Refer to *Chapter 8, Refactoring with Mockito*, to see how to use PowerMock to refactor legacy code

3
Creating Spies and Partial Mocks

In this chapter, we will cover the following recipes:

- ▸ Creating spies in code
- ▸ Creating spies with custom configuration
- ▸ Creating spies using annotations
- ▸ Creating partial mocks
- ▸ Creating partial mocks of final classes with `delegatesTo()`
- ▸ Creating spies of final classes with PowerMock

Introduction

Before going into the details regarding how to create a spy, let's first consider what a spy really is. It's an object that may have predefined answers to its method executions, whereas by default it calls the real implementation. It also records the method calls for further verification. So how does it differ from any other test double? Well, apart from the fact that you can stub its methods, you can also verify its behavior. From the theoretical point of view, a spy is nothing but a partial mock, whose advantages and risks have been described in greater depth in the introduction to the previous chapter.

In general, you should use neither spies nor partial mocks in a well-designed code base. If you do use them, it most likely means that you are violating the S in the SOLID principles (described in more depth in the previous chapter). Let's have another look at that principle as a reminder.

[**(S) Single responsibility principle**: a class should have only a single responsibility. In other words, your class should be dedicated to doing only one thing and should have only one reason to change.]

If you are stubbing only some methods from the mock and you'd prefer that the rest of them execute their real implementations, then it is most likely that your object is doing too much. Consider splitting it into pieces. There are some cases where you would like the real computation to take place by default but you might, however, want to verify whether a particular method was executed. (Imagine the business requirements where your company pays a lot of money for each web service call. I will talk about cases in which the verification of implementation does make sense in *Chapter 6, Verifying Test Doubles*.)

In this chapter, we will take a closer look at spies and partial mock creation.

[A standard reminder that you will see throughout the book is as follows:

Because I am very fond of behavior-driven development (`http://dannorth.net/introducing-bdd/` first introduced by Dan North), I'm using Mockito's `BDDMockito` and AssertJ's `BDDAssertions` static methods in all of the test cases to make the code even more readable and intuitive. Also, please read Szczepan Faber's blog (author of Mockito) about the given, when, then separation in your test methods, from `http://monkeyisland.pl/2009/12/07/given-when-then-forever/`, since these separation methods are omnipresent throughout the book.]

Some of the methods mentioned might not sound too clear, or the test code may look complicated, but don't worry – it will all be explained throughout the book. I don't want the book to become a duplication of the Mockito documentation. I would like you to take a look at nice tests and get acquainted with Mockito syntax from the very beginning. What is more, I'm using static imports in the code to make it even more readable, so if you get confused with any of the pieces of code, it would be best to consult the repository and the code.

Creating spies in code

In the following recipe, we will learn how to create a spy using Mockito code only (without annotations). As a reminder, you should have very legitimate reasons to use a spy in your code, otherwise it most likely signifies that there is something wrong with your code's design.

Getting ready

Our system under test for this recipe will be `TaxFactorProcessor`, which interacts with `TaxService`. Let's assume that the latter is part of some legacy system that, for the time being, you don't want to refactor. Also assume that `TaxService` does two things. First, it performs calculations of a tax factor, and second it sends a request via a web service to update tax data for a given person. If the person's country is not specified explicitly (and by default it's not in our examples), then a default tax factor value is returned from `TaxService`. In a proper code base, one should separate these two functionalities (calculation and data update) into separate classes, but for the sake of this example, let's leave it as it is. Have a look at the following code:

```
public class TaxFactorProcessor {

    public static final double INVALID_TAX_FACTOR = -1;

    private final TaxService taxService;

    public TaxFactorProcessor(TaxService taxService) {
        this.taxService = taxService;
    }

    public double processTaxFactorFor(Person person) {
        try {
            double taxFactor = taxService.
calculateTaxFactorFor(person);
            taxService.updateTaxData(taxFactor, person);
            return taxFactor;
        } catch (Exception e) {
            System.err.printf("Exception [%s] occurred
while trying to calculate tax factor for person
 [%s]%n", e, person.getName());
            return INVALID_TAX_FACTOR;
        }
    }

}
```

We will test our system to check that `TaxService` performs computations but does not call a web service in our unit test.

How to do it...

To create a spy of a given object using the Mockito API, you need to call the static `Mockito.spy(T object)` method with the instantiated object for which you want to create a spy.

The following test is written for JUnit. For a TestNG configuration, please refer to *Chapter 1, Getting Started with Mockito* (remember that I'm using the AssertJ's `BDDAssertions`. `then(...)` static method. Refer to *Chapter 7, Verifying Behavior with Object Matchers*, to know how to work with AssertJ or how to do the same with Hamcrest's `assertThat(...)`). Have a look at the following code:

```java
public class TaxFactorProcessorTest {

    TaxService taxService = spy(new TaxService());

    TaxFactorProcessor systemUnderTest = new
TaxFactorProcessor(taxService);

    @Test
    public void should_return_default_tax_factor_for_person
_from_undefined_country() {
        // given
        doNothing().when(taxService)
.updateTaxData(anyDouble(), any(Person.class));

        // when
        double taxFactor = systemUnderTest
.processTaxFactorFor(new Person());

        // then
        then(taxFactor).isEqualTo(TaxService.DEFAULT_TAX_FACTOR);
    }

}
```

What happens in the test is that we first create a spy for the `TaxService` instance (via the statically imported `Mockito.spy(...)` method), and next we create the system under test. In the body of our test, in the `//given` section, we are stubbing our spy so that it does nothing when the `updateTaxData(...)` method is called (don't worry if you haven't seen the stubbing syntax of spies before. You can read more about it in *Chapter 5, Stubbing Behavior of Spies*). In the `//when` section, we are executing the application logic, and in the `//then` part, we are verifying whether the processed tax factor is the default one from the application.

How it works...

Mockito internally runs the following when you execute the static `spy` method:

```
public static <T> T spy(T object) {
        return mock((Class<T>) object.getClass(), withSettings()
                .spiedInstance(object)
                .defaultAnswer(CALLS_REAL_METHODS));
    }
```

You can see that a spy is in fact a mock that by default calls real methods. Additionally, the `MockitoSpy` interface is added to that mock.

There are some gotchas regarding spy initialization with Mockito. Mockito creates a shallow copy of the original object so that tested code won't see or use the original object. That's important to know since any interactions on the original object will not get reflected on the spy, and vice versa (if you want to interact directly with the original object, you need to use the `AdditionalAnswers.delegateTo(...)` answer. To check how to stub methods with a custom answer, check *Chapter 4, Stubbing Behavior of Mocks*, or *Chapter 5, Stubbing Behavior of Spies*, for an explanation of a mock or spy's method stubbing.)

Another issue is final methods. Mockito can't stub final methods, so when you try to stub them, you will not even see a warning message and a real implementation will be called. Refer to *Chapter 5, Stubbing Behavior of Spies*, for more information on this. PowerMock related recipes to see how to deal with those methods (remember that using PowerMock suggests that there is most likely something really wrong with your code base, so you should use it with extreme caution).

See also

▶ The xUnit pattern's comparison of test doubles at `http://xunitpatterns.com/Mocks,%20Fakes,%20Stubs%20and%20Dummies.html`

▶ Mockito documentation on spying real instances at `http://docs.mockito.googlecode.com/hg/1.9.5/org/mockito/Mockito.html#13`

Creating spies with custom configuration

There might be some cases in which you would like to provide some additional configuration to your spy (for example, making the spy serializable or turning on Mockito logging). Even though Mockito doesn't provide a straightforward solution to do it, it is possible to pass such a configuration to the spy. As a reminder, you should have very legitimate reasons to use a spy in your code. Otherwise, it most likely signifies that there is something wrong with the design of your code.

Getting ready

As presented in the previous recipe, the `Mockito.spy` method has only a single parameter: the spied instance. But as we can see, internally, it's a mock that by default calls real methods. So what we can do is create the spy by ourselves together with some additional configuration (refer to the *Creating mocks with a custom configuration* recipe in *Chapter 2, Creating Mocks*, for a description of all possible configurations).

For this recipe, we will reuse the example from the previous recipe, but let's take another look at it. Our system under test for this recipe will be a `TaxFactorProcessor` class that interacts with `TaxService` in order to calculate the tax factor and update the tax data of a given person, as shown in the following code:

```
public class TaxFactorProcessor {

    public static final double INVALID_TAX_FACTOR = -1;

    private final TaxService taxService;

    public TaxFactorProcessor(TaxService taxService) {
        this.taxService = taxService;
    }

    public double processTaxFactorFor(Person person) {
        try {
            double taxFactor =
taxService.calculateTaxFactorFor(person);
            taxService.updateTaxData(taxFactor, person);
            return taxFactor;
        } catch (Exception e) {
            System.err.printf("Exception [%s] occurred while trying to
calculate tax factor for person [%s]%n", e, person.getName());
            return INVALID_TAX_FACTOR;
        }
    }

}
```

We will test our system to check that `TaxService` performs computations but does not call a web service in our unit test.

How to do it...

To create a spy with a custom configuration, you need to perform the following steps:

1. Call the static `Mockito.mock(...)` method and provide a custom configuration.

2. As for the custom configuration, add `MockSettings.spiedInstance(T object)` and `MockSettings.defaultAnswer(Mockito.CALLS_REAL_METHODS)` to create a spy of the given object.

3. To add more configurations, call additional `MockSettings` methods.

The following test is written for JUnit. For a TestNG configuration, please refer to *Chapter 1, Getting Started with Mockito* (remember that I'm using the AssertJ's `BDDAssertions.then(...)` static method. Refer to *Chapter 7, Verifying Behavior with Object Matchers*, to know how to work with AssertJ or how to do the same with Hamcrest's `assertThat(...)`). Have a look at the following code:

```java
public class TaxFactorProcessorTest {

    TaxService taxService = mock(TaxService.class, withSettings().
serializable().spiedInstance(new TaxService()).defaultAnswer(CALLS_
REAL_METHODS));

    TaxFactorProcessor systemUnderTest = new
TaxFactorProcessor(taxService);

    @Test
    public void should_return_default_tax_factor_for_person
_from_undefined_country() {
        // given
        doNothing().when(taxService)
.updateTaxData(anyDouble(), any(Person.class));

        // when
        double taxFactor =
systemUnderTest.processTaxFactorFor(new Person());

        // then
        then(taxFactor).isEqualTo(TaxService.DEFAULT_TAX_FACTOR);
        then(taxService).isInstanceOf(Serializable.class);
    }

}
```

 Mockito doesn't provide a standard way of spying with a custom configuration for a reason. In the vast majority of cases, you shouldn't have the need to do it.

How it works...

The body of the test is pretty straightforward and self-explanatory. The last assertion, regarding verification whether the mock implements the `serializable` interface, is done only to prove that the mock works as it is supposed to (don't write that in the real test code). The most interesting part, however, is the mock creation part, as follows:

```
TaxService taxService = mock(TaxService.class,
  withSettings().serializable().spiedInstance
(new TaxService()).defaultAnswer(CALLS_REAL_METHODS));
```

Since a spy is nothing but a mock that calls real implementations by default, we can create it manually, as presented in the test. The additional configuration in our case was to make the mock serializable.

See also

▶ The xUnit pattern's comparison of test doubles at `http://xunitpatterns.com/Mocks,%20Fakes,%20Stubs%20and%20Dummies.html`

▶ Mockito documentation on spying real instances at `http://docs.mockito.googlecode.com/hg/1.9.5/org/mockito/Mockito.html#13`

Creating spies using annotations

As usual, Mockito offers you the chance to remove a number of lines of code to make your tests more readable and clear. In this recipe, we will remove unnecessary code and convert it into annotations. As a reminder, you should have very legitimate reasons to use a spy in your code. Otherwise, it most likely signifies that there is something wrong with the design of your code.

Getting ready

For this recipe, we will reuse the example from the previous recipe. However, let's take another look at it. Our system under test for this recipe will be a `TaxFactorProcessor` class that interacts with a `TaxService` class in order to calculate the tax factor and update the tax data of a given person. Have a look at the following code:

```
public class TaxFactorProcessor {

    public static final double INVALID_TAX_FACTOR = -1;

    private final TaxService taxService;

    public TaxFactorProcessor(TaxService taxService) {
        this.taxService = taxService;
```

```
        }

    public double processTaxFactorFor(Person person) {
        try {
            double taxFactor = taxService.
calculateTaxFactorFor(person);
            taxService.updateTaxData(taxFactor, person);
            return taxFactor;
        } catch (Exception e) {
            System.err.printf("Exception [%s] occurred while trying to
calculate tax factor for person [%s]%n", e, person.getName());
            return INVALID_TAX_FACTOR;
        }
    }

}
```

We will test our system to check that `TaxService` performs computations but does not call a web service in our unit test.

How to do it...

To profit from Mockito's annotations, you need to perform the following steps:

1. For JUnit, annotate your test class with `@RunWith(MockitoJUnitRunner.class)`. For TestNG, copy the necessary TestNG listeners and annotate your test class with `@Listeners(MockitoTestNGListener.class)`. Refer to *Chapter 1, Getting Started with Mockito*, for more details on the TestNG setup.

2. Annotate the object you want to create a spy for with the `@Spy` annotation.

For both scenarios, remember that I'm using the AssertJ's `BDDAssertions.then(...)` static method. Refer to *Chapter 7, Verifying Behavior with Object Matchers*, to know how to work with AssertJ or how to do the same with Hamcrest's `assertThat(...)`.

Now, let's take a look at the test written for JUnit. Have a look at the following code:

```
@RunWith(MockitoJUnitRunner.class)
public class TaxFactorProcessorTest {

    @Spy TaxService taxService;

    @InjectMocks TaxFactorProcessor systemUnderTest;

    @Test
    public void should_return_default_tax_factor_for_person
_from_undefined_country() {
```

```
        // given
        doNothing().when(taxService)
.updateTaxData(anyDouble(), any(Person.class));

        // when
        double taxFactor =
systemUnderTest.processTaxFactorFor(new Person());

        // then
        then(taxFactor).isEqualTo(TaxService.DEFAULT_TAX_FACTOR);
    }

}
```

For TestNG, the test is written as follows:

```
@Listeners(MockitoTestNGListener.class)
public class TaxFactorProcessorTestNgTest {

    @Spy TaxService taxService;

    @InjectMocks TaxFactorProcessor systemUnderTest;

    @Test
    public void should_return_default_tax_factor_for_person
_from_undefined_country() {
        // given
        doNothing().when(taxService)
.updateTaxData(anyDouble(), any(Person.class));

        // when
        double taxFactor =
systemUnderTest.processTaxFactorFor(new Person());

        // then
        then(taxFactor).isEqualTo(TaxService.DEFAULT_TAX_FACTOR);
    }

}
```

How it works...

The creation of spies based on annotations works exactly the same as the mocks presented in the *Creating Mocks with annotations* recipe of *Chapter 2, Creating Mocks*. Please refer to that chapter for more details.

There's more...

Let's take another look at the `@Spy` annotated field from our test:

```
@Spy TaxService taxService
```

What if you want to create a spy of an object that you want to instantiate in a special way? What if, in our example, `TaxService` doesn't have a default constructor and we need to provide some explicit value to initialize it?

Before we answer that question, let's check how Mockito works for spy initialization. If you annotate a field with `@Spy`, Mockito will initialize it if its zero argument constructor can be found. The scope of the constructor doesn't need to be public; it can be private too. What Mockito can't do is instantiate local or inner interfaces and classes.

Coming back to the question, how can we create a spy and provide its initialization parameters? You need to explicitly call the object's constructor as follows:

```
@Spy TaxService taxService = new TaxService("Some value");
```

See also

- ▶ *Chapter 1, Getting Started with Mockito*, for annotation-based JUnit and TestNG configurations
- ▶ The `@Spy` annotation described in the Mockito documentation at `http://docs.mockito.googlecode.com/hg/1.9.5/org/mockito/Mockito.html#21`
- ▶ Automatic instantiation of `@Spies` and `@InjectMocks` in the Mockito documentation at `http://docs.mockito.googlecode.com/hg/1.9.5/org/mockito/Mockito.html#23`

Creating partial mocks

Using partial mocks generally should be considered a code smell. When writing good and clean code, you want it to be modular and follow all of the best practices, including the SOLID principles (please refer to the *Introduction* section of *Chapter 2, Creating Mocks*, for an elaborate explanation). When working with complex code, as a refactoring process, one tries to split the largest tasks into more modular ones. During that process, you may want to mock external dependencies of the system under test. You might come across a situation in which you do not want to mock the entire dependency but only a part of it while leaving the rest unstubbed. Such a mocked class is called a partial mock and creating one means that a class that you are mocking most likely does more than one thing, which is a pure violation of the single-responsibility principle.

Let's consider the example from the current chapter – the `TaxService` class. It has two responsibilities:

- ▸ Calculation of the tax factor for a person
- ▸ Updating the tax data for the person via a web service

The class both computes and updates data, so all-in-all it's not responsible for a single action, but two. If we split these responsibilities into two classes, since we don't want to really call a web service, we could create a mock only for the class responsible for updating the tax data. At the end of the day, that's how we will eliminate the need for creating a partial mock.

So why would you want to create a partial mock? You definitely would not need to do it in your new code base (because you are following the SOLID principles). However, there are cases where you will want to create partial mocks: when dealing with legacy code or third-party libraries. This would be code that you can't easily change or you can't change at all.

In this recipe, we will describe how to create partial mocks, but before that, let's have another look at the concept of a test double known as stub (based on Gerard Meszaros's definitions from the xUnit patterns). Stub is an object that has predefined answers to method executions made during the test.

The process of predefining those answers is called stubbing (refer to *Chapter 4*, *Stubbing Behavior of Mocks*, and *Chapter 5*, *Stubbing Behavior of Spies*, for more details), and you have already seen it being used with the following syntax throughout the book (an example for stubbing a method that returns a value using first the BDDMockito and then the Mockito syntax):

```
BDDMockito.given(...).willReturn(...)
Mockito.when(...).thenReturn(...)
```

Getting ready

For this recipe, we will reuse the example from the previous recipe, but let's take another look at it. Our system under test for this recipe will be a `TaxFactorProcessor` class that interacts with a `TaxService` class in order to calculate the tax factor and update the tax data of a given person. Have a look at the following code:

```
public class TaxFactorProcessor {

    public static final double INVALID_TAX_FACTOR = -1;

    private final TaxService taxService;

    public TaxFactorProcessor(TaxService taxService) {
        this.taxService = taxService;
    }
```

```
    public double processTaxFactorFor(Person person) {
        try {
            double taxFactor = taxService.
calculateTaxFactorFor(person);
            taxService.updateTaxData(taxFactor, person);
            return taxFactor;
        } catch (Exception e) {
            System.err.printf("Exception [%s] occurred while trying to
calculate tax factor for person [%s]%n", e, person.getName());
            return INVALID_TAX_FACTOR;
        }
    }

}
```

We will test our system to check that `TaxService` performs computations but does not call a web service in our unit test.

How to do it...

In order to create a partial mock, you need to perform the following steps:

1. Create a mock (either via code or annotations).
2. Stub the method execution so that it calls a real method (we want to execute the real logic).

The following tests illustrate the case for JUnit. For a TestNG configuration, please refer to *Chapter 1, Getting Started with Mockito*, (remember that I'm using the BDDMockito. `given(...)` and AssertJ's `BDDAssertions.then(...)` static methods. Refer to *Chapter 7, Verifying Behavior with Object Matchers*, to know how to work with AssertJ, or how to do the same with Hamcrest's `assertThat(...)`). Have a look at the following code:

```
@RunWith(MockitoJUnitRunner.class)
public class TaxFactorProcessorTest {

    @Mock TaxService taxService;

    @InjectMocks TaxFactorProcessor systemUnderTest;

    @Test
    public void should_return_default_tax_factor_for_person
_from_undefined_country() {
        // given
        given(taxService.calculateTaxFactorFor
(any(Person.class))).willCallRealMethod();
```

```
        // when
        double taxFactor =
    systemUnderTest.processTaxFactorFor(new Person());

        // then
        then(taxFactor).isEqualTo(TaxService.DEFAULT_TAX_FACTOR);
    }


}
```

What happens in the test is that we create a mock and inject it to our system under test via annotations. Next, we are stubbing the mock's `calculateTaxFactorFor(...)` method execution in the test itself so that it calls a real method of the `TaxService` class. The rest of the test is self-explanatory. First, we execute the system under a test method and then we assert that the behavior of the system is the same as we would expect it.

How it works...

The explanation of the internals related to stubbing the mocked object with the execution of a real implementation is covered in more depth in the next chapter, related to stubbing.

There's more...

You can make the mock call real methods by default by changing its default answer (check the corresponding recipe in *Chapter 2, Creating Mocks*, for more details), as presented in the following snippet:

```
@Mock(answer = Answers.CALLS_REAL_METHODS) TaxService taxService;
```

However, because each method will by default call a real method right now, coming back to our example, we need to stub the execution of the method that calls a web service so that it doesn't do it and the rest of the test remains the same. Have a look at the following code:

```
// given
doNothing().when(taxService)
.updateTaxData(anyDouble(), any(Person.class));
```

See also

▶ The xUnit pattern's comparison of test doubles at `http://xunitpatterns.com/Mocks,%20Fakes,%20Stubs%20and%20Dummies.html`

▶ Mockito's documentation on partial mocks at `http://docs.mockito.googlecode.com/hg/1.9.5/org/mockito/Mockito.html#16`

Creating partial mocks of final classes with delegatesTo()

The previous recipe showed an example of working with code that is not very trivial to mock. The obstacles might be as follows:

> ▸ There are cases where the classes to mock are final

> ▸ The object to be mocked is an already proxied object (Mockito will have issues with dealing with those)

The main feature described in this recipe focuses on the process of delegation of a method execution from a method of the implemented interface to the instantiated class (as you can see, there is a catch – the class to be mocked needs to implement an interface). As a reminder, you should have very legitimate reasons to use a partial mock in your code. Otherwise, it most likely signifies that there is something wrong with the design of your code.

Getting ready

For this recipe, we will reuse the example from the previous recipe, but let's take another look at it. Our system under test for this recipe will be a `TaxFactorProcessor` class that interacts with a `TaxService` class in order to calculate the tax factor and update the tax data of a given person. The difference between this and other examples is that `TaxService` is now an interface with the following API:

```
public interface TaxService {

    double calculateTaxFactorFor(Person person);

    void updateTaxData(double taxFactor, Person person);

}
```

The implementation of this interface is the `FinalTaxService` final class that performs some logic (for purposes of readability, we will not go into the details regarding the implementation). Have a look at the following code:

```
public final class FinalTaxService implements TaxService {
...
}
```

Our system under test, the `TaxFactorProcessor` class, as shown in the following code:

```
public class TaxFactorProcessor {

    public static final double INVALID_TAX_FACTOR = -1;
```

```
        private final TaxService taxService;

        public TaxFactorProcessor(TaxService taxService) {
            this.taxService = taxService;
        }

        public double processTaxFactorFor(Person person) {
            try {
                double taxFactor = taxService.
calculateTaxFactorFor(person);
                taxService.updateTaxData(taxFactor, person);
                return taxFactor;
            } catch (Exception e) {
                System.err.printf("Exception [%s] occurred while trying to
calculate tax factor for person [%s]%n", e, person.getName());
                return INVALID_TAX_FACTOR;
            }
        }

}
```

We will test our system to check that `TaxService` performs computations but does not call a web service in our unit test.

How to do it...

To delegate all method executions to the provided object, you need to perform the following steps:

1. Instantiate the object that you want to delegate calls to.

2. Create a mock whose default answer will be `AdditionalAnswers.delegatesTo(T delegate)`.

The following tests illustrate the case for JUnit. For a TestNG configuration, refer to *Chapter 1, Getting Started with Mockito* (remember that I'm using the `BDDMockito.given(...)` and AssertJ's `BDDAssertions.then(...)` static methods. Refer to *Chapter 7, Verifying Behavior with Object Matchers*, to know how to work with AssertJ, or how to do the same with Hamcrest's `assertThat(...)`). Have a look at the following code:

```
@RunWith(MockitoJUnitRunner.class)
public class TaxFactorProcessorTest {

    FinalTaxService finalTaxService = new FinalTaxService();
```

```
    TaxService taxService = mock(TaxService.class,
  delegatesTo(finalTaxService));

    TaxFactorProcessor systemUnderTest =
new TaxFactorProcessor(taxService);

    @Test
    public void should_return_default_tax_factor_for_person
_from_undefined_country() {
        // given
        doNothing().when(taxService)
.updateTaxData(anyDouble(), any(Person.class));

        // when
        double taxFactor =
systemUnderTest.processTaxFactorFor(new Person());

        // then
        then(taxFactor).isEqualTo
(FinalTaxService.DEFAULT_TAX_FACTOR);
    }

}
```

How it works...

To put it briefly, what happens under the hood of Mockito is that `AdditionalAnswers.delegatesTo(...)` internally uses the `ForwardsInvocations` answer that delegates the method invocation to the delegate object (in our case, to `FinalTaxService`).

There's more...

You may ask yourself this question: how does this solution differ from the standard spy? When Mockito creates a spy, this is what occurs:

- ▸ The object that is wrapped with the spy is used only when the mock is created. Next, the spied instance state gets copied to the spy.

- ▸ The spy contains all states from the spied instance.

- ▸ When you invoke a method on the spy, it gets invoked on the spy and not on the spied instance.

- ▸ When you call a method on a spy, and internally that method calls another method of the spy, both of them can be stubbed or you can perform the verification of execution of those methods.

If you use the `delegatesTo(...)` solution, then what happens is that you just delegate the execution from the mock to the real object. When you call a method on that mock, and internally that method calls another method of the mock, you can neither stub nor verify the method execution of that mock.

In other words, the mock with the default answer set to `delegatesTo(...)` can do less than a spy. On the other hand, if you have a final class, then you will not be able to create a spy using just Mockito. To achieve this, you will need to use PowerMock, and we will discuss those cases in the next recipe.

See also

▸ The Mockito documentation on delegating calls to a real instance at `http://docs.mockito.googlecode.com/hg/latest/org/mockito/Mockito.html#delegating_call_to_real_instance`

▸ The Mockito documentation on the `delegatesTo(...)` answer at `http://docs.mockito.googlecode.com/hg/latest/org/mockito/AdditionalAnswers.html#delegatesTo(java.lang.Object)`

Creating spies of final classes with PowerMock

Before going into the details of this recipe, if you haven't already done so, please read the *Creating mocks of final classes with PowerMock* recipe of *Chapter 2, Creating Mocks*. PowerMock is a powerful (thus dangerous) tool, that in the hands of an inexperienced developer, can lead to the creation of really bad test and production code.

Why would you want to use PowerMock? Mockito can't create mocks for classes that are final. The same problem exists when trying to create spies. If you have a properly written test-driven code, you shouldn't have the need to use either spies or partial mocks, nor have PowerMock in your project. If you need to use PowerMock to create spies of final classes, do it only as a last resort in order to refactor your code, and at the end remove PowerMock dependencies and only use Mockito. Refer to *Chapter 8, Refactoring with Mockito*, for examples of how to use PowerMock as a mean to refactor your code (and at the end of the day, remove PowerMock from your classpath).

Getting ready

Speaking of classpaths, in order to use PowerMock with Mockito, you need to add it to your classpath. Please refer to the *Creating Mocks of final classes with PowerMock* recipe of *Chapter 2, Creating Mocks*, to know how to add PowerMock to your project.

Our system under test will be a class whose responsibility is to calculate the tax factor for a given person. It interacts with `TaxService`, which happens to be a final class. (We'll omit its implementation since it's irrelevant for this recipe. The important thing is to remember that it's a final class.) Have a look at the following code:

```
public class TaxFactorProcessor {

    public static final double INVALID_TAX_FACTOR = -1;

    private final TaxService taxService;

    public TaxFactorProcessor(TaxService taxService) {
        this.taxService = taxService;
    }

    public double processTaxFactorFor(Person person) {
        try {
            double taxFactor = taxService.
calculateTaxFactorFor(person);
            taxService.updateTaxData(taxFactor, person);
            return taxFactor;
        } catch (Exception e) {
            System.err.printf("Exception [%s] occurred while trying to
calculate tax factor for person [%s]%n", e, person.getName());
            return INVALID_TAX_FACTOR;
        }
    }

}
```

How to do it...

To use PowerMock with JUnit to create a spy for final classes, you need to perform the following steps:

1. Annotate your test class with `@RunWith(PowerMockRunner.class)`.

2. Provide all of the classes that need to be prepared for testing (most likely byte-code manipulated) in the `@PrepareForTest` annotation (in the case of our scenario, it would be `@PrepareForTest(TaxService.class)` since `TaxService` is a final class). In general, the classes that need to be prepared for testing would include those with final, private, static, or native methods. These are classes that are final and should be spied on, and are also classes that should be returned as spies on instantiation.

3. Annotate the field to be spied with the `@Spy` annotation and instantiate that object (it differs from the standard Mockito approach, where if the spy has a default constructor, you wouldn't need to instantiate it).

Let's take a look at the JUnit test which will verify whether the tax factor is properly calculated (remember that I'm using the `BDDMockito.given(...)` and AssertJ's `BDDAssertions. then(...)` static methods. Refer to *Chapter 7, Verifying Behavior with Object Matchers*, to know how to work with AssertJ, or how to do the same with Hamcrest's `assertThat(...)`). Have a look at the following code:

```
@RunWith(PowerMockRunner.class)
@PrepareForTest(TaxService.class)
public class TaxFactorProcessorTest {

    static final double TAX_FACTOR = 10000;

    @Spy TaxService taxService = new TaxService();

    @InjectMocks TaxFactorProcessor systemUnderTest;

    @Test
    public void should_return_default_tax_factor_for_person
_from_undefined_country() {
        // given
        doReturn(TAX_FACTOR).when(taxService)
.calculateTaxFactorFor(Mockito.any(Person.class));

        // when
        double taxFactorForPerson = systemUnderTest.
processTaxFactorFor(new Person());

        // then
        then(taxFactorForPerson).isEqualTo(TAX_FACTOR);
    }

}
```

To use PowerMock with TestNG to create a spy for final classes, you need to perform the following steps:

1. Make your class extend the `PowerMockTestCase` class.

2. Implement a method annotated with the `@ObjectFactory` annotation that returns an instance of the `PowerMockObjectFactory` class (this object factory will be used for the creation of all object instances in the test).

3. Provide all of the classes that need to be prepared for testing (most likely byte-code manipulated) in the `@PrepareForTest` annotation (in the case of our scenario, it would be `@PrepareForTest(TaxService.class)` since `TaxService` is a final class). This includes classes with final, private, static, or native methods. These are classes that are final and that should be spied on; and are also classes that should return a spy on object instantiation.

4. Annotate the field to be spied with the `@Spy` annotation and instantiate that object (it differs from the standard Mockito approach, where if the spy has a default constructor, you wouldn't need to instantiate it).

Let's take a look at the TestNG test that will verify whether the tax factor is properly calculated (refer to the introduction to the preceding analogous JUnit example for more information on `BDDMockito` and `BDDAssertions` usage):

```
@PrepareForTest(TaxService.class)
public class TaxFactorProcessorTestNgTest extends PowerMockTestCase {

    static final double TAX_FACTOR = 10000;

    @Spy TaxService taxService = new TaxService();

    @InjectMocks TaxFactorProcessor systemUnderTest;

    @Test
    public void should_return_default_tax_factor_for_person
_from_undefined_country() {
        // given
        doReturn(TAX_FACTOR).when(taxService)
.calculateTaxFactorFor(Mockito.any(Person.class));

        // when
        double taxFactorForPerson = systemUnderTest.
processTaxFactorFor(new Person());

        // then
        then(taxFactorForPerson).isEqualTo(TAX_FACTOR);
    }

    @ObjectFactory
    public IObjectFactory getObjectFactory() {
        return new PowerMockObjectFactory();
    }

}
```

How it works...

The internals of PowerMock go far beyond the scope of this recipe, but the overall concept is such that a part of the `PowerMockRunner` logic is to create a custom classloader and byte-code manipulation for the classes defined using the `@PrepareForTest` annotation in order to mock them and to use these mocks with the standard Mockito API. Due to byte-code manipulations, PowerMock can ignore a series of constraints of the Java language, such as extending final classes.

See also

- The PowerMock website: `https://code.google.com/p/powermock/`
- *Chapter 8, Refactoring with Mockito*, to see how to use different approaches and tools like PowerMock to refactor bad code

4
Stubbing Behavior of Mocks

In this chapter, we will cover the following recipes:

- ► Using argument matchers for stubbing
- ► Stubbing methods that return values
- ► Stubbing methods so they throw exceptions
- ► Stubbing methods so they return custom answers
- ► Stubbing methods so they call real methods
- ► Stubbing void methods
- ► Stubbing void methods so they throw exceptions
- ► Stubbing void methods so they return custom answers
- ► Stubbing final methods with PowerMock
- ► Stubbing static methods with PowerMock
- ► Stubbing object instantiation with PowerMock

Introduction

As explained in the previous chapters, Mockito is all about creating mocks and stubbing their behavior. It's worth taking another look at the differences between mocks and stubs in order to properly distinguish possible actions that can be taken on either of them. In his xUnit patterns (`http://xunitpatterns.com/Test%20Double%20Patterns.html`), Gerard Meszaros describes stubs and mocks as follows:

- ► **Stub**: This is an object that has predefined answers to method executions made during the test

> ► **Mock**: This is an object that has predefined answers to method executions made during the test and that has recorded expectations of these executions

Mockito does not distinguish this separation, so each test double, regardless of its purpose, is considered to be a mock. This chapter will focus on showing you numerous ways of the stubbing behavior of mocks in order to simulate real interactions. We'll cover stubbing methods that return values and those that are void. We'll simulate returning results, throwing exceptions, and execution of custom logic. We'll also go down the path of dealing with static, final method, and object-initialization stubbing. (Hopefully you'll never need to use stubbing. Otherwise it means that something is wrong with your code or you're integrating it with some third-party piece of software that does not follow object-oriented principles.)

Before going further, let's take a closer look at two definitions: behavior of the application and its interactions.

Your system should be split into modules that have limited responsibilities. These responsibilities may be related to some computation, data storing or processing, and so on. You can compare the behavior to the outcome of these actions, so when you're testing the behavior, you will mostly be interested in whether your system has altered the input data or stored some values and not in how it was done (for instance, a particular method was executed). Often, it might not even involve a mock—you just want to test the output for the given input. (If you are writing a piece of software that adds two numbers, then why would you want to mock any collaborators? Just check whether by providing 1 and 1 as arguments, you get 2 as the result.)

Interactions are concrete calls between different parts of your system. In *Chapter 6, Verifying Test Doubles*, I will describe with greater depth the situations in which it is worth checking whether some particular piece of code was called. It's all about a sense of security and the business requirements.

In the forthcoming recipes, we will not verify interactions. Instead, we will verify whether the system under the test's logic does what it is supposed to do. You might ask why we are not performing such verifications on the mocked object. The reason is that what we want to test in the aforementioned examples is not whether a method has been called on a mock but whether the logic that was executed by the system under test works as we expect it to work.

Imagine that you change some algorithm inside the collaborating object but at the end of the day, you want the system under test to work in exactly the same manner. If you test your implementation and not the behavior, your test will fail. In other words, in the majority of cases, you don't want to know exactly how something is done. Instead, you want to know what its outcome is. You can check the Google testing article at `http://googletesting.blogspot.com/2013/08/testing-on-toilet-test-behavior-not.html` to see nice examples of why you should be interested in it and not how your system under test does what it is supposed to do.

If possible, verify the behavior and not the implementation.

While going through the examples in this chapter, you will see that there is some repetition and similarity of content. This is done on purpose to make the examples look alike so that the reader memorizes them fast. Since this is a cookbook, it is written in such a way that each recipe can be addressed separately in terms of the examples and solutions. This is why I always want to give you the business background of the tested system. You will not always read this book chapter by chapter. You might want to find a particular solution to your problem and then you wouldn't have to search through the book to check whether the system under test looks like some other system.

 The following is a standard reminder that you will see throughout the book:

As I am very fond of the Behavior Driven Development in all of the test cases, I'm using Mockito's `BDDMockito` and AssertJ's `BDDAssertions` static methods to make the code even more readable and intuitive. Also, please read Szczepan Faber's blog (the author of Mockito) about the given, when, then separation in your test methods; `http://monkeyisland.pl/2009/12/07/given-when-then-forever/`, since these methods are omnipresent throughout the book.

Even though you might not understand some of the preceding explanations, or the test code might look complicated, don't worry as it will all get explained throughout the book. I don't want the book to become a duplication of the Mockito documentation that is of high quality. Instead, I would like you to take a look at nice tests and get acquainted with the Mockito syntax from the early beginning. What is more, I'm using static imports in the code to make it even more readable, so if you get confused with any of the pieces of code, it would be best to refer to the repository and the code as such.

Using argument matchers for stubbing

Before going into detail regarding the different ways of stubbing method calls, we have to define the concept of argument matchers. When passing arguments to the mock's methods during the stubbing process, Mockito verifies argument values using the `equals()` method. In other words, when calling the following code:

```
Person smith = new Person();
given(taxFactorFetcher.getTaxFactorFor(smith).willReturn(10);
```

Mockito will check whether the person passed as an argument to the `getTaxFactorFor(...)` method equals to our person (in this case, Mr. Smith). If that is the case, only then will Mockito return `10` as the output of the `getTaxFactorFor(...)` method.

There are cases where you want to perform more complex verification of the passed argument. Mockito already gives you quite a few predefined argument matchers and also provides you with the integration with Hamcrest to create custom argument matchers (check *Chapter 7, Verifying Behavior with Object Matchers*, for more details on Hamcrest).

 In general, you should use equality or pass a matcher that starts with *any* prefix, which means you don't care about the passed value. If you are using more complex examples, then ensure your code isn't too complicated.

Getting ready

Let's take a look at the existing Mockito argument matchers that are present in the Matchers class:

- Examples of argument matchers that start with the any prefix are any(), any(Person.class), anyDouble(), anyList(), and so on.

- Examples of argument matchers that end with the That suffix are argThat(...), booleanThat(...), doubleThat(...), and so on. You can provide a custom Hamcrest matcher that matches the argument of the given type.

- The startsWith(...) and endsWith(...) argument matchers are used for string comparison.

- The eq(...) argument matcher checks for equality.

- The isNotNull(), isNull(), and notNull() argument matchers provide verification against null values.

- The refEq(...) argument matcher is used for reflection-equal verification (checks via reflection whether two objects are equal).

There is also the AdditionalMatchers class that contains some matchers, but it's better that you don't use it since it's only there to maintain compatibility with EasyMock.

Since using argument matchers is pretty straightforward, intuitive, and we have already been profiting from them throughout the book, we'll skip the business context of the test and move through a quick syntax example to a reminder regarding common mistakes while using argument matching.

How to do it...

To use Mockito's argument matchers, you have to ensure that when calling any method on a mock, you pass a matcher from the Matchers class instead of passing an argument.

Let's take a look at a couple of snippets that show us some of the possible matchers that Mockito has in the `Matchers` class in the example of a method that takes two parameters: an object of the `Person` type and a string:

```
/* match the method for any person and for the city of Warsaw */
given(irsDataFetcher.isIrsApplicable(any(Person.class),
eq("Warsaw"))).willReturn(true);

/* match the method for any person and for the city starting with 'W'
*/
given(irsDataFetcher.isIrsApplicable(any(Person.class),
startsWith("W"))).willReturn(true);

/* match the method for any Person and for the city ending with 'w' */
given(irsDataFetcher.isIrsApplicable(any(Person.class),
endsWith("w"))).willReturn(true);

/* match the method for any person and for any city */
given(irsDataFetcher.isIrsApplicable(any(Person.class), anyString())).
willReturn(true);

/* match the method for a person that equals another person and for
any city */
given(irsDataFetcher.isIrsApplicable(refEq(new Person()),
anyString())).willReturn(true);

/* match the method for the same reference of the person and for any
city */
given(irsDataFetcher.isIrsApplicable(same(person), anyString())).
willReturn(true);

/* match the method for a person called Lewandowski and for any city
(using Hamcrest matcher) */
given(irsDataFetcher.isIrsApplicable(argThat(new
ArgumentMatcher<Person>() {

        @Override
        public boolean matches(Object argument) {
            return "Lewandowski".equalsIgnoreCase(((Person)
argument).getName());
        }

    }), anyString())).willReturn(true);
```

How it works...

All of the methods of the `Matchers` class return dummy values so that the code gets compiled. Internally, Mockito places a matcher on a stack for further verification when a method gets executed on a mock or a method verification takes place.

There's more...

One of the most common mistakes when using argument matchers is that people tend to forget that if you are using a matcher for at least one argument, then you have to provide matchers for all of the arguments. In other words, the following example will result in `InvalidUseOfMatchersException` (notice that there is an `any(...)` matcher for the first argument and no matcher for the second argument):

```
given(irsDataFetcher.isIrsApplicable(any(Person.class), "Warsaw")).
willReturn(true);
```

The following code will work like a charm (notice the `any(...)` and `eq(...)` matchers):

```
given(irsDataFetcher.isIrsApplicable(any(Person.class),
eq("Warsaw"))).willReturn(true);
```

See also

▶ Refer to the Mockito documentation in terms of argument matchers at `http://docs.mockito.googlecode.com/hg/1.9.5/org/mockito/Mockito.html#3`

▶ Refer to the GitHub account of the book for more examples on argument matchers at `https://github.com/marcingrzejszczak/mockito-cookbook`

Stubbing methods that return values

In this recipe, we will stub a method that returns a value so that it returns our desired result.

Getting ready

For this recipe, our system under test will be `MeanTaxFactorCalculator`, which calls `TaxFactorFetcher` twice to get a tax factor for the given person and then calculates a mean value for those two results as follows:

```
public class MeanTaxFactorCalculator {

    private final TaxFactorFetcher taxFactorFetcher;

    public MeanTaxFactorCalculator(TaxFactorFetcher taxFactorFetcher)
{
```

```
        this.taxFactorFetcher = taxFactorFetcher;
    }

    public double calculateMeanTaxFactorFor(Person person) {
        double taxFactor = taxFactorFetcher.getTaxFactorFor(person);
        double anotherTaxFactor = taxFactorFetcher.
getTaxFactorFor(person);
        return (taxFactor + anotherTaxFactor) / 2;
    }

}
```

How to do it...

To stub nonvoid methods so they return a given value, you have to perform the following steps:

1. For the BDD approach, call `BDDMockito.given(mock.methodToStub())`. `willReturn(value)`, or in the standard way, call `Mockito.when(mock.methodToStub()).thenReturn(value)`.

2. Regardless of the chosen approach in the `given(...)` or `when(...)` methods, you have to provide the mock's method call, and in the `willReturn(...)` or `thenReturn(...)` methods, you have to provide the desired output.

3. Remember that the last passed value during the stubbing will be for each stubbed method call. In other words, say that you stub the mock as follows:

    ```
    given(taxFetcher.getTax()).willReturn(50, 100);
    ```

    Then, regardless of the number of `taxFetcher.getTax()` method executions, you will first return `50` and then, you will always receive `100` (until it's stubbed again).

Let's check the JUnit test. Refer to *Chapter 1, Getting Started with Mockito*, for the TestNG configuration (remember that I'm using `BDDMockito.given(...)` and AssertJ's `BDDAssertions.then(...)` static methods. Check out *Chapter 7, Verifying Behavior with Object Matchers*, for more details on how to work with AssertJ or how to do the same with Hamcrest's `assertThat(...)`):

```
@RunWith(MockitoJUnitRunner.class)
public class MeanTaxFactorCalculatorTest {

    @Mock TaxFactorFetcher taxFactorFetcher;

    @InjectMocks MeanTaxFactorCalculator systemUnderTest;

    @Test
    public void should_calculate_mean_tax_factor() {
        // given
```

```
        double expectedTaxFactor = 10;
        given(taxFactorFetcher.getTaxFactorFor(any(Person.class))).
willReturn(expectedTaxFactor);

        // when
        double meanTaxFactor = systemUnderTest.
calculateMeanTaxFactorFor(new Person());

        // then
        then(meanTaxFactor).isEqualTo(expectedTaxFactor);
    }

}
```

How it works...

What Mockito does internally when you stub methods is that it executes two main actions, validation and answer construction. When you call the `given(...)` or `when(...)` methods, the validation takes place for the following situations:

- ▸ Stubbing is not complete (when you forget to write `thenReturn(...)` or `willReturn(...)`)
- ▸ Argument matchers are misplaced (you can't use them outside of verification or stubbing)
- ▸ Stubbing is performed on an object that is not a mock
- ▸ Invalid checked exception is being thrown

As for the answer construction phase, it takes place on the execution of the `willReturn(...)` or `thenReturn(...)` method calls. Eventually, Mockito constructs the `Returns` answer with the passed value and then delegates the execution to it.

There's more...

Mockito allows for providing a series of possible stubbed results either by using the fluent interface API, or by means of varargs. The following snippet shows you how to stub a method and provide subsequent results by means of fluent API using JUnit (see *Chapter 1, Getting Started with Mockito,* for the TestNG configuration):

```
@RunWith(MockitoJUnitRunner.class)
public class MeanTaxFactorCalculatorTest {

    @Mock TaxFactorFetcher taxFactorFetcher;
```

```
    @InjectMocks MeanTaxFactorCalculator systemUnderTest;

    @Test
    public void should_calculate_mean_tax_factor_for_two_different_
tax_factors() {
        // given
        double taxFactor = 10;
        double anotherTaxFactor = 20;
        double expectedMeanTaxFactor =
(taxFactor + anotherTaxFactor) / 2;
        given(taxFactorFetcher.getTaxFactorFor(any(Person.class))).
willReturn(taxFactor).willReturn(anotherTaxFactor);

        // when
        double meanTaxFactor = systemUnderTest.
calculateMeanTaxFactorFor(new Person());

        // then
        then(meanTaxFactor).isEqualTo(expectedMeanTaxFactor);
    }

}
```

To achieve the same result using varargs, take the following code:

```
given(taxFactorFetcher.getTaxFactorFor(any(Person.class))).
willReturn(taxFactor).willReturn(anotherTaxFactor);
```

Then, change it to the following code:

```
given(taxFactorFetcher.getTaxFactorFor(any(Person.class))).
willReturn(taxFactor, anotherTaxFactor);
```

See also

- ▸ Refer to the Mockito documentation (especially, check argument matchers and stubbing consecutive calls) at `http://docs.mockito.googlecode.com/hg/1.9.5/org/mockito/Mockito.html`

Stubbing methods so that they throw exceptions

In this recipe, we will stub a method that returns a value so that it throws an exception of our choice. This way, you can simulate scenarios in which some connection issues might occur or some business exceptions have been thrown in your application.

In the behavior verification part of our test, we will check the thrown exception and since our goal is to write beautiful tests, we will use the catch-exception library (https://code.google.com/p/catch-exception/) to assert the caught exceptions. (We will use this library even though it's not maintained any more since in JDK 8, you can profit from the lambda expressions to achieve a similar goal.)

Getting ready

First, we have to add `catch-exception` to the classpath. To do that, let's use either Maven or Gradle (for manual installation, you can download the JAR files from https://code.google.com/p/catch-exception/downloads/list).

The following is the configuration for Gradle:

```
testCompile 'com.googlecode.catch-exception:catch-exception:1.2.0'
```

The following is the configuration for Maven:

```
<dependency>
    <groupId>com.googlecode.catch-exception</groupId>
    <artifactId>catch-exception</artifactId>
    <version>1.2.0</version>
    <scope>test</scope>
</dependency>
```

For this recipe, our system under test will again be `MeanTaxFactorCalculator`, which calls `TaxFactorFetcher` twice and calculates a mean value out of the received tax factor values as follows:

```
public class MeanTaxFactorCalculator {

    private final TaxFactorFetcher taxFactorFetcher;

    public MeanTaxFactorCalculator(TaxFactorFetcher taxFactorFetcher)
{
        this.taxFactorFetcher = taxFactorFetcher;
    }
```

```
public double calculateMeanTaxFactorFor(Person person) {
    double taxFactor = taxFactorFetcher.getTaxFactorFor(person);
    double anotherTaxFactor = taxFactorFetcher.
getTaxFactorFor(person);
    return (taxFactor + anotherTaxFactor) / 2;
}
```

How to do it...

To make the mock's nonvoid method throw an exception, you have to perform the following steps:

1. For the BDD approach, call `BDDMockito.given(mock.methodToStub())`. `willThrow(exception)`, or in the standard way, call `Mockito.when(mock. methodToStub()).thenThrow(exception)`.

2. Regardless of the chosen approach in the `given(...)` or `when(...)` method, you have to provide the mock's method call, and in the `willThrow(...)` or `thenThrow(...)` method, provide the desired exception to throw.

3. Remember that the last passed value during the stubbing will be thrown for each stubbed method call. In other words, you stub the mock as follows:

   ```
   given(taxFetcher.getTax()).willThrow(new Exception1(),
     new Exception2());
   ```

   Then, regardless of the number of `taxFetcher.getTax()` method executions, first `Exception1()` will be thrown and then you will always have `Exception2()` thrown (until it's stubbed again).

Let's check the JUnit test. See *Chapter 1, Getting Started with Mockito*, for the TestNG configuration (remember that I'm using `BDDMockito.given(...)` and AssertJ's `BDDAssertions.then(...)` static methods. Check out *Chapter 7, Verifying Behavior with Object Matchers*, for more details on how to work with AssertJ or how to do the same with Hamcrest's `assertThat(...)`). The `when(...)` method comes from the `CatchExceptionAssertJ` class. This way, I can use `CatchExceptionAssertJ. thenThrown(...)` without any unnecessary code in between, as shown in the following code:

```
@RunWith(MockitoJUnitRunner.class)
public class MeanTaxFactorCalculatorTest {

    @Mock TaxFactorFetcher taxFactorFetcher;

    @InjectMocks MeanTaxFactorCalculator systemUnderTest;

    @Test
    public void should_throw_exception_when_calculating_mean_tax_
factor() {
        given(taxFactorFetcher.getTaxFactorFor(any(Person.class))).
willThrow(new TaxServiceUnavailableException());
```

```
                    when(systemUnderTest).calculateMeanTaxFactorFor(new Person());

                    thenThrown(TaxServiceUnavailableException.class);
        }

    }
```

It's worth taking a look at what happens in this test. Assuming that we have all of the mocks set up and injected, let's move to the test's body. Over there, first, we stub the `taxFactorFetcher.getTaxFactorFor(...)` method execution so that it throws a `TaxServiceUnavailableException` exception. Then, we use the `CatchExceptionAssertJ.when(...)` method to allow the `catch-exception` library to catch the thrown exception (if there is one). Finally, we use the `CatchExceptionAssertJ.thenThrown(TaxServiceUnavailableException. class)` method to check whether the thrown exception was of a proper type.

How it works...

Please refer to the *Stubbing methods that return values* recipe for more information on the Mockito internals related to stubbing methods so that they throw exceptions.

It's worth mentioning that eventually, when the `willThrow(...)` or `thenThrow(...)` code is called, Mockito constructs the `ThrowsException` answer with the passed exception and delegates the execution to it.

There's more...

Mockito allows for providing a series of possible stubbed exceptions either by using the fluent interface API or by means of varargs. The following snippet shows you how to stub a method and provide subsequent exceptions to be thrown by means of fluent API using JUnit (see *Chapter 1, Getting Started with Mockito,* for the TestNG configuration):

```
@RunWith(MockitoJUnitRunner.class)
public class MeanTaxFactorCalculatorTest {

    @Mock TaxFactorFetcher taxFactorFetcher;

    @InjectMocks MeanTaxFactorCalculator systemUnderTest;

    @Test
    public void should_throw_exception_when_calculating_mean_tax_
factor() {
        given(taxFactorFetcher.getTaxFactorFor(any(Person.class))).
willThrow(new TaxServiceUnavailableException()).
willThrow(new InvalidTaxFactorException());
```

```
when(systemUnderTest).calculateMeanTaxFactorFor(new Person());

thenThrown(TaxServiceUnavailableException.class);

when(systemUnderTest).calculateMeanTaxFactorFor(new Person());

thenThrown(InvalidTaxFactorException.class);
    }

}
```

To achieve the same result using varargs, take the following code:

```
given(taxFactorFetcher.getTaxFactorFor(any(Person.class))).
willThrow(new TaxServiceUnavailableException()).
willThrow(new InvalidTaxFactorException());
```

Then, change it to the following code:

```
given(taxFactorFetcher.getTaxFactorFor(any(Person.class))).
willThrow(new TaxServiceUnavailableException(), new
InvalidTaxFactorException());
```

See also

▸   Refer to the `catch-exception` library home page at `https://code.google.com/p/catch-exception/`

▸   Refer to *JUnit ExpectedException Rule vs. Catch-Exception* by Tomasz Kaczanowski at `http://www.kaczanowscy.pl/tomek/2013-03/junit-expected-exception-rule-vs-catch-exception`

Stubbing methods so that they return custom answers

In this recipe, we will stub a method that returns a value so that it returns a custom answer of our choice.

Getting ready

For this recipe, our system under test will again be `MeanTaxFactorCalculator`, which calls `TaxFactorFetcher` twice to get a tax factor for the given person, and then calculates a mean value for those two results as follows:

```
public class MeanTaxFactorCalculator {
```

```
        private final TaxFactorFetcher taxFactorFetcher;

        public MeanTaxFactorCalculator(TaxFactorFetcher taxFactorFetcher)
    {
            this.taxFactorFetcher = taxFactorFetcher;
        }

        public double calculateMeanTaxFactorFor(Person person) {
            double taxFactor = taxFactorFetcher.getTaxFactorFor(person);
            double anotherTaxFactor = taxFactorFetcher.
    getTaxFactorFor(person);
            return (taxFactor + anotherTaxFactor) / 2;
        }

    }
```

Let's assume that depending on whether the person is from a defined or undefined country, the logic of calculating the factor by `TaxFactorFetcher` is different.

How to do it...

To stub nonvoid methods so they execute the logic from the custom answer, you have to perform the following steps:

1. For the BDD approach, call `BDDMockito.given(mock.methodToStub())`. `willAnswer(answer)`, or in the standard way, call `Mockito.when(mock.methodToStub()).thenAnswer(answer)`.

2. Regardless of the chosen approach in the `given(...)` or `when(...)` method, you have to provide the mock's method call, and in `willAnswer(...)` or `thenAnswer(...)`, you have to provide the desired `Answer` implementation.

3. Remember that the last passed value during the stubbing will be returned for each stubbed method call. In other words, you stub the mock as follows:

   ```
   given(taxFetcher.getTax()).willAnswer(new Answer1(), new
   Answer2());
   ```

   Then, regardless of the number of `taxFetcher.getTax()` method executions, first `Answer1` will be executed, and then you will always have `Answer2` executed (until it is stubbed again).

Now, let's move to the JUnit test. See *Chapter 1, Getting Started with Mockito*, for the TestNG configuration (remember that I'm using `BDDMockito.given(...)` and AssertJ's `BDDAssertions.then(...)` static methods; check out *Chapter 7, Verifying Behavior with Object Matchers*, to learn how to work with AssertJ or how to do the same with Hamcrest's `assertThat(...)`):

```
@RunWith(MockitoJUnitRunner.class)
public class MeanTaxFactorCalculatorTest {
```

```java
    @Mock TaxFactorFetcher taxFactorFetcher;

    @InjectMocks MeanTaxFactorCalculator systemUnderTest;

    @Test
    public void should_return_tax_factor_incremented_by_additional_
factor_when_calculating_mean_tax_factor() {
        // given
      final double additionalTaxFactor = 100;
      final double factorForPersonFromUndefinedCountry = 200;
      given(taxFactorFetcher.getTaxFactorFor(any(Person.class)))
.willAnswer(new Answer<Object>() {
            @Override
            public Object answer(InvocationOnMock invocation) throws
Throwable {
                if (invocation.getArguments().length > 0) {
                    Person person = (Person) invocation.getArguments()
[0];

                    if (!person.isCountryDefined()) {
                        return additionalTaxFactor +
factorForPersonFromUndefinedCountry;
                    }
                }
                return additionalTaxFactor;
            }
        });

        // when
        double meanTaxFactor = systemUnderTest.
calculateMeanTaxFactorFor(new Person());

        // then
        then(meanTaxFactor).isEqualTo(additionalTaxFactor +
factorForPersonFromUndefinedCountry);
    }

}
```

 Another thing to remember is that most likely, you won't have the need to create any special answers. If that is the case, it's highly probable that your scenario is getting too complicated. For additional information regarding Answers, please refer to *Chapter 2, Creating Mocks*.

How it works...

Please refer to the *Stubbing methods that return values* recipe for more information on the Mockito internals related to stubbing methods so that they throw exceptions.

It's worth mentioning that eventually, when the `willThrow(...)` or `thenThrow(...)` code is called, Mockito constructs the `ThrowsException` answer with the passed exception and then delegates further execution to it.

There's more...

Mockito provides a series of possible answers to be executed either by using the fluent interface API, or by means of varargs.

You can perform stubbing via a fluent API as follows:

```
given(...).willAnswer(answer1).willAnswer(answer2)
...willAnswer(answer3)
```

Or, with the varargs style, you can perform the stubbing as follows:

```
given(...).willAnswer(answer1, answer2, …. answerN)
```

Please refer to the *There's more...* section of the *Stubbing methods so that they throw exception* recipe from this chapter for analogous test examples.

See also

▶   Refer to the Mockito documentation regarding stubbing with callbacks (answers) at `http://docs.mockito.googlecode.com/hg/1.9.5/org/mockito/Mockito.html#11`

Stubbing methods so that they call real methods

In this recipe, we will stub a method that returns a value so that it calls a real method. This way, we will construct a partial mock (to read more about partial mocking, please refer to *Chapter 2, Creating Mocks*).

Getting ready

For this recipe, our system under test will be `MeanTaxFactorCalculator`, which calls `TaxFactorFetcher` twice to get a tax factor for the given person and then calculates a mean value for those two results as follows:

```
public class MeanTaxFactorCalculator {

    private final TaxFactorFetcher taxFactorFetcher;

    public MeanTaxFactorCalculator(TaxFactorFetcher taxFactorFetcher)
{
        this.taxFactorFetcher = taxFactorFetcher;
    }

    public double calculateMeanTaxFactorFor(Person person) {
        double taxFactor = taxFactorFetcher.getTaxFactorFor(person);
        double anotherTaxFactor = taxFactorFetcher.
getTaxFactorFor(person);
        return (taxFactor + anotherTaxFactor) / 2;
    }

}
```

Unlike the previous recipes, `TaxFactorFetcher` will not be an interface but a concrete class.

How to do it...

To stub nonvoid methods so that they execute the logic from the custom answer, you have to perform the following steps:

1. For the BDD approach, call `BDDMockito.given(mock.methodToStub())`. `willCallRealMethod()`, or in the standard way, call `Mockito.when(mock.methodToStub()).thenCallRealMehod()`.

2. Regardless of the chosen approach in the `given(...)` or `when(...)` method, you have to provide the mock's method call.

3. Remember that the last passed value during the stubbing will be returned for each stubbed method call. In other words, say that you stub the mock as follows:

   `given(taxFetcher.getTax()).willReturn(2). willCallRealMethod()`

   Then, regardless of the number of `taxFetcher.getTax()` method executions, first 2 will be returned, and then you will always have the real logic executed (until it is stubbed again).

Now, let's move to the JUnit test. See *Chapter 1, Getting Started with Mockito*, for the TestNG configuration (remember that I'm using `BDDMockito.given(...)` and AssertJ's `BDDAssertions.then(...)` static methods. Check out *Chapter 7, Verifying Behavior with Object Matchers*, for more details on how to work with AssertJ or how to do the same with Hamcrest's `assertThat(...)`):

```
@RunWith(MockitoJUnitRunner.class)
public class MeanTaxFactorCalculatorTest {
```

```
@Mock TaxService taxService;

@InjectMocks MeanTaxFactorCalculator systemUnderTest;

@Test
public void should_return_mean_tax_factor() {
    // given
    double taxFactor = 15000;
    double expectedMeanTaxFactor = (TaxService.NO_COUNTRY_TAX_
FACTOR + taxFactor) / 2;
    given(taxService.getTaxFactorFor(any(Person.class))).
willCallRealMethod().willReturn(taxFactor);

    // when
    double meanTaxFactor = systemUnderTest.
calculateMeanTaxFactorFor(new Person());

    // then
    then(meanTaxFactor).isEqualTo(expectedMeanTaxFactor);
}

}
```

Another thing to remember is that if you need to create a partial mock, and if you really don't have some strong arguments to back that decision up, then you should rethink the architecture of your program or your tests since it is not of the best quality, most likely.

It's always crucial to remember the boy scout rule and the process of refactoring. You should work on your code and the code of your colleagues in an iterative manner, trying to make small improvements each time you operate on it.

See also

▸ Refer to the Mockito documentation on partial mocks at `http://docs.mockito.googlecode.com/hg/1.9.5/org/mockito/Mockito.html#16`

▸ Refer to *Chapter 3, Creating Spies and Partial Mocks*, for more details on partial mocks

Stubbing void methods

In this recipe, we will stub a void method that doesn't return a value. The trick with void methods is that Mockito assumes that they do nothing by default, so there is no need to explicitly stub them (although you may do it).

How to do it...

If you do not want your void method to execute logic, you need to perform the following steps:

1. Do nothing: Mockito stubs the method for you so that it does nothing.

2. Explicitly tell Mockito that the void method does nothing; for the BDD approach, call `BDDMockito.willNothing().given(mock).methodToStub()`, or in the standard way, call `Mockito.doNothing().when(mock).methodToStub()`.

3. Regardless of the chosen approach in the `given(...)` or `when(...)` method, you have to provide the mock object (and not the method call in the case of methods that return values).

4. Remember that the last passed value during the stubbing will be returned for each stubbed method call. In other words, say that you stub the mock as follows (the `willThrow` answer will be described in more detail in the next recipe):

   ```
   willThrow(new Exception1()).willNothing().given(personSaver).
   savePerson(smith);
   ```

   Then, regardless of the number of `personSaver.savePerson(...)` method executions, first an exception will be thrown, and then you will always have no action taken (until it is stubbed again).

How it works...

What Mockito does internally when you start stubbing using the methods starting with `do...(...)` or `will...(...)` is that the `MockitoCore.doAnswer(...)` method is executed with a proper answer, which, in the case of void methods that don't do anything, is the `DoesNothing` answer.

It's worth mentioning that as a result of the execution of the `doAnswer(...)` method, we have the `Stubber` interface returned, which has several fluent API methods (that return `Stubber` itself), for example, the following one:

```
Stubber doNothing();
```

It also provides us with a method that returns the stubbed object, the `when` method (`BDDMockito` delegates method execution to the `when` method as well).

```
<T> T when(T mock);
```

This is why you can profit from Mockito's fluent API, and when you call the when method, you have access to the mocked object's methods.

See also

▶ Refer to the Mockito documentation on the doReturn()|doThrow()|doAnswer())|doNothing()|doCallRealMethod() family of methods from http://docs. mockito.googlecode.com/hg/1.9.5/org/mockito/Mockito.html#12

Stubbing void methods so that they throw exceptions

In this recipe, we will stub a void method that doesn't return a value, so it throws an exception.

Getting ready

For this recipe, our system under test will be a PersonProcessor class that, for simplicity, does only one thing: it delegates the process of saving person to the PersonSaver class. As shown in the following code, in case of success, true is returned; otherwise, false is returned:

```java
public class PersonProcessor {

    private final PersonSaver personSaver;

    public PersonProcessor(PersonSaver personSaver) {
        this.personSaver = personSaver;
    }

    public boolean process(Person person) {
        try {
            personSaver.savePerson(person);
            return true;
        } catch (FailedToSavedPersonDataException e) {
            System.err.printf("Exception occurred while trying save
person data [%s]%n", e);
            return false;
        }
    }

}
```

How to do it...

If you want your void method to throw an exception upon calling, you need to perform the following steps:

1. Explicitly tell Mockito that the void method should throw an exception. For the BDD approach, call `BDDMockito.willThrow(exception).given(mock).methodToStub()`, or in the standard way, call `Mockito.doThrow(exception).when(mock).methodToStub()`.

2. Regardless of the chosen approach in the `given(...)` or `when(...)` method, you have to provide the mock object (and not the method call in the case of methods that return values).

3. Remember that the last passed value during the stubbing will be returned for each stubbed method call. In other words, say that you stub the mock as follows:

    ```
    willThrow(new Exception1()).willThrow(new Exception2()).
    given(personSaver).savePerson(smith);
    ```

    Then, regardless of the number of `personSaver.savePerson(...)` method executions, first `Exception1` will be thrown, and then you will always have `Exception2` thrown (until it is stubbed again).

Let's check the JUnit test. See *Chapter 1, Getting Started with Mockito*, for the TestNG configuration (remember that I'm using `BDDMockito.given(...)` and AssertJ's `BDDAssertions.then(...)` static methods. Check out *Chapter 7, Verifying Behavior with Object Matchers*, for more details on how to work with AssertJ or how to do the same with Hamcrest's `assertThat(...)`):

```
@RunWith(MockitoJUnitRunner.class)
public class PersonProcessorTest {

    @Mock PersonSaver personSaver;

    @InjectMocks PersonProcessor systemUnderTest;

    @Test
    public void should_fail_to_save_person_data_when_exception_
occurs() {
        // given
        willThrow(FailedToSavedPersonDataException.class)
.given(personSaver).savePerson(any(Person.class));

        // when
        boolean updateSuccessful =
systemUnderTest.process(new Person());

        // then
```

```
            then(updateSuccessful).isFalse();
    }

}
```

How it works...

Please refer to the *Stubbing void methods* recipe for more information on the Mockito internals that are related to stubbing void methods.

What's worth mentioning is that the answers that take part in the Mockito internal delegation process are either `ThrowsExceptionClass` or `ThrowsException` answers.

See also

▶ Refer to the Mockito documentation on the `doReturn()|doThrow()|doAnswer ()|doNothing()|doCallRealMethod()` family of methods at `http://docs. mockito.googlecode.com/hg/1.9.5/org/mockito/Mockito.html#12`

Stubbing void methods so that they return custom answers

In this recipe, we will stub a void method that doesn't return a value, so it returns a custom answer.

Getting ready

For this recipe, our system under test will be the same class as the one in the previous recipe, but let's take another look at it so that you don't need to scroll around to see the source code. The `PersonProcessor` class does only one thing for simplicity: it delegates the process of saving `person` to the `PersonSaver` class. As shown in the following code, in case of success, true is returned; otherwise, false is returned:

```
public class PersonProcessor {

    private final PersonSaver personSaver;

    public PersonProcessor(PersonSaver personSaver) {
        this.personSaver = personSaver;
    }

    public boolean process(Person person) {
        try {
```

```
            personSaver.savePerson(person);
            return true;
        } catch (FailedToSavedPersonDataException e) {
            System.err.printf("Exception occurred while trying save
person data [%s]%n", e);
            return false;
        }
    }

}
```

How to do it...

If you want your void method to throw an exception upon calling, you need to perform the following steps:

1. Explicitly tell Mockito that the void method does nothing. For the BDD approach, call `BDDMockito.willAnswer(answer).given(mock).methodToStub()`, or in the standard way, call `Mockito.doAnswer(answer).when(mock).methodToStub()`.

2. Regardless of the chosen approach in the `given(...)` or `when(...)` method, you have to provide the mock object (and not the method call like in the case of methods that return values).

3. Remember that the last passed value during the stubbing will be returned for each stubbed method call. In other words, say that you stub the mock as follows:

   ```
   willAnswer(answer1).willAnswer(answer2).given(personSaver).
   savePerson(smith);
   ```

   Then, regardless of the number of `personSaver.savePerson(...)` method executions, first `answer1` logic will be executed, and then you will always have the `answer2` logic executed (until it is stubbed again).

Let's check the JUnit test. See *Chapter 1, Getting Started with Mockito,* for the TestNG configuration (remember that I'm using `BDDMockito.given(...)` and AssertJ's `BDDAssertions.then(...)` static methods. Check out *Chapter 7, Verifying Behavior with Object Matchers,* for more details on how to work with AssertJ or how to do the same with Hamcrest's `assertThat(...)`):

```
@RunWith(MockitoJUnitRunner.class)
public class PersonProcessorTest {

    @Mock PersonSaver personSaver;

    @InjectMocks PersonProcessor systemUnderTest;

    @Test
```

```
        public void should_fail_to_save_person_data_due_to_having_
undefined_country() {
            // given
            willAnswer(new Answer() {
                @Override
                public Object answer(InvocationOnMock invocation) throws
Throwable {
                    if (invocation.getArguments().length > 0) {
                        Person person = (Person) invocation.getArguments()
[0];
                        if (!person.isCountryDefined()) {
                            throw new FailedToSavedPersonDataException("Un
defined country");
                        }
                    }
                    return null;
                }
            }).given(personSaver).savePerson(any(Person.class));

            // when
            boolean updateSuccessful =
systemUnderTest.process(new Person());

            // then
            then(updateSuccessful).isFalse();
        }

    }
```

How it works...

Please refer to the *Stubbing void methods* recipe for more information on the Mockito internals related to stubbing void methods.

As you can see, the `Answer` interface has the following method:

```
public Object answer(InvocationOnMock invocation) throws Throwable
```

Note that since we have a void method to stub, we don't care about the answer's returned value. That is why we return null in the answer's body.

▸ Refer to the Mockito documentation on the `doReturn()|doThrow()|doAnswer()|doNothing()|doCallRealMethod()` family of methods at `http://docs.mockito.googlecode.com/hg/1.9.5/org/mockito/Mockito.html#12`

▸ Refer to the Mockito documentation on the stubbing with callbacks at `http://docs.mockito.googlecode.com/hg/1.9.5/org/mockito/Mockito.html#11`

Stubbing void methods so that they call real methods

In this recipe, we will stub a method that is a void method. It doesn't return a value, so it calls a real method. This way, we will construct a partial mock (to read more about partial mocking, please refer to *Chapter 2, Creating Mocks*).

Getting ready

For this recipe, our system under test will be the same class as in the previous recipe, but let's take another look at it so that you don't need to scroll around to see the source code. The `PersonProcessor` class, for simplicity, does only one thing: it delegates the process of saving `person` to the `PersonSaver` class. As shown in the following code, in case of success, true is returned; otherwise, false is returned:

```java
public class PersonProcessor {

    private final PersonSaver personSaver;

    public PersonProcessor(PersonSaver personSaver) {
        this.personSaver = personSaver;
    }

    public boolean process(Person person) {
        try {
            personSaver.savePerson(person);
            return true;
        } catch (FailedToSavedPersonDataException e) {
            System.err.printf("Exception occurred while trying save
person data [%s]%n", e);
            return false;
        }
    }

}
```

Contrary to the previous recipe, `PersonSaver` is a class and not an interface. This verifies whether the person's origin is defined. If that is not the case, then `FailedToSavedPersonDataException` will be thrown.

How to do it...

If you want your void method to call real methods upon calling the void method, you need to perform the following steps:

1. Explicitly tell Mockito that the void method should call the real implementation. For the BDD approach, call `BDDMockito.willCallRealMethod().given(mock).methodToStub()`, or in the standard way, call `Mockito.doCallRealMethod().when(mock).methodToStub()`.

2. Regardless of the chosen approach in the `given(...)` or `when(...)` method, you have to provide the mock object (and not the method call like in case of methods that return values).

3. Remember that the last passed value during the stubbing will be returned for each stubbed method call. In other words, say that you stub the mock as follows:

    ```
    willCallRealMethod().willNothing().given(personSaver)
    .savePerson(smith);
    ```

    This example shows you how to make your void method call the real method only once, and then do nothing, by default. Regardless of the number of `personSaver.savePerson(...)` method executions, first the real implementation will be called, and then you will always have no further execution (until it is stubbed again).

Let's check the JUnit test. See *Chapter 1, Getting Started with Mockito*, for the TestNG configuration (remember that I'm using `BDDMockito.given(...)` and AssertJ's `BDDAssertions.then(...)` static methods. Check out *Chapter 7, Verifying Behavior with Object Matchers*, for more details on how to work with AssertJ or how to do the same with Hamcrest's `assertThat(...)`):

```
@RunWith(MockitoJUnitRunner.class)
public class PersonProcessorTest {

    @Mock PersonSaver personSaver;

    @InjectMocks PersonProcessor systemUnderTest;

    @Test
    public void should_fail_to_save_person_data_due_to_having_
undefined_country() {
        // given
        willCallRealMethod().given(personSaver).
savePerson(any(Person.class));

        // when
```

```
        boolean updateSuccessful = systemUnderTest.
updatePersonData(new Person());

        // then
        then(updateSuccessful).isFalse();
    }


}
```

Remember that if you need to create a partial mock, and if you really don't have some strong arguments to back that decision up, then you should rethink the architecture of your program or your tests since it most likely is not the best quality. Please refer to *Chapter 3, Creating Spies and Partial Mocks*, for more details.

How it works...

Please refer to the *Stubbing void methods* recipe for more information on the Mockito internals related to stubbing void methods.

What's worth mentioning is that the answer-taking part in the Mockito internal delegation process is the `CallsRealMethod` answer.

See also

▶ Refer to the Mockito documentation on the `doReturn()|doThrow()|doAnswer()|doNothing()|doCallRealMethod()` family of methods at `http://docs.mockito.googlecode.com/hg/1.9.5/org/mockito/Mockito.html#12`

Stubbing final methods with PowerMock

In this recipe, we will stub a final method and verify the behavior of the system under test. Since Mockito can't stub methods that are final, we'll use PowerMock to do it.

Remember that it absolutely isn't good practice to use PowerMock in your well-written code. If you follow all of the SOLID principles (please refer to *Chapter 2, Creating Mocks*, for the explanation of each of these principles), then you should not resort to stubbing final methods. PowerMock can come in hand when dealing with the legacy code or stubbing third-party libraries (you can check *Chapter 8, Refactoring with Mockito*, to see how to use PowerMock to refactor the badly written code).

Getting ready

To use PowerMock, you have to add it to your classpath. Please check the *Creating mocks of final classes with PowerMock* recipe in *Chapter 2, Creating Mocks*, for more details on how to add PowerMock to your project.

For this recipe, our system under test will be `MeanTaxFactorCalculator`, which calls a `TaxFactorFetcher` object twice to get a tax factor for the given person and then calculates a mean value for those two results:

```
public class MeanTaxFactorCalculator {

    private final TaxFactorFetcher taxFactorFetcher;

    public MeanTaxFactorCalculator(TaxFactorFetcher taxFactorFetcher)
{
        this.taxFactorFetcher = taxFactorFetcher;
    }

    public double calculateMeanTaxFactorFor(Person person) {
        double taxFactor = taxFactorFetcher.getTaxFactorFor(person);
        double anotherTaxFactor = taxFactorFetcher.
getTaxFactorFor(person);
        return (taxFactor + anotherTaxFactor) / 2;
    }

}
```

Let's assume that `TaxFactorFetcher` is a class that returns a proper tax factor (for readability purposes, we'll omit going through its implementation since it's irrelevant for this recipe) based on the person's origin. One thing worth noting is that `TaxFactorFetcher.getTaxFactorFor(...)` is a final method.

How to do it...

To use PowerMock with JUnit to stub a final method, you have to perform the following steps:

1. Annotate your test class with `@RunWith(PowerMockRunner.class)`.
2. Provide all of the classes that need to be prepared for testing (most likely, bytecode manipulated classes) in the `@PrepareForTest` annotation (in the case of our scenario, it would be `@PrepareForTest(TaxFactorFetcher .class)` since `TaxFactorFetcher` has a final method that we want to stub). In general, the class that needs to be prepared for testing would include classes with final, private, static or native methods, classes that are final and that should be spied, and also classes that should be returned as spies on instantiation.
3. Use Mockito annotations in a standard way to set up test doubles.

Let's take a look at the JUnit test which will verify whether the tax factor is properly calculated (remember that I'm using `BDDMockito.given(...)` and AssertJ's `BDDAssertions.then(...)` static methods. Check out *Chapter 7, Verifying Behavior with Object Matchers*, for details on how to work with AssertJ or how to do the same with Hamcrest's `assertThat(...)`):

```
@RunWith(PowerMockRunner.class)
@PrepareForTest(TaxFactorFetcher.class)
public class MeanTaxFactorCalculatorTest {

    @Mock TaxFactorFetcher taxFactorFetcher;

    @InjectMocks MeanTaxFactorCalculator systemUnderTest;

    @Test
    public void should_calculate_tax_factor_for_a_player_with_
undefined_country() {
        // given
      double expectedMeanTaxFactor = 10;
        given(taxFactorFetcher.
getTaxFactorFor(any(Person.class))).willReturn(5.5, 14.5);

        // when
        double meanTaxFactor = systemUnderTest.
calculateMeanTaxFactorFor(new Person());

        // then
        then(meanTaxFactor).isEqualTo(expectedMeanTaxFactor);
    }

}
```

To use PowerMock with TestNG to create a spy for final classes, you have to perform the following steps:

1. Make your class extend the `PowerMockTestCase` class.
2. Implement a method annotated with the `@ObjectFactory` annotation that returns an instance of the `PowerMockObjectFactory` class (this object factory will be used for the creation of all object instances in the test).
3. Provide all of the classes that need to be prepared for testing (most likely bytecode manipulated classes) in the `@PrepareForTest` annotation (in the case of our scenario, this would be `@PrepareForTest(TaxFactorFetcher .class)` since `TaxFactorFetcher` has a final method that we want to stub).
4. Use Mockito annotations in a standard way to set up test doubles.

5. Let's take a look at the TestNG test which will verify whether the tax factor is properly calculated (refer to the introduction to the analogous JUnit example in terms of the BDDMockito and BDDAssertions usage):

```
@PrepareForTest(TaxFactorFetcher.class)
public class MeanTaxFactorCalculatorTestNgTest extends
PowerMockTestCase {

    @Mock TaxFactorFetcher taxFactorFetcher;

    @InjectMocks MeanTaxFactorCalculator systemUnderTest;

    @Test
    public void should_calculate_tax_factor_for_a_player_with_
undefined_country() {
        // given
        double expectedTaxFactor = 10;
        given(taxFactorFetcher.getTaxFactorFor(any(Person.class))).
willReturn(5.5, 14.5);

        // when
        double taxFactorForPerson = systemUnderTest.
calculateMeanTaxFactorFor(new Person());

        // then
        then(taxFactorForPerson).isEqualTo(expectedTaxFactor);
    }

    @ObjectFactory
    public IObjectFactory getObjectFactory() {
        return new PowerMockObjectFactory();
    }
}
```

In the majority of cases, if working on a well-written code base, you should not have the need to use PowerMock at all. There are cases, however, when dealing with the legacy code or third-party dependencies that you would like to mock where using PowerMock comes in handy.

The best approach with using PowerMock is to make it a mean to refactor your codebase into one that doesn't need any of PowerMock's tweaking.

How it works...

The internals of PowerMock go far beyond the scope of this recipe. However, the overall concept is such that part of the PowerMockRunner's logic is to create a custom classloader and byte-code manipulation for the classes defined using the `@PrepareForTest` annotation in order to mock them and use these mocks with the standard Mockito API. Due to bytecode manipulations, PowerMock can ignore a series of constraints of the Java language, such as extending final classes.

See also

- ► Refer to the PowerMock website at `https://code.google.com/p/powermock/`
- ► Refer to *Chapter 8, Refactoring with Mockito,* to see how to use different approaches and tools such as PowerMock to refactor bad code

Stubbing static methods with PowerMock

The current recipe will be about stubbing a static method in order to properly verify the behavior of the system under test. Unfortunately, Mockito can't stub static methods, and that's why we will use PowerMock to do that.

I'd like to yet again remind you that it absolutely isn't good practice to use PowerMock in your well-written code. If you follow all of the SOLID principles (please refer to *Chapter 2, Creating Mocks,* for the explanation of each of these principles), then you should not resort to stubbing static methods. PowerMock can come in hand when dealing with legacy code or stubbing third-party libraries (you can check *Chapter 8, Refactoring with Mockito,* to see how to use PowerMock to refactor the badly written code).

Getting ready

To use PowerMock, you have to add it to your classpath. Please check the *Creating mocks of final classes with PowerMock* recipe in *Chapter 2, Creating Mocks,* for more details on how to add PowerMock to your project.

For this recipe, our system under test will be `MeanTaxFactorCalculator`, which calls a `TaxFactorFetcher` object's static methods twice to get a tax factor for the given person and then calculates a mean value for these two results, as follows:

```
public class MeanTaxFactorCalculator {

    public double calculateTaxFactorFor(Person person) {
        double taxFactor = TaxFactorFetcher.getTaxFactorFor(person);
        double anotherTaxFactor = TaxFactorFetcher.
getTaxFactorFor(person);
```

```
        return (taxFactor + anotherTaxFactor) / 2;
    }

}
```

Let's assume that `TaxFactorFetcher` is a class that checks what country the person is from, and depending on that piece of information, it returns a proper tax factor (for readability purposes, we will not go into any details regarding this). Note that `TaxFactorFetcher.getTaxFactorFor(...)` is a static method.

How to do it...

To use PowerMock with JUnit to stub a static method, you have to perform the following steps:

1. Annotate your test class with `@RunWith(PowerMockRunner.class)`.

2. Provide all of the classes that need to be prepared for testing (most likely, bytecode manipulated classes) in the `@PrepareForTest` annotation (in the case of our scenario, this would be `@PrepareForTest(TaxFactorFetcher .class)` since `TaxFactorFetcher` has a static method that we want to stub).

3. Before stubbing a static method, you have to call the `PowerMockito.mockStatic(...)` method to start the stubbing of static methods in the class.

4. Stub static methods in a standard way as you would while using objects.

5. Use Mockito annotations in a standard way to set up test doubles.

Let's take a look at the JUnit test which will verify whether the tax factor is properly calculated (remember that I'm using `BDDMockito.given(...)` and AssertJ's `BDDAssertions.then(...)` static methods. Check out *Chapter 7, Verifying Behavior with Object Matchers*, for more details on how to work with AssertJ or how to do the same with Hamcrest's `assertThat(...)`):

```
@RunWith(PowerMockRunner.class)
@PrepareForTest(TaxFactorFetcher.class)
public class MeanTaxFactorCalculatorTest {

    MeanTaxFactorCalculator systemUnderTest =
new MeanTaxFactorCalculator();

    @Test
    public void should_calculate_tax_factor_for_a_player_with_
undefined_country() {
        // given
      double expectedMeanTaxFactor = 10;
        mockStatic(TaxFactorFetcher.class);
        given(TaxFactorFetcher.getTaxFactorFor
(any(Person.class))).willReturn(5.5, 14.5);
```

```
        // when
        double taxFactorForPerson = systemUnderTest.
calculateTaxFactorFor(new Person());

        // then
        then(taxFactorForPerson).
isEqualTo(expectedMeanTaxFactor);
    }

}
```

To use PowerMock with TestNG to create a spy for final classes, you have to perform the following steps:

1. Make your class extend the `PowerMockTestCase` class.
2. Implement a method annotated with the `@ObjectFactory` annotation that returns an instance of the `PowerMockObjectFactory` class (this object factory will be used for the creation of all object instances in the test).
3. Provide all of the classes that need to be prepared for testing (most likely, bytecode manipulated classes) in the `@PrepareForTest` annotation (in the case of our scenario, this would be `@PrepareForTest(TaxFactorFetcher .class)` since `TaxFactorFetcher` has a final method that we want to stub).
4. Before stubbing a static method, you have to call the `PowerMockito. mockStatic(...)` method to start the stubbing of static methods in the class.
5. Stub static methods in a standard way as you would while using objects.
6. Use Mockito annotations in a standard way to set up test doubles.

Let's take a look at the TestNG test which will verify whether the tax factor is properly calculated (refer to the introduction to the analogous JUnit example, as discussed earlier, in terms of the `BDDMockito` and `BDDAssertions` usage):

```
@PrepareForTest(TaxFactorFetcher.class)
public class MeanTaxFactorCalculatorTestNgTest extends
PowerMockTestCase {

    MeanTaxFactorCalculator systemUnderTest = new
MeanTaxFactorCalculator();

    @Test
    public void should_calculate_tax_factor_for_a_player_with_
undefined_country() {
        // given
        double expectedMeanTaxFactor = 10;
        mockStatic(TaxFactorFetcher.class);
        given(TaxFactorFetcher.
getTaxFactorFor(any(Person.class))).willReturn(5.5, 14.5);
```

```
        // when
        double taxFactorForPerson = systemUnderTest.
calculateTaxFactorFor(new Person());

        // then
        then(taxFactorForPerson).isEqualTo(expectedMeanTaxFactor);
    }

    @ObjectFactory
    public IObjectFactory getObjectFactory() {
        return new PowerMockObjectFactory();
    }

}
```

In the majority of cases, if working on a well-written codebase, you should not need to use PowerMock at all. There are cases, however, when dealing with legacy code or third-party dependencies that you would like to mock where using PowerMock can be handy.

The best approach when using PowerMock is to make it a mean to refactor your codebase into the one that doesn't need any of PowerMock's tweaking.

How it works...

The internals of PowerMock go far beyond the scope of this recipe. However, the overall concept is such that part of the logic of `PowerMockRunner` is to create a custom classloader and bytecode manipulation for the classes defined using the `@PrepareForTest` annotation in order to mock them and use these mocks with the standard Mockito API. Due to bytecode manipulations, PowerMock can ignore a series of constraints of the Java language, such as extending final classes.

See also

▸ Refer to the PowerMock website at `https://code.google.com/p/powermock/`

▸ Refer to *Chapter 8, Refactoring with Mockito*, to see how to use different approaches and tools such as PowerMock to refactor bad code

Stubbing object instantiation using PowerMock

In some badly written code, you can find cases in which the system under test's collaborators are not passed into the object in any way (for example, by the constructor), but the object itself instantiates them via the `new` operator. The best practice would be to not write like this in the first place. But let's assume that you have inherited such a code and, since we follow the boy scout rule, that you should leave the code that you've encountered in a better state than you the one in which you have found it in the first place. We have to do something about this.

The very step of the refactoring of such a scenario is presented in *Chapter 8, Refactoring with Mockito*. This is why, in the current recipe, we will just learn how to stub object initialization in such a way that instead of creating a new instance of an object, a mock will be returned. Unfortunately, Mockito can't perform such stubbing, and that's why we will use PowerMock to do that.

Even though you might have already seen this warning, I'd like to yet again remind you that it absolutely isn't a good practice to use PowerMock in your well-written code. If you follow all of the SOLID principles (please refer to *Chapter 2, Creating Mocks*, for the explanation of each of those principles), then you should not resort to stubbing static methods. PowerMock can come in handy when dealing with the legacy code or stubbing third-party libraries (you can check *Chapter 8, Refactoring with Mockito*, to see how to use PowerMock to refactor the badly written code).

Getting ready

To use PowerMock, you have to add it to your classpath. Please check the *Creating mocks of final classes with PowerMock* recipe in *Chapter 2, Creating Mocks*, for more details on how to add PowerMock to your project.

For this recipe, our system under test will be `MeanTaxFactorCalculator`, which calls a `TaxFactorFetcher` object's static methods twice to get a tax factor for the given person and then calculates a mean value for those two results as follows:

```
public class MeanTaxFactorCalculator {

    public double calculateMeanTaxFactorFor(Person person) {
       TaxFactorFetcher taxFactorFetcher = new TaxFactorFetcher();
        double taxFactor = taxFactorFetcher.getTaxFactorFor(person);
        double anotherTaxFactor = taxFactorFetcher.
getTaxFactorFor(person);
        return (taxFactor + anotherTaxFactor) / 2;
    }

}
```

Let's assume that `TaxFactorFetcher` is a class that calculates a person's tax factor in a different way depending on his or her origin.

How to do it...

To use PowerMock with JUnit to stub object instantiation, you have to perform the following steps:

1. Annotate your test class with `@RunWith(PowerMockRunner.class)`.

2. Provide all of the classes that need to be prepared for testing (most likely, bytecode manipulated classes) in the `@PrepareForTest` annotation (in the case of our scenario, this would be `@PrepareForTest(MeanTaxFactorCalculator.class)` since that class needs to be manipulated in order to stub the execution of the `TaxFactorFetcher` constructor).

3. Stub object initialization by calling the `PowerMockito.whenNew(ClassToStub.class)` method together with additional stubbing configuration (whether the constructor has no arguments or has precisely provided parameters, and so on).

4. Use Mockito annotations in a standard way to set up test doubles.

Let's take a look at the JUnit test which will verify whether the tax factor is properly calculated (remember that I'm using `BDDMockito.given(...)` and AssertJ's `BDDAssertions.then(...)` static methods. Check out *Chapter 7, Verifying Behavior with Object Matchers*, for more details on how to work with AssertJ or how to do the same with Hamcrest's `assertThat(...)`):

```
@RunWith(PowerMockRunner.class)
@PrepareForTest(MeanTaxFactorCalculator.class)
public class MeanTaxFactorCalculatorTest {

    @Mock TaxFactorFetcher taxFactorFetcher;

   MeanTaxFactorCalculator systemUnderTest = new
MeanTaxFactorCalculator();

    @Test
    public void should_calculate_tax_factor_for_a_player_from_
undefined_country() throws Exception {
        // given
      double expectedMeanTaxFactor = 10;
      whenNew(TaxFactorFetcher.class).withNoArguments()
.thenReturn(taxFactorFetcher);
        given(taxFactorFetcher.getTaxFactorFor
(any(Person.class))).willReturn(5.5, 14.5);

        // when
```

```
        double meanTaxFactor = systemUnderTest.
calculateMeanTaxFactorFor(new Person());

        // then
        then(meanTaxFactor).isEqualTo(expectedMeanTaxFactor);
    }

}
```

To use PowerMock with TestNG to create a spy for final classes, you have to perform the following steps:

1. Make your class extend the `PowerMockTestCase` class.

2. Implement a method annotated with the `@ObjectFactory` annotation that returns an instance of the `PowerMockObjectFactory` class (this object factory will be used for the creation of all object instances in the test).

3. Provide all of the classes that need to be prepared for testing (most likely bytecode manipulated) in the `@PrepareForTest` annotation (in the case of our scenario, this would be `@PrepareForTest(MeanTaxFactorCalculator.class)` since that class needs to be manipulated in order to stub the execution of the `TaxFactorFetcher` constructor).

4. Stub object initialization by calling the `PowerMockito.whenNew(ClassToStub.class)` method together with the additional stubbing configuration (whether the constructor has no arguments or has precisely provided parameters, and so on).

5. Use Mockito annotations in a standard way to set up test doubles.

Let's take a look at the TestNG test which will verify whether the tax factor is properly calculated (refer to the introduction to the analogous JUnit example discussed earlier in terms of the `BDDMockito` and `BDDAssertions` usage):

```
@PrepareForTest(MeanTaxFactorCalculator.class)
public class MeanTaxFactorCalculatorTestNgTest extends
PowerMockTestCase {

  @Mock TaxFactorFetcher taxFactorFetcher;

  MeanTaxFactorCalculator systemUnderTest = new
MeanTaxFactorCalculator();

  @Test
  public void should_calculate_tax_factor_for_a_player_from_undefined_
country() throws Exception {
    // given
    double expectedMeanTaxFactor = 10;
    whenNew(TaxFactorFetcher.class).withNoArguments()
.thenReturn(taxFactorFetcher);
```

```
        given(taxFactorFetcher.getTaxFactorFor
    (any(Person.class))).willReturn(5.5, 14.5);

        // when
        double meanTaxFactor = systemUnderTest.
    calculateMeanTaxFactorFor(new Person());

        // then
        then(meanTaxFactor).isEqualTo(expectedMeanTaxFactor);
    }


    @ObjectFactory
    public IObjectFactory getObjectFactory() {
        return new PowerMockObjectFactory();
    }

}
```

Please remember that you should resort to stubbing object instantiation only if you absolutely know what you are doing: you are familiar with the SOLID principles and you are going to follow them. There are cases (dealing with the legacy code or third-party dependencies) that you would like to mock where using PowerMock can be handy.

Use PowerMock to write the tests for the bad code and then refactor it so that you no longer need to have PowerMock on the classpath.

How it works...

The internals of PowerMock go far beyond the scope of this recipe, but the overall concept is such that part of the logic of `PowerMockRunner` is to create a custom classloader and bytecode manipulation for the classes defined using the `@PrepareForTest` annotation in order to mock them and use these mocks with the standard Mockito API. Due to bytecode manipulations, PowerMock can ignore a series of constraints of the Java language, such as extending final classes.

See also

▶ Refer to the PowerMock website at `https://code.google.com/p/powermock/`

▶ Refer to *Chapter 8, Refactoring with Mockito*, to see how to use different approaches and tools such as PowerMock to refactor bad code

5
Stubbing Behavior of Spies

In this chapter, we will cover the following recipes:

- ▶ Stubbing methods that return values
- ▶ Stubbing methods so that they throw exceptions
- ▶ Stubbing methods so that they return custom answers
- ▶ Stubbing void methods
- ▶ Stubbing void methods so that they throw exceptions
- ▶ Stubbing void methods so that they return custom answers
- ▶ Stubbing final methods with PowerMock

Introduction

As presented in previous chapters, Mockito is all about creating mocks and stubbing their behavior. In comparison to the previous chapter, which focused on mocks, in this chapter we will take a look at partial mocks, also known as spies. Spies are mocks that by default call real implementations. Additionally, you can also perform verification on such objects.

Remember that usually you shouldn't have the need to create a spy. You might want to create a spy as an exception to the rule because partial mocks do not fit into the paradigm of single responsibility—the S from SOLID principles that we described in depth in *Chapter 2, Creating Mocks*. In other words, you should only use that technique when there is no other option. If you need to create a partial mock and stub a part of its logic, it most likely means that your architecture is wrong. In the vast majority of cases, for a new, well designed, test-driven system, there should be no need to create spies. I encourage you to check *Chapter 3, Creating Spies and Partial Mocks*, to see the danger related to using spies and partial mocks. The need to create a partial mock most likely signifies that your class is doing too much work; check out the *Refactoring classes that do too much* recipe of *Chapter 8, Refactoring with Mockito*, to see an example of how to refactor a class.

After reading this chapter, you will be able to stub spy methods that either return values or are void. You will learn how to provide stubbed results or how to throw exceptions. We will also show how to stub final methods of spies (hopefully, you'll never need to use this; if you do, it means that something is wrong with your code or you're integrating with some third-party piece of software that is badly written).

The purpose of all these examples is to show how to work with spies, but the tests could and, in fact, should be written without them. Let's assume that what we are trying to achieve is a partial mock for functional tests where we don't want to set up a database; instead, we'll stub the responses from the database and the rest of the object until test functionalities work as they should. The test should be rewritten keeping in mind that an in-memory database is used.

As done in the previous chapter, we will not verify implementation (check if a method on a mock has been executed a defined number of times or in a given sequence) but verify whether the object under the test's logic does what it is supposed to do. Imagine that you change some algorithm inside the collaborator but at the end of the day you want the object under test to work in exactly the same manner; if you test the implementation of your methods and not the behavior of your system, your test will fail. In other words, in the majority of cases, you don't want to know exactly how something is done; you want to know what is its outcome.

 Remember, whenever possible, verify behavior and not implementation.

Stubbing methods that return values

In this recipe, we will stub a method that returns a value so that it returns our desired result.

Getting ready

For this recipe, our system under test will be `AverageTaxFactorCalculator` along with the `TaxFactorFetcher` class. Together, they form a unit whose purpose is to calculate the average factor. The `TaxFactorFetcher` class is called twice: once to get a tax factor from DB and once to get a tax factor for a given person. Then, it calculates an average out of those values. Have a look at the following code:

```
public class AverageTaxFactorCalculator {

    private final TaxFactorFetcher taxFactorFetcher;

    public AverageTaxFactorCalculator(TaxFactorFetcher
taxFactorFetcher) {
        this.taxFactorFetcher = taxFactorFetcher;
    }

    public double calculateAvgTaxFactorFor(Person person) {
        double taxFactor = taxFactorFetcher.
getTaxFactorFromDb(person);
        double anotherTaxFactor = taxFactorFetcher.
getTaxFactorFor(person);
        return (taxFactor + anotherTaxFactor) / 2;
    }

}
```

The implementation of the `TaxFactorFetcher` looks as follows:

```
public class TaxFactorFetcher {

    static final double NO_COUNTRY_TAX_FACTOR = 0.3;
    static final double DEFAULT_TAX_FACTOR = 0.5;
    static final double DB_TAX_FACTOR = 0.8;

    public double getTaxFactorFor(Person person) {
        if (person.isCountryDefined()) {
            return DEFAULT_TAX_FACTOR;
        }
        return NO_COUNTRY_TAX_FACTOR;
    }

    public double getTaxFactorFromDb(Person person) {
        // simulation of DB access
        return DB_TAX_FACTOR;
    }
}
```

How to do it...

We would like to test our system as a whole without calling the database, so we will have to only partially stub `TaxFactorFetcher`. To do this, perform the following steps:

1. For the BDD approach, call `BDDMockito.willReturn(value).given(spy).methodToStub()`. Or, in the standard manner, call `Mockito.doReturn(value).when(spy).methodToStub()`.

2. Whichever approach you've chosen, you have to provide the desired output in the `willReturn(...)` or `thenReturn(...)` method, and pass the spy itself in the `given(...)` or `when(...)` method.

3. Remember that the last passed value during stubbing will be returned for each stubbed method call. Have a look at the following code:

   ```
   willReturn(50,100).given(taxFetcher).getTax();
   ```

   As shown in the preceding line of code, regardless of the number of `taxFetcher.getTax()` method executions, you will first return `50` and then always receive `100` (until stubbed again).

 You have to bear in mind that if you try to stub a method with the `BDDMockito.given(...).willReturn(...)` call or in the standard manner—with the `Mockito.when(...).thenReturn(...)` call—then you will actually call the spy's method that you want to stub!

The following snippet depicts the aforementioned scenario for JUnit. See *Chapter 1, Getting Started with Mockito,* for the TestNG configuration (I'm using the `BDDMockito.given(...)` and AssertJ's `BDDAssertions.then(...)` static methods. Check out *Chapter 7, Verifying Behavior with Object Matchers,* for more details on how to work with AssertJ or how to do the same with Hamcrest's `assertThat(...)`). Have a look at the following snippet:

```
@RunWith(MockitoJUnitRunner.class)
public class AverageTaxFactorCalculatorTest {

    @Spy TaxFactorFetcher taxFactorFetcher;

    @InjectMocks AverageTaxFactorCalculator systemUnderTest;

    @Test
    public void should_calculate_avg_tax_factor_for_person_without_a_
country() {
        // given
        double storedTaxFactor = 10;
        double expectedAvgTaxFactor = 12;
```

```
        willReturn(storedTaxFactor).given(taxFactorFetcher).
getTaxFactorFromDb(any(Person.class));

        // when
        double avgTaxFactor = systemUnderTest.
calculateAvgTaxFactorFor(new Person());

        // then
        then(avgTaxFactor).isEqualTo(expectedAvgTaxFactor);
    }


}
```

How it works...

A spy is a special case of a mock. Refer to the *Stubbing methods that return values* recipe of *Chapter 4*, *Stubbing Behavior of Mocks*, for more information.

There's more...

Mockito allows you to provide a series of possible stubbed results either by using the fluent interface API or by means of varargs.

If you need to pass a series of return values to the stubbed spy's method using the fluent API, you will have to stub the method invocation as follows:

```
willReturn(obj1).willReturn(obj2).given(spy).methodToStub()
```

Or, if you want to use varargs, you will have do it as follows:

```
willReturn(obj1, obj2).given(spy).methodToStub()
```

See also

▶ Refer to the xUnit pattern's comparison of test doubles at
  `http://xunitpatterns.com/Mocks,%20Fakes,%20Stubs%20and%20Dummies.html`

▶ Refer to the Mockito documentation on spying real instances at
  `http://docs.mockito.googlecode.com/hg/1.9.5/org/mockito/Mockito.html#13`

Stubbing methods so that they throw exceptions

In this recipe, we will stub a method that returns a value so that it throws an exception. Since we want our code to be beautiful, we'll use the `catch-exception` library to catch and check the exceptions thrown in our system.

Getting ready

Ensure that you have the `catch-exception` library on your classpath; refer to the *Stubbing methods so that they throw exceptions* recipe of *Chapter 4, Stubbing Behavior of Mocks*, for details on how to add `catch-exception` to your project.

This recipe will reuse the example from the previous recipe. We have a class that calculates an average value of tax factors (`AverageTaxFactorCalculator`) and `TaxFactorFetcher` is the provider of those values. One of the values is picked from the database (and we'll stub that method). We will test those two classes as a unit. For your convenience (so that you don't scroll around the book too much), I'm showing you the classes here (don't worry, they're really small):

```
public class AverageTaxFactorCalculator {

    private final TaxFactorFetcher taxFactorFetcher;

    public AverageTaxFactorCalculator(TaxFactorFetcher
taxFactorFetcher) {
        this.taxFactorFetcher = taxFactorFetcher;
    }

    public double calculateAvgTaxFactorFor(Person person) {
        double taxFactor = taxFactorFetcher.
getTaxFactorFromDb(person);
        double anotherTaxFactor = taxFactorFetcher.
getTaxFactorFor(person);
        return (taxFactor + anotherTaxFactor) / 2;
    }

}
```

And its collaborator, `TaxFactorFetcher`, is as follows:

```
public class TaxFactorFetcher {

    static final double NO_COUNTRY_TAX_FACTOR = 0.3;
```

```
    static final double DEFAULT_TAX_FACTOR = 0.5;
    static final double DB_TAX_FACTOR = 0.8;

    public double getTaxFactorFor(Person person) {
        if (person.isCountryDefined()) {
            return DEFAULT_TAX_FACTOR;
        }
        return NO_COUNTRY_TAX_FACTOR;
    }

    public double getTaxFactorFromDb(Person person) {
        // simulation of DB access
        return DB_TAX_FACTOR;
    }
}
}
```

How to do it...

To make your spy throw an exception instead of executing the real logic, you have to follow these simple steps:

1. For the BDD approach, call `BDDMockito.willReturn(value).given(spy).methodToStub()`. Or, in the standard manner, call `Mockito.doReturn(value).when(spy).methodToStub()`.

2. Whichever approach you've chosen, you have to provide the desired output in `willReturn(...)` or `thenReturn(...)`, and pass the spy itself in the `given(...)` or `when(...)` method.

3. Remember that the value that was passed last during stubbing will be returned for each stubbed method call. Have a look at the following line of code:

   `willThrow(exception1, exception2).given(taxFetcher).getTax();`

   As shown in the preceding line of code, regardless of the number of `taxFetcher.getTax()` method executions, you will first throw `exception1` and then always throw `exception2` (until stubbed again).

 You have to bear in mind that if you try to stub a method with the `BDDMockito.given(...).willReturn(...)` call or in the standard manner—you stub a method with the `Mockito.when(...).thenReturn(...)` call—then you will actually call the spy's method that you want to stub!

Let's check the JUnit test; see *Chapter 1, Getting Started with Mockito,* for the TestNG configuration (I'm using the `BDDMockito.given(...)` and AssertJ's `BDDAssertions.then(...)` static methods. Check out *Chapter 7, Verifying Behavior with Object Matchers,* for more details on how to work with AssertJ or how to do the same with Hamcrest's `assertThat(...))`. The `when(...)` method comes from the `CatchExceptionAssertJ` class; you can use `CatchExceptionAssertJ.thenThrown(...)` without any unnecessary code in between, as follows:

```
@RunWith(MockitoJUnitRunner.class)
public class AverageTaxFactorCalculatorTest {

    @Spy TaxFactorFetcher taxFactorFetcher;

    @InjectMocks AverageTaxFactorCalculator systemUnderTest;

    @Test
    public void should_throw_exception_while_trying_to_calculate_mean_
tax_factor() {
        willThrow(new TaxFactorFetchException()).
given(taxFactorFetcher)
.getTaxFactorFor(any(Person.class));

        when(systemUnderTest).calculateAvgTaxFactorFor
(new Person());

        thenThrown(TaxFactorFetchException.class);
    }

}
```

How it works...

A spy is a special case of a mock. Refer to the *Stubbing methods so that they throw exceptions* recipe of *Chapter 4, Stubbing Behavior of Mocks,* for more information.

There's more...

Mockito allows you to provide a series of possible thrown exceptions to the stubbed method, either by using the fluent interface API or by means of varargs.

If you need to throw a series of exceptions from the stubbed spy's method using the fluent API, you will have to stub the method invocation as follows:

```
willThrow(ex1).willThrow(ex2).given(spy).methodToStub()
```

Or, if you want to use varargs, you have do it as follows:

```
willThrow(ex1, ex2).given(spy).methodToStub()(ex1, exj2).given(spy).
methodToStub()
```

 Note that we are not passing an additional `expected` parameter to the `@Test` annotation (the `expected` parameter suggests that if a test ends by throwing an exception of the given type, then the test has ended successfully). In the majority of cases, you would want to control where the exception is thrown from (otherwise, your test could pass when it shouldn't). That is why, either you should use the try-catch approach (if an exception has not been thrown, the test should fail with a given message), the `ExpectedException` JUnit rule, or the `catch-exception` library.

See also

▸ Refer to the catch-exception library homepage at `https://code.google.com/p/catch-exception/`

▸ Refer to the article `JUnit ExpectedException Rule vs. Catch-Exception` by Tomasz Kaczanowski, at `http://www.kaczanowscy.pl/tomek/2013-03/junit-expected-exception-rule-vs-catch-exception`

Stubbing methods so that they return custom answers

In this recipe, we will stub a method that returns a value so that it returns a custom answer of our choice.

Getting ready

This recipe is the last that will reuse the example from the previous recipe, which is related to a class that calculates an average value of tax factors. The starting point is the `AverageTaxFactorCalculator` class and its collaborator is `TaxFactorFetcher`, which is the provider of those values. The latter class picks one of the tax factors from the database (we'll stub that method). We will test those two classes as a unit. For your convenience, even though it violates the **don't repeat yourself** (**DRY**) principle, we will see the classes as follows so that you don't have to scroll around the book too much:

```
public class AverageTaxFactorCalculator {

    private final TaxFactorFetcher taxFactorFetcher;
```

```
    public AverageTaxFactorCalculator(TaxFactorFetcher
taxFactorFetcher) {
        this.taxFactorFetcher = taxFactorFetcher;
    }

    public double calculateAvgTaxFactorFor(Person person) {
        double taxFactor = taxFactorFetcher.
getTaxFactorFromDb(person);
        double anotherTaxFactor = taxFactorFetcher.
getTaxFactorFor(person);
        return (taxFactor + anotherTaxFactor) / 2;
    }

}
```

You can find the `TaxFactorFetcher` collaborator class in the following code:

```
public class TaxFactorFetcher {

    static final double NO_COUNTRY_TAX_FACTOR = 0.3;
    static final double DEFAULT_TAX_FACTOR = 0.5;
    static final double DB_TAX_FACTOR = 0.8;

    public double getTaxFactorFor(Person person) {
        if (person.isCountryDefined()) {
            return DEFAULT_TAX_FACTOR;
        }
        return NO_COUNTRY_TAX_FACTOR;
    }

    public double getTaxFactorFromDb(Person person) {
        // simulation of DB access
        return DB_TAX_FACTOR;
    }
}
```

How to do it...

We'll stub the method that accesses the database in such a way that we will register a callback (an answer) that will check if the person has provided information about his country of origin. Based on that piece of data, we will return a specific value. To do this, you have to perform the following steps:

1. For the BDD approach, call `BDDMockito.willAnswer(answer).
    given(spy).methodToStub()`. Or, in the standard manner, call `Mockito.
    doAnswer(answer).when(spy).methodToStub()`.

2. Whichever approach you've chosen, you have to provide the answer to be executed in
    `willAnswer(...)` or `doAnswer(...)`, and pass the spy itself in the `given(...)`
    or `when(...)` method.

3. Remember that the exception that was passed last during stubbing will be thrown for
    each stubbed method call. Have a look at the following line of code:

    ```
    willAnswer(answer1, answer2).given(taxFetcher).getTax();
    ```

    As shown in the preceding line of code, regardless of the number of `taxFetcher.`
    `getTax()` method executions, you will first throw `exception1` and then always
    throw `exception2` (until stubbed again).

>
> You have to bear in mind that if you try to stub a method with
> the `BDDMockito.given(...).willReturn(...)`
> call or in the standard manner—you stub a method with the
> `Mockito.when(...).thenReturn(...)` call—then you
> will actually call the spy's method that you want to stub!

Let's check the JUnit test. See *Chapter 1, Getting Started with Mockito,* for the TestNG
configuration (I'm using the `BDDMockito.given(...)` and AssertJ's `BDDAssertions.`
`then(...)` static methods; check out *Chapter 7, Verifying Behavior with Object Matchers,*
on how to work with AssertJ or how to do the same with Hamcrest's `assertThat(...)`).
Have a look at the following code:

```
@RunWith(MockitoJUnitRunner.class)
public class AverageTaxFactorCalculatorTest {

  @Spy TaxFactorFetcher taxFactorFetcher;

  @InjectMocks AverageTaxFactorCalculator systemUnderTest;

    @Test
public void should_return_incremented_tax_factor_while_trying_to_
calculate
_mean_tax_factor_for_a_person_from_undefined_country() {
        // given
        final double expectedTaxFactor = 107;
        willAnswer(withTaxFactorDependingOnPersonOrigin())
.given(taxFactorFetcher).getTaxFactorFromDb(any(Person.class));

        // when
        double avgTaxFactor = systemUnderTest.
calculateAvgTaxFactorFor(new Person());

        // then
```

```
        then(avgTaxFactor).isEqualTo(expectedTaxFactor);
    }

    private Answer<Object> withTaxFactorDependingOnPersonOrigin() {
        return new Answer<Object>() {
            @Override
            public Object answer(InvocationOnMock invocation) throws
    Throwable {
                double baseTaxFactor = 50;
                double incrementedTaxFactor = 200;
                if (invocation.getArguments().length > 0) {
                    Person person = (Person) invocation.getArguments()[0];
                    if (!person.isCountryDefined()) {
                        return incrementedTaxFactor;
                    }
                }
                return baseTaxFactor;
            }
        };
    }

}
```

How it works...

A spy is a special case of a mock. Refer to the *Stubbing methods so that they return custom answers* recipe of *Chapter 4, Stubbing Behavior of Mocks*, for more information.

There's more...

Mockito allows you to provide a series of possible answers to the stubbed method, either by using the fluent interface API or by means of varargs.

If you need to execute a series of answers from the stubbed spy's method using the fluent API, you will have to stub the method invocation as follows:

```
willAnswer(answer1).willAnswer(answer2).given(spy).methodToStub()
```

Or, if you want to use varargs, you'd have do it as follows:

```
willAnswer(answer1, answer2).given(spy).methodToStub()
```

See also

- ▶ Refer to the Mockito documentation on the `doReturn()|doThrow()|doAnswer()|doNothing()|doCallRealMethod()` family of methods at `http://docs.mockito.googlecode.com/hg/1.9.5/org/mockito/Mockito.html#12`
- ▶ Refer to the Mockito documentation on stubbing with callbacks at `http://docs.mockito.googlecode.com/hg/1.9.5/org/mockito/Mockito.html#11`

Stubbing void methods

In this recipe, we will stub a void method. A void method is one that doesn't return a value. Remember that since we want to partially stub a mock, it most likely means that our class is doing too much, and that is quite true for this scenario. It is best practice to not write such code – always try to follow the SOLID principles.

Getting ready

For this recipe, our system under test will be the `PersonDataUpdator` class, which delegates most of the work to its collaborator, `TaxFactorService`. The latter calculates the mean value of the tax factor (for simplicity, it's a fixed value) and then updates the person's tax data via a web service (since it's a simple example, we do not have any real web service calls):

```java
public class PersonDataUpdator {

  private final TaxFactorService taxFactorService;

  public PersonDataUpdator(TaxFactorService taxFactorService) {
    this.taxFactorService = taxFactorService;
  }

  public boolean processTaxDataFor(Person person) {
    try {
      double meanTaxFactor = taxFactorService.
calculateMeanTaxFactor();
      taxFactorService.updateMeanTaxFactor(person, meanTaxFactor);
      return true;
    } catch (ConnectException exception) {
      System.err.printf("Exception occurred while
trying update person data [%s]%n", exception);
      throw new TaxFactorConnectionException(exception);
    }
  }

}
```

The `TaxFactorService` class is shown in the following code (note that `updateMeanTaxFactor` is throwing a checked exception, `ConnectException`):

```
public class TaxFactorService {

    private static final double MEAN_TAX_FACTOR = 0.5;

    public void updateMeanTaxFactor(Person person,
double meanTaxFactor) throws ConnectException {
        System.out.printf("Updating mean tax factor [%s] for
person with defined country%n", meanTaxFactor);
    }

    public double calculateMeanTaxFactor() {
      return MEAN_TAX_FACTOR;
    }

}
```

How to do it...

To stub a spy's void method in such a way that it does nothing, you have to perform the following steps:

1. For the BDD approach, call the `BDDMockito.willDoNothing().given(spy).methodToStub()`. Or, in the standard manner, call `Mockito.doNothing().when(spy).methodToStub()`.

2. Whichever approach you've chosen, `willDoNothing()` or `doNothing()`, you will pass the spy itself in the `given(...)` or `when(...)` method.

3. Remember that the exception that was passed last during stubbing will be thrown for each stubbed method call. Have a look at the following code:

   ```
   willDoNothing().willThrow(exception).given(taxFetcher)
   .getTax();
   ```

   As shown in the preceding code, regardless of the number of `taxFetcher.getTax()` method executions, the method will first do nothing and then always throw an exception (until stubbed again).

The following snippet depicts the aforementioned scenario for JUnit. See *Chapter 1, Getting Started with Mockito*, for the TestNG configuration (I'm using the `BDDMockito.given(...)` and AssertJ's `BDDAssertions.then(...)` static methods. Check out *Chapter 7, Verifying Behavior with Object Matchers*, on how to work with AssertJ or how to do the same with Hamcrest's `assertThat(...)`). Have a look at the following snippet:

```
@RunWith(MockitoJUnitRunner.class)
public class PersonDataUpdatorTest {
```

```
    @Spy TaxFactorService taxFactorService;

    @InjectMocks PersonDataUpdator systemUnderTest;

    @Test
    public void should_successfully_update_tax_factor_
for_person() throws ConnectException {
        // given
        willDoNothing().given(taxFactorService).
updateMeanTaxFactor(any(Person.class), anyDouble());

        // when
        boolean success = systemUnderTest.
processTaxDataFor(new Person());

        // then
        then(success).isTrue();
    }

}
```

How it works...

A spy is a special case of a mock. Refer to the *Stubbing void methods* recipe of *Chapter 4, Stubbing Behavior of Mocks,* for more information.

There's more...

Say you want to make a method first throw an exception and do that only once; after that, you want the method to do nothing. Take a look at the following snippet, which shows how to achieve this:

```
    willThrow(exception).willNothing().given(spy).methodToSpy();
```

See also

▶   Refer to the Mockito documentation on the doReturn()|doThrow()|doAnswer
   ()|doNothing()|doCallRealMethod() family of methods at http://docs.
   mockito.googlecode.com/hg/1.9.5/org/mockito/Mockito.html#12

Stubbing void methods so that they throw exceptions

In this recipe, we will stub a void method. It doesn't return a value, so it throws an exception.

Getting ready

We'll reuse the example from the previous recipe, but let's take a fast look at it again. We have a system under test that combines two classes: a `PersonDataUpdator` class that delegates work to `TaxFactorService`. The latter is a nice example of violating the single responsibility principle (S from SOLID; refer to *Chapter 2, Creating Mocks*, for more details) and it does too much, it calculates a mean value of tax factors (in our case, it's fixed) and then it updates the person's information via a web service. In this scenario, we will verify how our system works when an exception related to connectivity issues occurs:

```
public class PersonDataUpdator {

  private final TaxFactorService taxFactorService;

  public PersonDataUpdator(TaxFactorService taxFactorService) {
    this.taxFactorService = taxFactorService;
  }

  public boolean processTaxDataFor(Person person) {
    try {
      double meanTaxFactor = taxFactorService.
calculateMeanTaxFactor();
        taxFactorService.updateMeanTaxFactor(person, meanTaxFactor);
        return true;
    } catch (ConnectException exception) {
        System.err.printf("Exception occurred while trying update person
data [%s]%n", exception);
        throw new TaxFactorConnectionException(exception);
    }
  }

}
```

In the following code snippet, you can find the internals of `TaxFactorService`. It's important to remember that the `updateMeanTaxFactor` method is throwing a checked exception, `ConnectException`.

```
public class TaxFactorService {

    private static final double MEAN_TAX_FACTOR = 0.5;
```

```
    public void updateMeanTaxFactor(Person person, double
meanTaxFactor) throws ConnectException {
        System.out.printf("Updating mean tax factor [%s] for person with
defined country%n", meanTaxFactor);
    }

    public double calculateMeanTaxFactor() {
        return MEAN_TAX_FACTOR;
    }

}
```

How to do it...

To stub a spy's void method in such a way that it throws an exception, you have to perform the following steps:

1. For the BDD approach, call `BDDMockito.willThrow(exception).given(spy).methodToStub()`. Or, in the standard manner, call `Mockito.doThrow(exception).when(spy).methodToStub()`.

2. Whichever approach you've chosen, you have to provide the exception to be thrown in `willThrow(...)` or `doThrow(...)`, and pass the spy itself in the `given(...)` or `when(...)` method.

3. Remember that the last passed exception during stubbing will be thrown for each stubbed method call. Have a look at the following line of code:

   `willThrow(ex1).willThrow(ex2).given(taxFetcher).getTax();`

   As shown in the preceding line of code, regardless of the number of `taxFetcher.getTax()` method executions, first `exception1` will be thrown and then always `exception2` will be thrown (until stubbed again).

Let's check the JUnit test. See _Chapter 1, Getting Started with Mockito_, for the TestNG configuration (remember that I'm using the `BDDMockito.given(...)` and AssertJ's `BDDAssertions.then(...)` static methods. Check out _Chapter 7, Verifying Behavior with Object Matchers_, for details on how to work with AssertJ or how to do the same with Hamcrest's `assertThat(...)`). The `when(...)` method comes from the `CatchExceptionAssertJ` class; this way, I can use `CatchExceptionAssertJ.thenThrown(...)` without any unnecessary code in between. Last but not least, the `CatchException.caughtException()` method gives you access to the exception that was thrown last. Have a look at the following code:

```
@RunWith(MockitoJUnitRunner.class)
public class PersonDataUpdatorTest {

    @Spy TaxFactorService taxFactorService;
```

```
    @InjectMocks PersonDataUpdator systemUnderTest;

    @Test
    public void should_fail_to_update_tax_factor_for_person_due_to_
connection_issues() throws ConnectException {
        willThrow(ConnectException.class).given(taxFactorService)
.updateMeanTaxFactor(any(Person.class), anyDouble());

        when(systemUnderTest).processTaxDataFor(new Person());

        then(caughtException()).hasCauseInstanceOf
(ConnectException.class);
    }

}
```

How it works...

A spy is a special case of a mock. Refer to the *Stubbing methods so that they return custom answers* recipe of *Chapter 4, Stubbing Behavior of Mocks*, for more information.

As for the assertion part of the test, we use AssertJ to work on `Throwables` and we check whether the cause of the exception is indeed `ConnectException`. To do that, we can use AssertJ's `ThrowableAssert` assertions.

See also

▸ Refer to the catch-exception library home page at `https://code.google.com/p/catch-exception/`

▸ Refer to the article *JUnit ExpectedException Rule vs. Catch-Exception* by Tomasz Kaczanowski at `http://www.kaczanowscy.pl/tomek/2013-03/junit-expected-exception-rule-vs-catch-exception`

Stubbing void methods so that they return custom answers

In this recipe, we will stub a void method. It doesn't return a value, so it returns a custom answer.

Getting ready

In this recipe, we'll reuse the example from the previous recipes. A quick reminder again – we have a system under test that consists of two objects: a `PersonDataUpdator` class that delegates work to `TaxFactorService`. The output of the system is a calculation of a mean value of tax factors (we have a fixed value for that). The person's data then gets updated via a web service. In this scenario, we will verify how our system works when an exception related to connectivity issues occurs. Have a look at the following code:

```
public class PersonDataUpdator {

  private final TaxFactorService taxFactorService;

  public PersonDataUpdator(TaxFactorService taxFactorService) {
    this.taxFactorService = taxFactorService;
  }

  public boolean processTaxDataFor(Person person) {
    try {
      double meanTaxFactor = taxFactorService.
calculateMeanTaxFactor();
      taxFactorService.updateMeanTaxFactor(person, meanTaxFactor);
      return true;
    } catch (ConnectException exception) {
      System.err.printf("Exception occurred while trying update person
data [%s]%n", exception);
      throw new TaxFactorConnectionException(exception);
    }
  }

}
```

Its collaborator, `TaxFactorService`, whose `updateMeanTaxFactor` method throws a checked exception, `ConnectException`, is shown in the following code:

```
public class TaxFactorService {

  private static final double MEAN_TAX_FACTOR = 0.5;

  public void updateMeanTaxFactor(Person person, double
meanTaxFactor) throws ConnectException {
    System.out.printf("Updating mean tax factor [%s] for person with
defined country%n", meanTaxFactor);
  }

  public double calculateMeanTaxFactor() {
```

```
        return MEAN_TAX_FACTOR;
    }


}
```

How to do it...

To stub a spy's void method in such a way that it executes your callback, you have to perform the following steps:

1. For the BDD approach, call `BDDMockito.willAnswer(answer)`. `given(spy).methodToStub()`. Or, in the standard manner, call `Mockito.doAnswer(answer).when(spy).methodToStub()`.

2. Whichever approach you've chosen, you have to provide the answer to be executed in `willAnswer(...)` or `doAnswer(...)`, and pass the spy itself in the `given(...)` or `when(...)` method.

3. Remember that the answer that was passed last during stubbing will be executed for each stubbed method call. Have a look at the following line of code:

   ```
   willAnswer(answ1).willAnswer(answ2).given(taxFetcher).getTax();
   ```

   As shown in the preceding line of code, regardless of the number of `taxFetcher.getTax()` method executions, first `answ1` will be executed and then always `answ2` will be called (until stubbed again).

Let's check the JUnit test. See *Chapter 1, Getting Started with Mockito*, for the TestNG configuration (remember that I'm using the `BDDMockito.given(...)` and AssertJ's `BDDAssertions.then(...)` static methods. Check out *Chapter 7, Verifying Behavior with Object Matchers*, for details on how to work with AssertJ or how to do the same with Hamcrest's `assertThat(...)`). The `when(...)` method comes from the `CatchExceptionAssertJ` class; this way, I can use `CatchExceptionAssertJ.thenThrown(...)` without any unnecessary code in between. Last but not least, the `CatchException.caughtException()` method gives you access to the exception that was thrown last, as shown in the following code:

```
@RunWith(MockitoJUnitRunner.class)
public class PersonDataUpdatorTest {

  @Spy TaxFactorService taxFactorService;

    @InjectMocks PersonDataUpdator systemUnderTest;

    @Test
    public void should_fail_to_update_tax_factor_for_person_due_to_
having
_undefined_country() throws ConnectException {
```

```
            willAnswer(withExceptionForPersonWithUndefinedCountry())
.given(taxFactorService).updateMeanTaxFactor
(any(Person.class), anyDouble());

            when(systemUnderTest).processTaxDataFor(new Person());

        then(caughtException()).isInstanceOf
(UndefinedCountryException.class);
    }

  private Answer withExceptionForPersonWithUndefinedCountry() {
    return new Answer() {
        @Override
        public Object answer(InvocationOnMock invocation) throws
Throwable {
            if (invocation.getArguments().length > 0) {
                Person person = (Person) invocation.getArguments()[0];
                if (!person.isCountryDefined()) {
                    throw new UndefinedCountryException
("Undefined country");
                }
            }
            return null;
        }
    };
  }

}
```

 Another thing to remember is that you most likely won't need to create any special answers; if that is the case, it's highly probable that your scenario is getting too complicated. For additional information regarding both `Answers` and the `AdditionalAnswers`—classes that hold quite a few predefined answers—refer to *Chapter 2, Creating Mocks*.

How it works...

A spy is a special case of a mock. Refer to the *Stubbing methods so that they return custom answers* recipe of *Chapter 4, Stubbing Behavior of Mocks*, for more information.

 ▶ Refer to the Mockito documentation on the `doReturn()|doThrow()|doAnswer
 ()|doNothing()|doCallRealMethod()` family of methods at `http://docs.
 mockito.googlecode.com/hg/1.9.5/org/mockito/Mockito.html#12`

 ▶ Refer to the Mockito documentation on stubbing with callbacks at `http://docs.
 mockito.googlecode.com/hg/1.9.5/org/mockito/Mockito.html#11`

Stubbing final methods with PowerMock

In this recipe, we will stub a final method and verify the object under test's behavior using JUnit. Since Mockito can't stub final methods, we'll use PowerMock to do it.

As usual, when dealing with PowerMock, you have to be really sure of what you are doing. You shouldn't need to use it with well-written code. Just follow the SOLID principles (see *Chapter 2*, *Creating Mocks*, for more information) and you shouldn't have the need to use this library.

PowerMock can be useful when dealing with legacy code or stubbing third-party libraries (you can check *Chapter 8*, *Refactoring with Mockito*, to see how to use PowerMock to refactor legacy code).

Getting ready

To use PowerMock, you have to add it to your classpath. Check the *Creating mocks of final classes with PowerMock* recipe in *Chapter 2*, *Creating Mocks*, for details on how to add PowerMock to your project.

As shown in the following code, for this recipe, our system under test will be a unit of a `PersonProcessor` class and its collaborator, the `PersonSaver` class. The latter is responsible for logging warnings while validating the person and for persisting the person in the database:

```
public class PersonProcessor {

    private final PersonSaver personSaver;

    public PersonProcessor(PersonSaver personSaver) {
        this.personSaver = personSaver;
    }

    public boolean process(Person person) {
        try {
            personSaver.validatePerson(person);
```

```
        personSaver.savePerson(person);
        return true;
    } catch (Exception exception) {
        System.err.printf("Exception occurred while trying save
person [%s]%n", exception);
        return false;
    }
}

}
```

Now, let's take a look at the `PersonSaver` class that has a single final method that we want to stub:

```
public class PersonSaver {

    public void validatePerson(Person person) {
        if (!person.isCountryDefined()) {
        System.out.printf("Warning person [%s] has undefined
country%n", person.getName());
        }
    }

    public final void savePerson(Person person) {
      // simulating web service call
      System.out.println("Storing person in the db");
    }

}
```

How to do it...

To use PowerMock with JUnit to stub a final method, you have to perform the following steps:

1. Annotate your test class with `@RunWith(PowerMockRunner.class)`.

2. Provide all the classes that need to be prepared for testing (most likely byte-code manipulated) in the `@PrepareForTest` annotation (in the case of our scenario, it would be `@PrepareForTest(PersonSaver.class)` since `PersonSaver` has a final method that we want to stub). In general, the class that needs to be prepared for testing will include classes with final, private, static, or native methods; classes that are final and that should be spied on; and also classes that should be returned as spies on instantiation.

3. Since we are creating a PowerMock spy, we can't profit from Mockito's annotations and need to create a spy using the `PowerMockito.spy(...)` method.

The following snippet depicts the aforementioned scenario for JUnit. See *Chapter 1, Getting Started with Mockito,* for the TestNG configuration (I'm using the `BDDMockito.given(...)` and AssertJ's `BDDAssertions.then(...)` static methods. Check out *Chapter 7, Verifying Behavior with Object Matchers,* for details on how to work with AssertJ or how to do the same with `Hamcrest's assertThat(...)`). Have a look at the following code:

```
@RunWith(PowerMockRunner.class)
@PrepareForTest(PersonSaver.class)
public class PersonProcessorTest {

    PersonSaver personSaver = PowerMockito.spy(new PersonSaver());

    PersonProcessor systemUnderTest = new
PersonProcessor(personSaver);

    @Test
    public void should_successfully_proces_person_with_defined_
country() {
        // given
        willDoNothing().given(personSaver).savePerson(any(Person.
class));

        // when
        boolean result = systemUnderTest.process(new
Person("POLAND"));

        // then
        then(result).isTrue();
    }

}
```

Now, let's see how to configure our class to work with TestNG:

1. Make your class extend the `PowerMockTestCase` class.

2. Implement a method annotated with `@ObjectFactory` that returns an instance of the `PowerMockObjectFactory` class (this object factory will be used for the creation of all object instances in the test).

3. Provide all the classes that need to be prepared for testing (most likely bytecode manipulated) in the `@PrepareForTest` annotation (in the case of our scenario, it would be `@PrepareForTest(PersonSaver.class)` since `PersonSaver` has a final method that we want to stub). In general, the class that needs to be prepared for testing would include classes with final, private, static or native methods; classes that are final and that should be spied on; and also classes that should be returned as spies on instantiation.

4. Since we are creating a PowerMock spy, we can't profit from Mockito's annotations and need to create a spy using the `PowerMockito.spy(…)` method.

Let's check the following TestNG test (see the JUnit example for the warnings in terms of static imports and the BDD approach):

```java
@PrepareForTest(PersonSaver.class)
public class PersonProcessorTestNgTest extends PowerMockTestCase {

    PersonSaver personSaver;

    PersonProcessor systemUnderTest;

  @BeforeMethod
  public void setup() {
    personSaver = PowerMockito.spy(new PersonSaver());
    systemUnderTest = new PersonProcessor(personSaver);
  }

    @Test
    public void should_successfully_proces_person_with_defined_
country() {
        // given
        willDoNothing().given(personSaver).savePerson(any(Person.
class));

        // when
        boolean result = systemUnderTest.process(new
Person("POLAND"));

        // then
        then(result).isTrue();
    }


  @ObjectFactory
  public IObjectFactory getObjectFactory() {
    return new PowerMockObjectFactory();
  }

}
```

How it works...

The internals of PowerMock go far beyond the scope of this recipe, but the overall concept is that a part of the `PowerMockRunner` logic is to create a custom classloader and bytecode manipulation for the classes defined using the `@PrepareForTest` annotation in order to mock them, and to use these mocks with the standard Mockito API. Due to bytecode manipulations, PowerMock can ignore a series of constraints of the Java language, such as extending final classes.

See also

▸   Refer to the PowerMock website at `https://code.google.com/p/powermock/`

▸   Refer to *Chapter 8, Refactoring with Mockito,* to see how to use different approaches and tools such as PowerMock to refactor bad code

6

Verifying Test Doubles

In this chapter, we will cover the following topics:

- Verifying the method invocation count with `times()`
- Verifying the method invocation count with `atLeast()`
- Verifying the method invocation count with `atMost()`
- Verifying that interactions never happened
- Verifying that interactions stopped happening
- Verifying the order of interactions
- Verifying interactions and ignoring stubbed methods
- Verifying the method invocation within the specified time

Introduction

In the previous two chapters, you've been shown how to stub the mocked object's behavior in a number of ways. You can also see the verification approach that favors the assertion of what should happen instead of how it should happen, by telling you to verify the behavior, if possible, and not the implementation.

The preceding suggestion always starts heated discussions. Martin Fowler, in his article, *Mocks aren't Stubs* (`http://martinfowler.com/articles/mocksArentStubs.html`) defines that in general, there are two approaches in terms of verification: verifying state and verifying behavior. A part of this article is about coupling tests to the implementation. Fowler talks about one of the key problems behind such a binding of tests to the actual code—the interference in refactoring. Having such brittle tests could make them fail each time you refactor, even though the final behavior remains the same.

The importance of refactoring as an indispensable process in software development should not be put under any discussion or doubt. It increases the code quality, readability, and understandability. There are numerous ways to improve the actual code to make it more modular and clear for the developer. The same approach can be applied to the testing code. Throughout the book, I'm promoting the approach of asserting behavior instead of implementation. One may ask the question whether the book follows the most advantageous approach.

The answer to this is not trivial and, in fact, I'd say that the answer is quite subjective. From my experience, I have rarely seen cases in which I wanted to verify whether a certain piece of code was actually called, but still there were such scenarios. I was told by a software architect that you should pick such test types (unit, integration, and so on) so that you feel confident that your application does what it is supposed to do. Of course, you should also follow the concept of the test pyramid presented in *Succeeding with Agile, Mike Cohn* (the essential point of this concept is to have many more unit tests than high-level, end-to-end ones that go through the UI). It's crucial to remember this since developers often tend to think that if their tools show a high degree of code coverage, it will automatically mean that their code does what it should do. Josh Bloch once wrote that coverage won't ensure that an application works correctly, only what is expected from tests.

The complexity of business problems that software developers have to solve on a daily basis doesn't make it any easier for the programmers to choose proper ways of testing their software. Summing it all up, one must not say that only one approach is good and the other is bad—it's not a black or white approach—it all depends on your experience, your approach to testing, and when you feel that your code is properly tested. Like Andrew Hunt said, "Context is king!". As developers, we have to take responsibility to test our software. It's up to us to define whether the execution of precisely defined methods is essential to say that the application works in a correct manner or is it just an implementation detail.

Throughout this book, I'm suggesting that it is better not to tightly couple your testing code to the actual implementation. My hint contained the "if possible" part that we will deal with in more depth in the upcoming recipes. Sometimes, you might feel much more certain if some part of your code gets verified in terms of method invocation count and order. You may even want to check whether an argument passed to a method of your mock contains precisely defined values. At the end of the day, you just want your application to work fine, right?

Verifying the method invocation count with times()

In this recipe, we will verify whether a method on a mock was executed for exactly the given number of times.

Getting ready

For this recipe, our system under test will be `TaxUpdater`, which calls `TaxService` (let's assume that it is a web-service client) to update the mean tax factor for two people. Unfortunately, this system is old and can accept a single call at a time. For simplicity, the `calculateMeanTaxFactor()` method, shown in the following code, returns a fixed value but in reality, there could be some complex logic:

```
public class TaxUpdater {

    static final double MEAN_TAX_FACTOR = 10.5;

    private final TaxService taxService;

    public TaxUpdater(TaxService taxService) {
        this.taxService = taxService;
    }

    public void updateTaxFactorFor(Person brother, Person sister) {
        taxService.updateMeanTaxFactor(brother,
calculateMeanTaxFactor());
        taxService.updateMeanTaxFactor(sister,
calculateMeanTaxFactor());
    }

    private double calculateMeanTaxFactor() {
        return MEAN_TAX_FACTOR;
    }

}
```

How to do it...

To verify whether the mocked object's method was called the exact number of times as specified in the code, you have to call `Mockito.verify(mock, VerificationMode.times(count)).methodToVerify(...)`.

Let's check the JUnit test that verifies whether the web service's method has been called exactly twice (see *Chapter 1, Getting Started with Mockito*, for the TestNG configuration):

```
@RunWith(MockitoJUnitRunner.class)
public class TaxUpdaterTest {

    @Mock TaxService taxService;
```

```
    @InjectMocks TaxUpdater systemUnderTest;

    @Test
    public void should_send_exactly_two_messages_through_the_web_
service() {
        // when
        systemUnderTest.updateTaxFactorFor(new Person(),
 new Person());

        // then
        verify(taxService, times(2))
.updateMeanTaxFactor(any(Person.class), anyDouble());
    }

}
```

How it works...

When you run the `verify` method, Mockito internally delegates its call to `MockitoCore.verify(T mock, VerificationMode mode)`. The verification mode in our example is the `Times` object that is the result of the execution of the static `VerificationMode.times(2)` method. In general, the `Times` object has two responsibilities:

  ▶ It stores the expected number of invocations
  ▶ It delegates the verification of whether the verified method got executed for the expected number of times

You may get negative results for the following reasons (a proper exception will be thrown by Mockito):

  ▶ Too few actual invocations
  ▶ Never wanted but invoked
  ▶ Too many actual invocations

Otherwise, the method invocation gets marked as verified. It's pretty important in terms of greedy verification. (We'll go back to this in more detail in the later parts of the chapter.)

There's more...

To verify whether the method has been called once, you can write it in the following way (because Mockito assumes a single method execution by default):

```
verify(taxService).updateMeanTaxFactor
(any(Person.class), anyDouble());
```

▶ Refer to the Mockito documentation on *Verifying number of method invocations* at `http://docs.mockito.googlecode.com/hg/1.9.5/org/mockito/Mockito.html#4`

▶ Refer to *Test Driven Development: By example, Kent Beck,* available at `http://books.google.co.uk/books/about/Test_driven_Development.html?id=gFgnde_vwMAC`

Verifying the method invocation count with atLeast()

In this recipe, we will verify whether a method on a mock was executed for at least a specified number of times.

Getting ready

For this recipe, our system under test will be the same, `TaxUpdater`, as presented in the previous recipe; let's take another look at it:

```
public class TaxUpdater {

    static final double MEAN_TAX_FACTOR = 10.5;

    private final TaxService taxService;

    public TaxUpdater(TaxService taxService) {
        this.taxService = taxService;
    }

    public void updateTaxFactorFor(Person brother, Person sister) {
        taxService.updateMeanTaxFactor
(brother, calculateMeanTaxFactor());
        taxService.updateMeanTaxFactor
(sister, calculateMeanTaxFactor());
    }

    private double calculateMeanTaxFactor() {
        return MEAN_TAX_FACTOR;
    }

}
```

How to do it...

To verify whether the mocked object's method was called at least a given number of times, call `Mockito.verify(mock, VerificationMode.atLeast(count)).methodToVerify(...)`.

Let's check the JUnit test that verifies whether the web service's method has been called at least twice (see *Chapter 1, Getting Started with Mockito*, for the TestNG configuration):

```
@RunWith(MockitoJUnitRunner.class)
public class TaxUpdaterTest {

    @Mock TaxService taxService;

    @InjectMocks TaxUpdater systemUnderTest;

    @Test
    public void should_send_at_least_two_messages_through_the_web_
service() {
        // when
        systemUnderTest.updateTaxFactorFor
(new Person(), new Person());

        // then
        verify(taxService, atLeast(2))
.updateMeanTaxFactor(any(Person.class), anyDouble());
    }

}
```

How it works...

Since the `atLeast(...)` verification works in a similar way to the `times(...)` verification, please refer to the *How it works...* section of the previous recipe for more details.

The difference between the two is that in this recipe, we have the AtLeast VerificationMode that first stores the expected number of method invocations and then, on verification, checks if that method actually got executed at least that many times. If that isn't the case, an exception will be thrown.

There's more...

To verify whether the method has been executed at least once, you can write it as follows:

```
verify(taxService, atLeastOnce())
.updateMeanTaxFactor(any(Person.class), anyDouble());
```

- Refer to the Mockito documentation on *Verifying number of method invocations* at `http://docs.mockito.googlecode.com/hg/1.9.5/org/mockito/Mockito.html#4`

- Refer to *Test-Driven Development: By example, Kent Beck* available at `http://books.google.co.uk/books/about/Test_driven_Development.html?id=gFgnde_vwMAC`

Verifying the method invocation count with atMost()

In this recipe, we will verify whether a method on a mock was executed, at most, a specified number of times.

Getting ready

As shown in the following code, our system under test is `TaxUpdater` (the same as that presented in the previous recipes):

```
public class TaxUpdater {

    static final double MEAN_TAX_FACTOR = 10.5;

    private final TaxService taxService;

    public TaxUpdater(TaxService taxService) {
        this.taxService = taxService;
    }

    public void updateTaxFactorFor(Person brother, Person sister) {
        taxService.updateMeanTaxFactor
(brother, calculateMeanTaxFactor());
        taxService.updateMeanTaxFactor
(sister, calculateMeanTaxFactor());
    }

    private double calculateMeanTaxFactor() {
        return MEAN_TAX_FACTOR;
    }

}
```

How to do it...

To verify whether the mock's method was invoked at most a given number of times, call `Mockito.verify(mock, VerificationMode.atMost(count)).methodToVerify(...)`.

Let's check the JUnit test that verifies whether the web service's method has been called at most twice (see *Chapter 1, Getting Started with Mockito*, for the TestNG configuration):

```
@RunWith(MockitoJUnitRunner.class)
public class TaxUpdaterTest {

    @Mock TaxService taxService;

    @InjectMocks TaxUpdater systemUnderTest;

    @Test
    public void should_send_at_most_two_messages_through_the_web_
service() {
        // when
        systemUnderTest.updateTaxFactorFor
(new Person(), new Person());

        // then
        verify(taxService, atMost(2))
.updateMeanTaxFactor(any(Person.class), anyDouble());
    }

}
```

How it works...

Since the `atMost(...)` verification works in a similar way to the `times(...)` verification, please refer to the *How it works...* section of the *Verifying the method invocation count with times()* recipe for more details.

The difference between the two is that in this recipe, we have the AtMost VerificationMode that first stores the expected number of method invocations and then, on verification, it checks whether that method actually got executed at most that many times. If that isn't the case, an exception will be thrown.

▶ Refer to the Mockito documentation on *Verifying number of method invocations* at `http://docs.mockito.googlecode.com/hg/1.9.5/org/mockito/Mockito.html#4`

▶ Refer to *Test-Driven Development: By example, Kent Beck* available at `http://books.google.co.uk/books/about/Test_driven_Development.html?id=gFgnde_vwMAC`

Verifying that interactions never happened

In this recipe, we will verify the following two cases:

▶ A specified method on a mock was never executed

▶ The methods on the mock were executed

You might wonder whether there is any reason to check that a method on a mock was never executed. Well, imagine that your company is paying plenty of money for a bank transfer (let's assume that it's done via a web service). Having such business requirements where if some initial conditions were not met the bank transfer should not take place, you can check whether the method was executed.

If you actually need to verify that no more interactions took place on the mock, then perhaps you shouldn't actually have done this (check the link, `http://monkeyisland.pl/2008/07/12/should-i-worry-about-the-unexpected/`, for Szczepan Faber's article on that topic). If it's not a business requirement, you should not worry about the unexpected; perhaps, some additional methods of the mock can actually be executed if it doesn't change the way the application works. If you do a TDD, then you won't have this issue since you would write only the piece of code that is really necessary.

Getting ready

Our system under test will be a `TaxTransferer` class that will transfer tax for a non-null person as follows:

```
public class TaxTransferer {

    private final TaxService taxService;

    public TaxTransferer(TaxService taxService) {
        this.taxService = taxService;
    }
```

```
public void transferTaxFor(Person person) {
    if (person == null) {
        return;
    }
    taxService.transferTaxFor(person);
}

}
```

How to do it...

To verify whether the mock's method was not invoked, call `Mockito.verify(mock, VerificationMode.never()).methodToVerify(...)`.

Let's check the JUnit test that verifies whether the web service's method has been called at most twice (see *Chapter 1, Getting Started with Mockito*, for the TestNG configuration):

```
@RunWith(MockitoJUnitRunner.class)
public class TaxTransfererTest {

    @Mock TaxService taxService;

    @InjectMocks TaxTransferer systemUnderTest;

    @Test
    public void should_not_call_web_service_method_if_person_is_null()
    {
        // when
        systemUnderTest.transferTaxFor(null);

        // then
        verify(taxService, never()).transferTaxFor(any(Person.class));
    }

}
```

How it works...

Since the `never()` verification works in the same way as the `times(0)` verification, please refer to the *How it works...* section of the *Verifying the method invocation count with times()* recipe for more details.

There's more...

You can use the `Mockito.verifyZeroInteractions(...)` method to specify that you do not wish interactions to take place with a mock.

However, it will involve all the existing calls on the mock (even those from the setup phase of your test). So, we could rewrite the aforementioned test in another, less user friendly and readable way; for example, for JUnit, you can use the following code:

```
@RunWith(MockitoJUnitRunner.class)
public class TaxTransfererTest {

    @Mock TaxService taxService;

    @InjectMocks TaxTransferer systemUnderTest;

    @Test
    public void should_not_interact_with_web_service_in_any_way_if_
person_is_null() {
        // when
        systemUnderTest.transferTaxFor(null);

        // then
        verifyZeroInteractions(taxService);
    }
}
```

You can call either the `verifyZeroInteractions(...)` or `verifyNoMoreInteractions(...)` method and get the same result since both do the same task (they call the same methods under the hood).

See also

▶ Refer to the Mockito documentation on *Making sure interaction(s) never happened on mock* at `http://docs.mockito.googlecode.com/hg/1.9.5/org/mockito/Mockito.html#7`

▶ Refer to *Test-Driven Development: By example, Kent Beck* available at `http://books.google.co.uk/books/about/Test_driven_Development.html?id=gFgnde_vwMAC`

Verifying that interactions stopped happening

In this recipe, we will verify that a specified method on a mock was executed and then any interactions stopped taking place.

Getting ready

For this recipe, our system under test will be a `TaxTransferer` class that will transfer tax for a non-null person. If the passed person value is null, then an error report is sent:

```
public class TaxTransferer {

    private final TaxService taxService;

    public TaxTransferer(TaxService taxService) {
        this.taxService = taxService;
    }

    public void transferTaxFor(Person person) {
        if (person == null) {
            taxService.sendErrorReport();
            return;
        }
        taxService.transferTaxFor(person);
    }

}
```

How to do it...

To verify that the only method executed on a mock is the one provided by us, you have to call `Mockito.verify(mock, VerificationMode.only()).methodToVerify(...)`.

Let's check the JUnit test that verifies whether the web service's method has been called at most twice (see *Chapter 1, Getting Started with Mockito*, for the TestNG configuration):

```
@RunWith(MockitoJUnitRunner.class)
public class TaxTransfererTest {

    @Mock TaxService taxService;

    @InjectMocks TaxTransferer systemUnderTest;
```

```
    @Test
    public void should_only_send_error_report_if_person_is_null() {
        // when
        systemUnderTest.transferTaxFor(null);

        // then
        verify(taxService, only()).sendErrorReport();
    }
}
```

How it works...

When using the `only()` verification mode in the `Mockito.verify(…)` method, we are delegating the verification to the class named `Only`. This class verifies whether there was a single invocation of the verified method and no other interactions with the mock took place. Mockito will throw a verification exception under the following conditions:

▸ An interaction with a mock took place even though it shouldn't

▸ A method that we wanted to be executed has never been called

If neither of these cases are applicable, then the method invocation gets marked as verified. It's pretty important in terms of greedy verification. (We'll go back to this in more detail in the later parts of this chapter.)

There's more...

You can also define that interactions should stop happening by using a less elegant approach. The following code sample is presented only for you to know that you can refactor it to the one presented earlier:

```
@RunWith(MockitoJUnitRunner.class)
public class TaxTransfererTest {

    @Mock TaxService taxService;

    @InjectMocks TaxTransferer systemUnderTest;

    @Test
    public void should_only_send_error_report_if_person_is_null_in_an_
ugly_way() {
        // when
        systemUnderTest.transferTaxFor(null);
```

```
        // then
        verify(taxService).sendErrorReport();
        verifyNoMoreInteractions (taxService);
    }
}
```

See also

▶ Refer to the Mockito documentation on *Making sure interaction(s) never happened on mock* at `http://docs.mockito.googlecode.com/hg/1.9.5/org/mockito/Mockito.html#7`

▶ Refer to *Test-Driven Development: By example, Kent Beck* available at `http://books.google.co.uk/books/about/Test_driven_Development.html?id=gFgnde_vwMAC`

▶ Refer to Szczepan Faber's article *Should I worry about the unexpected?* at `http://monkeyisland.pl/2008/07/12/should-i-worry-about-the-unexpected`

Verifying the order of interactions

In this recipe, we will verify that a set of methods get executed in the specified order.

Getting ready

For this recipe, our system under test will be `TaxUpdator` which is a simplified version of a facade that calls the `TaxService` methods (let's assume that it is a web service) to update tax-related data and perform a series of tax transfers. Let's assume that this web service is a legacy, a badly-written system, and we have to synchronously call it in a precisely defined sequence.

Let's take a look at the implementation of the `TaxUpdator` class:

```
public class TaxUpdator {

    public static final int TAX_FACTOR = 100;

    private final TaxService taxService;

    public TaxUpdator(TaxService taxService) {
        this.taxService = taxService;
    }

    public void transferTaxFor(Person person) {
        taxService.updateTaxFactor(person, calculateTaxFactor(1));
```

```
        taxService.transferTaxFor(person);
        taxService.transferTaxFor(person);
        taxService.updateTaxFactor(person, calculateTaxFactor(2));
        taxService.transferTaxFor(person);
    }

    private double calculateTaxFactor(double ratio) {
        return TAX_FACTOR * ratio;
    }

}
```

How to do it...

To verify whether the mock's method execution took place in a specified order, perform the following steps:

1. Start the verification in order using `InOrder inOrder = Mockito.`
   `inOrder(mock1, mock2, ... , mockn);`, where `mock1`, `mock2`, and `mockn` are the objects that might be used in the verification process.

2. Then, you can call either of the following presented methods in a specified sequence to verify that their execution took place in the specified order:

   ```
   inOrder.verify(mock).method(...);
   inOrder.verify(mock, verificationMode).method(...);
   inOrder.verifyNoMoreInteractions()
   ```

Let's check the JUnit test that verifies whether the web service's method has been called at most twice (see *Chapter 1, Getting Started with Mockito*, for the TestNG configuration):

```
@RunWith(MockitoJUnitRunner.class)
public class TaxUpdaterTest {

    @Mock TaxService taxService;

    @InjectMocks TaxUpdater systemUnderTest;

    @Test
    public void should_update_tax_factor_and_transfer_tax_in_
specified_order() {
        // given
        Person person = new Person();

        // when
        systemUnderTest.transferTaxFor(person);
```

```
        // then
        InOrder inOrder = Mockito.inOrder(taxService);
        inOrder.verify(taxService)
.updateTaxFactor(eq(person), anyDouble());
        inOrder.verify(taxService, times(2)).transferTaxFor(person);
        inOrder.verify(taxService)
.updateTaxFactor(eq(person), anyDouble());
        inOrder.verify(taxService).transferTaxFor(person);
    }
}
```

How it works...

When you create the `InOrder` object and define the desired order of execution, Mockito stores the expected order and then verifies it against the actual execution. During the iteration over the actual method invocations, depending on the passed verification mode (`times(...)`, `atLeast(...)`, and so on), Mockito marks either a single or multiple actual method executions as verified.

Let's try to depict this scenario using our test example. Having the `inOrder.verify(taxService, times(2)).transferTaxFor(person);` verification in order means that we are asking Mockito to mark two subsequent invocations of the `transferTaxFor(...)` method as verified and throw an exception if there were no such two subsequent calls.

The `times(...)` method returns a verification mode that is not greedy, which means that it will verify subsequent calls only. Take a look at the following code:

```
    inOrder.verify(taxService, times(2)).transferTaxFor(person);
    inOrder.verify(taxService).updateTaxFactor(eq(person), anyDouble());
    inOrder.verify(taxService).transferTaxFor(person);
```

When Mockito goes past the first line, it will mark only two methods of `transferTaxFor(...)` as verified. If there are any other `transferTaxFor(...)` methods, Mockito will not mark them as verified. This will happen in the third line, where an additional verification takes place.

> There is an interesting case of the `calls(...)` method that behaves in a different manner from the analogous `times(...)` and `atLeast(...)` methods that return `VerificationMode`. Let's have a look at the examples:

- ▸ `times(2)`: This method verifies that a method was executed exactly two times (it will fail if a method was invoked once or, for example, three times).

- ▶ `atLeast(2)`: This method verifies that the method was executed at least twice (it will fail if a method was invoked once. It marks all the subsequent method executions as verified).

- ▶ `calls(2)`: This method allows a non-greedy verification (check the *There's more...* section of this recipe for more information). If a method is executed three times, then `calls(2)` will not fail, unlike the analogous `times(3)`. Also, it will not mark the third invocation as verified, unlike `atLeast(2)`.

There's more...

As stated in the previous section, there are verification modes that are greedy; they will mark all the matching method executions as verified.

Let's imagine the following scenario (the test is based on the previous example):

```
@Test
    public void should_fail_at_updating_second_tax_factor_in_
specified_order_due_to_greedy_at_least() {
        // given
        Person person = new Person();

        // when
        systemUnderTest.transferTaxFor(person);

        // then
        InOrder inOrder = Mockito.inOrder(taxService);
        inOrder.verify(taxService)
.updateTaxFactor(eq(person), anyDouble());
        inOrder.verify(taxService, atLeastOnce()).
transferTaxFor(person);
        inOrder.verify(taxService)
.updateTaxFactor(eq(person), anyDouble());
        inOrder.verify(taxService).transferTaxFor(person);
    }
```

As you can see, the only difference between the tests is the following line (the difference is that we had `times(2)` and now we have `atLeastOnce()`):

```
inOrder.verify(taxService, atLeastOnce()).transferTaxFor(person);
```

This test won't succeed, which can seem very odd at first glance.

Let's have a look at the execution sequence of the system under the test's method in which we have all the mocked object's method executions:

```
taxService.updateTaxFactor(person, calculateTaxFactor(1));
taxService.transferTaxFor(person);
taxService.transferTaxFor(person);
taxService.updateTaxFactor(person, calculateTaxFactor(2));
taxService.transferTaxFor(person);
```

You may think that when we provide the atLeastOnce() method, Mockito will mark all the subsequent executions of the transferTaxFor method (in our case, there are two subsequent executions: lines two and three of the snippet) and then, the next verification step will be of the updateTaxFactor method, in line four of the snippet.

Since atLeastOnce() is greedy (atLeast() is always greedy in the InOrder verification), the following tasks take place:

1. When the first transferTaxFor method is verified against the AtLeast verification mode, it marks all three transferTaxFor methods as verified (lines two, three, and five).

2. Then, it starts the next step of verification after the last line (after line five) of our snippet (moving over line four). In our test code, the next step of verification is inOrder.verify(taxService).updateTaxFactor(eq(person), anyDouble()).

3. Bear in mind that due to the greedy nature of the AtLeast verification mode, we moved to the last execution of the transferTaxFor method.

4. Now, we need to execute the updateTaxFactor method.

5. We will get a Mockito VerificationInOrderFailure exception since there is no such method. The message will look more or less like the one shown as follows:

```
Wanted but not invoked:
taxService.updateTaxFactor(
    Person@183b1e8b,
    <any>
);
-> at ExplainingTheGreedyAlgorithm.should_fail_at_updating
_second_tax_factor_in_specified_order_due_to_greedy
_at_least(ExplainingTheGreedyAlgorithm.java:56)
Wanted anywhere AFTER following interaction:
taxService.transferTaxFor(
    Person@183b1e8b
);
```

If you are only interested in the fact that a given method gets executed in a precise order and you don't care about the rest, you just have to explicitly define only those interactions that you are interested in. In other words, you must use the following methods:

```
taxService.transferTaxFor(person);
taxService.updateTaxFactor(person, taxFactor);
taxService.transferTaxFor(person);
```

If you are only interested in the fact that the `transferTaxFor` methods get executed one after another (ignore the `updateTaxFactor` method), you would just have to write the following code:

```
InOrder inOrder = Mockito.inOrder(taxService);
inOrder.verify(taxService).transferTaxFor(person);
inOrder.verify(taxService).transferTaxFor(person);
```

See also

▸ Refer to the Mockito Wiki on the *greedy algorithm* at `https://github.com/mockito/mockito/wiki/Greedy-algorithm-of-verfication-InOrder`

▸ Refer to the Mockito documentation on the *Verification in order* at `http://docs.mockito.googlecode.com/hg/1.9.5/org/mockito/Mockito.html#6`

Verifying interactions and ignoring stubbed methods

In this recipe, we will perform the verification of the interaction with a mock, but at the same time, we will ignore the stubbed methods from this verification.

Getting ready

For this recipe, our system under test will be a `TaxTransferer` class that will transfer tax through the web service for the given person if this person is not null. It will send a statistics report regardless of the fact whether the transfer took place or not:

```
public class TaxTransferer {

    private final TaxService taxService;

    public TaxTransferer(TaxService taxService) {
        this.taxService = taxService;
    }
```

```
public boolean transferTaxFor(Person person) {
    if(person != null) {
        taxService.transferTaxFor(person);
    }
    return taxService.sendStatisticsReport();
}

}
```

How to do it...

To verify a mock's behavior in such a way that Mockito ignores the stubbed methods, you have to either call `Mockito.verifyNoMoreInteractions(Mockito.ignoreStubs(mocks...));` or `InOrder.verifyNoMoreInteractions(Mockito.ignoreStubs(mocks...));`.

Let's test the system under test using JUnit; see *Chapter 1, Getting Started with Mockito*, for the TestNG configuration (I'm using the `BDDMockito.given(...)` and AssertJ's `BDDAssertions.then(...)` static methods; check out *Chapter 7, Verifying Behavior with Object Matchers*, for details on how to work with AssertJ or how to do the same with Hamcrest's `assertThat(...)` method):

```
@RunWith(MockitoJUnitRunner.class)
public class TaxTransfererTest {

    @Mock TaxService taxService;

    @InjectMocks TaxTransferer systemUnderTest;

    @Test
  public void should_verify_that_ignoring_stubbed_method_there_was_a
_single_interaction_with_mock() {
        // given
        Person person = new Person();
        given(taxService.sendStatisticsReport()).willReturn(true);

        // when
        boolean success = systemUnderTest.transferTaxFor(person);

        // then
        verify(taxService).transferTaxFor(person);
        verifyNoMoreInteractions(ignoreStubs(taxService));
        then(success).isTrue();
    }
}
```

How it works...

When you call `Mockito.ignoreStubs(Object... mocks)`, Mockito goes through all the provided mocks and then marks invocations on their methods so that if they get stubbed, then they should be ignored for verification.

See also

▸ Refer to the Mockito documentation on *Verification ignoring stubs* at `http://docs.mockito.googlecode.com/hg/1.9.5/org/mockito/Mockito.html#25`

Verifying the method invocation within the specified time

Testing asynchronous code is a very broad topic, and we will not go into great details here. The fact is that the best way to test this kind of code is to make it synchronous and test it separately; this is crucial in terms of performance and execution time of unit tests. Imagine having quite a few such cases where you have to wait for a second or so for the test to complete. It would definitely increase the overall time of your tests and you wouldn't want that to happen.

You might, however, have a business requirement where it is crucial to verify whether some particular business feature was executed within the specified time (for example, a request has been sent within one second). In this recipe, we will take a closer look at what Mockito offers in this regard, and we'll do the same using the `Awaitility` library.

Getting ready

We will test the `PersonProcessor` class that performs some data processing and then delegates the saving of the person to a `PersonSaver` class.

Let's imagine that `PersonProcessor` is an endpoint that receives a `Person` request. We'll assume that the business requirement is to save a person within one second from the time of receiving a request. We would like to write a test that will ensure that the `savePerson(...)` method is executed within this specified time boundary.

All the logic done by `PersonProcessor` is done in a separate thread. For simplicity, we will not use any `ExecutorServices`; instead, we will start a thread manually. Also, we are not doing any real computations; instead, we are making the thread sleep for some time as shown in the following code:

```
public class PersonProcessor {

    private final PersonSaver personSaver;
```

```
        public PersonProcessor(PersonSaver personSaver) {
            this.personSaver = personSaver;
        }

        public void process(final Person person) {
            new Thread(new Runnable() {
              @Override
              public void run() {
                try {
                  // simulating time consuming actions
                  Thread.sleep(500);
                } catch (InterruptedException e) {
                  System.err.printf("The thread got interrupted
    [%s]%n", e);
                }
                personSaver.savePerson(person);
              }
            }).start();
        }

    }
```

How to do it...

To verify whether a method was executed within the given time, you have to call
`Mockito.verify(mock, Mockito.timeout(millis)).methodToVerify();`.

You can find a JUnit test of our system under test in the following code; see *Chapter 1,
Getting Started with Mockito*, for the TestNG configuration:

```
    @RunWith(MockitoJUnitRunner.class)
    public class PersonProcessorTest {

      @Mock PersonSaver personSaver;

      @InjectMocks PersonProcessor systemUnderTest;

      @Test
      public void should_process_person_within_specified_time() {
        // when
        systemUnderTest.process(new Person());

        // then
        verify(personSaver, timeout(1000)).savePerson(any(Person.class));
      }

    }
```

How it works...

The `timeout(...)` method instantiates the `Timeout` object that implements the `VerificationWithTimeout` interface. By default, when you call `timeout(...)`, you set the expectation that the method will be executed only once.

What about the situations in which you would like to check whether the method got invoked, for example, at least twice? `VerificationWithTimeout` gives you additional methods to do this: `times(...)`, `never()`, `atLeastOnce()`, `atLeast(...)`, and `only()`. So, to check whether the method was executed twice, you would have to write the following code:

```
verify(personSaver, timeout(1000)
.atLeast(2)).savePerson(any(Person.class));
```

There's more...

The preceding example is a very simple one, and Mockito doesn't offer you too much flexibility in terms of providing more advanced time conditions for the verification. There are libraries that are dedicated to this purpose. We'll have a look at the `Awaitility` library (https://code.google.com/p/awaitility/). To put it briefly, `Awaitility` is an open source library founded by JayWay, which gives you a **Domain Specific Language (DSL)** that allows you to define the expectations of an asynchronous system in a very elegant manner.

Before going further, we have to add `Awaitility` to the classpath. To do this, let's use either Maven or Gradle (for manual installation, you can download the JAR files from https://code.google.com/p/awaitility/wiki/Downloads).

The following is the configuration for Gradle:

```
testCompile 'com.jayway.awaitility:awaitility:1.6.0'
```

The following is the configuration for Maven:

```
<dependency>
    <groupId>com.jayway.awaitility</groupId>
    <artifactId>awaitility</artifactId>
    <version>1.6.0</version>
    <scope>test</scope>
</dependency>
```

Although there is no special integration of `Awaitility` and Mockito, you can use it for the sake of verification. Let's try to rewrite our previous test using `Awaitility` (we have statically imported the `Awaitility.await()` method):

```
@RunWith(MockitoJUnitRunner.class)
public class PersonProcessorTest {
```

```
@Mock PersonSaver personSaver;

@InjectMocks PersonProcessor systemUnderTest;

@Test
public void should_process_person_within_specified_time() {
  // when
  systemUnderTest.process(new Person());

  // then
  await().atMost(1, SECONDS).until(personIsSaved());
}

private Callable<Boolean> personIsSaved() {
  return new Callable<Boolean>() {
    @Override
    public Boolean call() throws Exception {
      try {
        verify(personSaver).savePerson(any(Person.class));
        return true;
      } catch (AssertionError assertionError) {
        return false;
      }
    }
  };
}

}
```

In this example, `Awaitility` will execute the body of the instantiated `Callable`'s `call()` method each 100 ms (the default poll value) and wait for a positive result for, at most, one second. In `Callable`, we have to catch the Mockito `AssertionError` because `Awaitility` will re-throw this exception and the test will fail. In that case, we just need to return `false` so that `Awaitility` knows that it should retry the method execution until it receives a positive result.

See also

▶ Refer to the Mockito documentation on *Verification with timeout* at `http://docs.mockito.googlecode.com/hg/1.9.5/org/mockito/Mockito.html#22`

▶ Refer to the `Awaitility` project's home page at `https://code.google.com/p/awaitility/`

7
Verifying Behavior with Object Matchers

In this chapter, we will cover the following recipes:

- ▸ Using Hamcrest matchers for assertions
- ▸ Creating custom Hamcrest matchers
- ▸ Using Hamcrest matchers for stubbing and verification
- ▸ Using AssertJ for assertions
- ▸ Creating custom AssertJ assertions
- ▸ Capturing and asserting the argument

Introduction

In this chapter, you will learn how to use both Hamcrest matchers (https://github.com/hamcrest/JavaHamcrest) and AssertJ assertions (http://joel-costigliola.github.io/assertj/assertj-core.html) in order to properly check the output of your system under test. Now, let's take a quick look at both of the libraries and check their pros and cons.

Hamcrest is a library that is incorporated inside one of the most frequently used testing libraries: JUnit. More importantly, it is used by plenty of other libraries and thus, makes it easy to re-use your current custom assertions in various tools. It allows you to construct **domain-specific language** (**DSL**) like statements to combine assertions and make your tests such that they can be read nicely and intuitively. They become a living documentation of your code and become much easier to maintain. As for the disadvantages, unfortunately, the latest version of Hamcrest is 1.3 (April 2014) and the latest release took place in 2012. The Hamcrest community is not too active in comparison to the AssertJ community. The real drawback of Hamcrest is the fact that your IDE will not help you much with code completion in order to pick the matchers that are acceptable for the current type of the passed argument. You need to find all of them yourself.

AssertJ (created by Joel Costigliola) is a fork of the FEST (created by Alex Ruiz; see `https://code.google.com/p/fest/`) library of assertions, and it is as its authors state: community driven. The release of Version 1.0.0 took place in 2013, and there have been releases of new versions more or less every two months, with Version 1.6.0 released in March 2014. The core version of AssertJ contains more assertions than the core version of Hamcrest. Also, the IDE will help you with code completion since it's based on the fluent interface API. AssertJ allows you to create fantastic DSL-like test code and very intuitively extends the assertions by providing your custom implementations. To show that AssertJ is gaining more and more users, I can say that Mockito developers are planning to move their tests' assertions to AssertJ (part of Issue 459). As for the cons of AssertJ, it is still not a library that is heavily incorporated into other frameworks, and you might end up with both Hamcrest and AssertJ on your classpath.

AssertJ and Hamcrest differ in syntax and in the ease of using the language of the domain (the so-called ubiquitous language—this notion comes from **domain-driven design** (**DDD**); please refer to *Domain-Driven Design: Tackling Complexity in the Heart of Software*, *Eric Evans*, at `http://www.amazon.com/Domain-Driven-Design-Tackling-Complexity-Software/dp/0321125215`). Now that we generally know how AssertJ and Hamcrest differ, we can move on to looking at each of them in more depth.

We will start off by showing you how to add Hamcrest to your project (if you are using JUnit, it's most likely to be there already). We will then create some custom examples of a unit test that uses some of the matchers that you can find in the Hamcrest core and Hamcrest's additional libraries. Then, we will create a custom Hamcrest matcher that will hide the assertion logic and will make the test code readable, like in a book.

Next, we will see a similar project setup and test, but we will perform the resulting object's assertions using AssertJ. We will then go through the most elementary examples of its core features in two ways: the standard approach that uses the `assertThat` static method and the one based on the **behavior-driven development** (**BDD**) approach that uses the `then` syntax. Next, we will create a custom AssertJ assertion and bind it to the globally available ones.

The system under test for all of the presented recipes in this chapter will be a system that grants a person a new identity (it will create a person with a new name, age, and siblings). Of course, the presented assertions are exaggerated to present the possibilities of both libraries. I'm testing far too many details that could be easily merged into a smaller and more readable version. Please do not write assertions such as these in your codebase.

Using Hamcrest matchers for assertions

In this recipe, we will add Hamcrest to your classpath (or check if it's already there) and look at a test that shows the concept that lies behind the `Hamcrest` library.

Getting ready

First, let's check the differences between the various Hamcrest JAR files:

- `hamcrest-core.jar`: This file contains the core functionality and a set of common matchers
- `hamcrest-library.jar`: This file contains a set of additional Hamcrest matchers
- `hamcrest-generator.jar`: This file generates code that combines many matcher implementations into a single class with static methods
- `hamcrest-integration.jar`: This file contains the integration of Hamcrest and other testing `toolsrary.jar` files
- `hamcrest-all.jar`: This file contains one JAR file containing all other JAR files

Most likely, you will use either `hamcrest-core` or `hamcrest-all`, depending on your needs.

If you are using JUnit 4 (from at least 4.9), you have the core version of Hamcrest already bound to JUnit. If you are using a dependency manager that connects to Maven's central repository, then you can get your dependencies as follows (an example for `hamcrest-all` for Maven and Gradle):

The following is the code for `hamcrest-all` (Maven):

```
<dependency>
    <groupId>org.hamcrest</groupId>
    <artifactId>hamcrest-all</artifactId>
    <version>1.3</version>
    <scope>test</scope>
</dependency>
```

The following is the code for `hamcrest-all` (Gradle):

```
testCompile('org.hamcrest:hamcrest-all:1.3')
```

If you are not using any of the dependency managers, you have to download either of the aforementioned JARS and add them to your classpath.

For this recipe, our system under test will be a `NewPersonGenerator` class that will call an external service, `NewIdentityCreator`, to generate a new identity for the current person, as shown in the following code:

```
public class NewPersonGenerator {

    private final NewIdentityCreator newIdentityCreator;

    public NewPersonGenerator(NewIdentityCreator newIdentityCreator) {
        this.newIdentityCreator = newIdentityCreator;
    }

    public Person generateNewIdentity(Person person) {
        String newName = newIdentityCreator.createNewName(person);
        int newAge = newIdentityCreator.createNewAge(person);
        List<Person> newSiblings =
newIdentityCreator.createNewSiblings(person);
        return new Person(newName, newAge, newSiblings);
    }
}
```

How to do it...

To use Hamcrest matchers to assert the behavior of your system under test, you have to perform the following steps for JUnit:

1. Use either JUnit's `Assert.assertThat(T object, Matcher<? super T> matcher)` or Hamcrest's `MatcherAssert.assertThat(T object, Matcher<? super T> matcher)` (if you don't want to depend on JUnit's classes). For TestNG, you will need to use Hamcrest's `MatcherAssert.assertThat(T object, Matcher<? super T> matcher)`.

2. The previous step shows how to solve the first part of the puzzle, whereas the following snippet depicts its second part (for readability purposes, I've left only the imports related to Hamcrest):

```
import static org.hamcrest.CoreMatchers.*;
import static org.hamcrest.CoreMatchers.endsWith;
import static org.hamcrest.CoreMatchers.startsWith;
import static org.hamcrest.beans.HasPropertyWithValue.*;
import static org.hamcrest.number.OrderingComparison.*;
import static org.junit.Assert.*;
```

```
@RunWith(MockitoJUnitRunner.class)
public class NewPersonGeneratorTest {

    @Mock NewIdentityCreator newIdentityCreator;

    @InjectMocks NewPersonGenerator systemUnderTest;

    @Test
    public void should_return_person_with_new_identity() {
        // given
        Person person = new Person("Robert", 25, asList(new
Person("John", 10), new Person("Maria", 12)));
        given(newIdentityCreator.createNewName(person))
.willReturn("Andrew");
        given(newIdentityCreator.createNewAge(person))
.willReturn(45);
        given(newIdentityCreator.createNewSiblings(person))
.willReturn(asList(new Person("Amy", 20),
 new Person("Alex", 25)));

        // when
        Person newPerson =
systemUnderTest.generateNewIdentity(person);

        // then
        // core matchers - comes with JUnit 4.9+
        assertThat(newPerson, allOf(notNullValue(),
 is(not(person)))));
        assertThat(newPerson.getName(),
 both(startsWith("And")).and(endsWith("rew")));
        assertThat(newPerson.getSiblings(),
 hasItems(new Person("Amy", 20), new Person("Alex", 25)));
        // for more matchers attach
org.hamcrest:hamcrest-all
        assertThat(newPerson.getAge(), greaterThan(25));
        assertThat(newPerson, hasProperty
("name", equalTo("Andrew")));
    }

}
```

How it works...

First, we'll check out how Hamcrest works internally. Then, we will check out the code. Each Hamcrest matcher interface implementation needs to implement the following two methods:

- `boolean matches(Object item)`: This method executes the matching algorithm and returns with the response as to whether the item matches our assumptions (for example, if the item is equal to another one)

- `void describeMismatch(Object item, Description mismatchDescription)`: This method defines why the object didn't successfully pass the matching algorithm

  - What can seem odd is that this method is void. The `mismatchDescription` object is not returned but it's mutated.

  - The `Description` interface has several methods out of which you most probably will use either `appendText(...)` and `appendValue(...)`. The first method will append the given text to the exception description. The latter takes an object as a parameter and the result of its `toString()` method will be put inside the < and > characters.

When calling JUnit's `Assert.assertThat()` version, what happens under the hood is that the Hamcrest's `MatcherAssert.assertThat()` method is executed. The latter first executes the passed matcher's matching logic via the `matches(...)` method. If the result of its execution is `false`, then the following takes place:

- The `Description` object is built. It contains the default `Expected...` but `was...` message filled with the logic defined in the `describeMismatch(...)` method of the matcher.

- An `AssertionError` message is thrown with this description.

Now, since we know how Hamcrest matchers work, let's go through the test code and check each matcher.

The following matchers are present in the core version of the `Hamcrest` library:

- `CoreMatchers.allOf(...)`: This matcher checks whether all of the passed matcher's execution of the `matches` method result to `true`. An example of this matcher is given as follows:

  `assertThat(newPerson, allOf(notNullValue(), is(not(person))));`

- `CoreMatchers.notNullValue()`: This matcher checks if the asserted object is not null.

- `CoreMatchers.is(...)`: This matcher adds syntactic sugar—does nothing but makes the code more intuitive to read.

- `CoreMatchers.not(...)`: This matcher checks whether the asserted object is not equal to the given object.

- `CoreMatchers.both(...).and(...)`: This matcher evaluates whether both of the passed matchers's execution of the `matches` method result to `true`. An example of this matcher is given as follows:

```
assertThat(newPerson.getName(),
 both(startsWith("And")).and(endsWith("rew")));
```

- `CoreMatchers.startsWith(...)`: This matcher checks if the passed string starts with the provided one.

- `CoreMatchers.endsWith(...)`: This matcher checks if the passed string ends with the provided one.

- `CoreMatchers.hasItems(...)`: This matcher evaluates whether the passed collection contains the passed items, as shown in the following code:

```
assertThat(newPerson.getSiblings(), hasItems
(new Person("Amy", 20), new Person("Alex", 25)));
```

The following matchers are present in the additional `Hamcrest` libraries (all of them are there in `hamcrest-all`):

- `OrderingComparison.greaterThan(...)`: This matcher evaluates whether the asserted comparable is greater than the passed item, as shown in the following code:

```
assertThat(newPerson.getAge(), greaterThan(25));
```

- `HasPropertyWithValue.hasProperty(...)`: This matcher finds the passed property on the asserted object and calls the passed matcher's logic on its value as follows:

```
assertThat(newPerson, hasProperty("name", equalTo("Andrew")));
```

- `CoreMatchers.equalTo(...)`: This matcher evaluates whether the asserted object is equal to the passed parameter. If neither are arrays, then the `equals` method is called to compare those objects. If they are arrays, then lengths and elements are checked for equality.

There's more...

Hamcrest contains numerous matchers for different types and logic, so if you can't find the matcher that suits your needs, please double check that you are not reinventing the wheel as there is a probability that it exists already.

See also

- ▶ Refer to the Hamcrest home page at `http://hamcrest.org/`
- ▶ Refer to the Java Hamcrest on GitHub at `https://github.com/hamcrest/JavaHamcrest`
- ▶ Refer to the Hamcrest tutorial at `https://code.google.com/p/hamcrest/wiki/Tutorial`
- ▶ Refer to the Hamcrest Java User Group at `https://groups.google.com/forum/?fromgroups#!forum/hamcrest-java`
- ▶ Refer to the Hamcrest API reference documentation at `http://hamcrest.org/JavaHamcrest/javadoc/1.3/`

Creating custom Hamcrest matchers

In this recipe, we will create a custom Hamcrest matcher. Please refer to the previous recipe in terms of the presented assertions in the test because in the current recipe, we will combine them in our custom matchers.

Getting ready

For this recipe, our system under test will be a `NewPersonGenerator` class that will call an external service, `NewIdentityCreator`, to generate a new identity for the current person, as shown in the following code:

```
public class NewPersonGenerator {

    private final NewIdentityCreator newIdentityCreator;

    public NewPersonGenerator(NewIdentityCreator newIdentityCreator) {
        this.newIdentityCreator = newIdentityCreator;
    }

    public Person generateNewIdentity(Person person) {
        String newName = newIdentityCreator.createNewName(person);
        int newAge = newIdentityCreator.createNewAge(person);
        List<Person> newSiblings =
newIdentityCreator.createNewSiblings(person);
        return new Person(newName, newAge, newSiblings);
    }
}
```

How to do it...

If you want to create a custom Hamcrest matcher, you have to attach your Hamcrest dependencies (if necessary). Depending on your needs, you can extend either of the classes (BaseMatcher, TypeSafeMatcher, TypeSafeDiagnosingMatcher, or DiagnosingMatcher).

The following snippet shows the test of our system using JUnit. It calls static methods that return custom Hamcrest matchers (please refer to *Chapter 1, Getting Started with Mockito*, and the previous recipe for information on how to configure your test for TestNG):

```
@SuppressWarnings("unchecked")
@RunWith(MockitoJUnitRunner.class)
public class NewPersonGeneratorTest {

    @Mock NewIdentityCreator newIdentityCreator;

    @InjectMocks NewPersonGenerator systemUnderTest;

    @Test
    public void should_return_person_with_new_identity() {
        // given
        Person person = new Person("Robert", 25, asList
(new Person("John"), new Person("Maria")));
        given(newIdentityCreator.createNewName(person)).
willReturn("Andrew");
        given(newIdentityCreator.createNewAge(person)).willReturn(45);
        given(newIdentityCreator.createNewSiblings(person))
        .willReturn(asList(new Person("Amy", 20), new Person
        ("Alejandro Gonzales", 25)));

        // when
        Person newPerson =
systemUnderTest.generateNewIdentity(person);

        // then
        assertThat(newPerson, allOf(is(not(equalTo(person))),
                                    hasNameEqualTo("Andrew"),
                                    hasAgeGreaterThan(25),
                                    containsSiblings
(new Person("Amy", 20), new Person("Alejandro Gonzales", 25))));
    }

}
```

The class that contains the static methods that create Hamcrest matchers is shown in the following code:

```java
public class PersonMatchers {

  public static Matcher hasNameEqualTo(final String name) {
    return new BaseMatcher() {
      @Override
      public boolean matches(Object item) {
        if (!(item instanceof Person)) {
          return false;
        }
        Person person = (Person) item;
        return bothNamesAreNull(person) || bothNamesMatch(person);
      }

      private boolean bothNamesMatch(Person person) {
        return (name != null && name.equals(person.getName()));
      }

      private boolean bothNamesAreNull(Person person) {
        return (name == null && person.getName() == null);
      }

      @Override
      public void describeTo(Description description) {
        description.appendText
("Name should be equal to ").appendValue(name);
      }
    };
  }

  public static Matcher<Person> hasAgeGreaterThan(final int age) {
    return new TypeSafeMatcher<Person>() {
      @Override
      protected boolean matchesSafely(Person person) {
        return person.getAge() > age;
      }

      @Override
      public void describeTo(Description description) {
        description.appendText
("Age should be greater than ").appendValue(age);
      }
```

```
    };
  }


  public static Matcher<Person> containsSiblings
(final Person... siblings) {
    return new TypeSafeDiagnosingMatcher<Person>() {
      @Override
      public void describeTo(Description description) {
        description.appendText
("Person should have siblings ").appendValue(siblings);
      }

      @Override
      protected boolean matchesSafely
(Person person, Description mismatchDescription) {
        if (!person.getSiblings().containsAll(Arrays.
asList(siblings))) {
          mismatchDescription.appendText
("The person has size of siblings equal to ")
            .appendValue(person.getSiblings().size())
            .appendText(" and the person has siblings ")
            .appendValue(person.getSiblings());
          return false;
        }
        return true;
      }
    };
  }
}
```

There are three main ways of creating custom Hamcrest matchers:

- Extend the `BaseMatcher` class as follows:

  1. Verify the types and casting (check the `hasNameEqualTo(...)` method from the preceding example).

  2. Provide the matching logic and the description that will be appended to the core Hamcrest assertion error message.

- Extend the `TypeSafeMatcher` class as follows:

  1. You don't have to take care of the casting (check the `hasAgeGreaterThan(...)` method from the previous example).

  2. Provide the matching logic and the description that will be appended to the core Hamcrest assertion error message.

- ▶ Extend the `TypeSafeDiagnosingMatcher` or `DiagnosingMatcher` class as follows:

    1. Provide the matching logic.

    2. What differs from `TypeSafeMatcher` is that you have access to the `Description` object that you can already manipulate at this point (check the `containsSiblings(...)` method from the previous example).

    3. Provide the description that will be appended to the core Hamcrest assertion error.

How it works...

To check how Hamcrest works internally, please check the previous recipe.

 Remember, before you start writing your custom matcher, do not implement the `Matcher` interface. Instead, always extend the abstract `BaseMatcher` class or another class that has already implemented it.

There's more...

Hamcrest allows you to create a class that combines all of your matchers in one place. If you are interested in this feature, please refer to the documentation at `https://code.google.com/p/hamcrest/wiki/Tutorial#Sugar_generation`.

See also

- ▶ Refer to the Hamcrest home page at `http://hamcrest.org/`
- ▶ Refer to the Hamcrest creating custom matchers at `https://code.google.com/p/hamcrest/wiki/Tutorial#Writing_custom_matchers`

Using Hamcrest matchers for stubbing and verification

In this recipe, we will use Hamcrest matchers in the stubbing and verification phases.

In this recipe, the system under test will be the `NewPersonGenerator` class that generates new identities for the given list of people. Also, we will send a web service message with the generated list of people, so their data gets updated, as shown in the following code:

```
public class NewPersonGenerator {

    private final NewIdentityCreator newIdentityCreator;

    public NewPersonGenerator
(NewIdentityCreator newIdentityCreator) {
        this.newIdentityCreator = newIdentityCreator;
    }

    public List<Person> generateNewIdentities
(List<Person> people) {
        List<Person> newPeople = new ArrayList<Person>();
        for(Person person : people) {
        String newName = newIdentityCreator.createNewName(person);
        int newAge = newIdentityCreator.createNewAge(person);
        List<Person> newSiblings =
newIdentityCreator.createNewSiblings(person);
        Person newPerson = new Person
(newName, newAge, newSiblings);
        newPeople.add(newPerson);
        }
        newIdentityCreator.updateDataFor(newPeople);
        return newPeople;
    }

}
```

How to do it...

If you want to create a custom Hamcrest matcher, you have to perform the following steps:

1. Attach your Hamcrest dependencies (if necessary).

2. If method arguments are objects, just pass the `Mockito.argThat(...)` method as a stubbed/verified method parameter. If method arguments are primitives, pass the respective `intThat(...)` or `booleanThat(...)` method as a stubbed/verified method parameter.

3. Pass Hamcrest matchers as arguments to the `Mockito.argThat(...)` method, regardless of the fact that you are stubbing or verifying methods.

The following snippet shows the test of our system using JUnit. It calls static methods that return custom Hamcrest matchers (please refer to *Chapter 1, Getting Started with Mockito,* and the previous recipe for information on how to configure your test for TestNG):

```
@RunWith(MockitoJUnitRunner.class)
public class NewPersonGeneratorTest {

    @Mock NewIdentityCreator newIdentityCreator;

    @InjectMocks NewPersonGenerator systemUnderTest;

    @Test
    public void should_update_data_for_a_single_generated_mature_
person() {
        // given
        Person robert = new Person("Robert", 25);
        Person anna = new Person("Anna", 35);
      List<Person> oldPeople = asList(robert, anna);
        given(newIdentityCreator.createNewAge
(argThat(hasAgeGreaterThan(30)))).willReturn(18);

        // when
        systemUnderTest.generateNewIdentities(oldPeople);

        // then
        verify(newIdentityCreator).updateDataFor(numberOfMaturePeop
le(1));
    }

}
```

The `hasAgeGreaterThan(...)` method is shown in the following code:

```
public static Matcher<Person> hasAgeGreaterThan(final int age) {
    return new TypeSafeMatcher<Person>() {
        @Override
        protected boolean matchesSafely(Person person) {
          return person.getAge() > age;
        }

        @Override
        public void describeTo(Description description) {
            description.appendText
("Age should be greater than ").appendValue(age);
        }
    };
}
```

The `peopleNotContaining(...)` method is shown in the following code
(`Mockito.argThat(...)` is statically imported):

```
    public static List<Person> numberOfMaturePeople(int count) {
    return argThat(containsNumberOfMaturePeople(count));
}


  static Matcher<List<Person>> containsNumberOfMaturePeople
(final int count) {
    return new TypeSafeMatcher<List<Person>>() {
      @Override
      protected boolean matchesSafely(List<Person> item) {
        return count == countMaturePeople(item);
      }

      @Override
      public void describeTo(Description description) {
        description.appendText
("Number of mature people should be equal to ")
                .appendValue(count);
      }

      private int countMaturePeople(List<Person> people) {
        int maturePeopleCount = 0;
        for(Person person : people) {
          if (person.getAge() >= 18) {
            maturePeopleCount = maturePeopleCount + 1;
          }
        }
        return maturePeopleCount;
      }
    };
}
```

What happens in this test can be summarized as follows:

1. We stub the creation of age only for people whose age is greater than 30.
2. The code gets executed.
3. We verify that the `newIdentityCreator.updateDataFor(...)` method gets
   executed with a list of people containing only one person who has an age greater
   than or equal to 18.

How it works...

When you pass a matcher as an argument of the verified method, then behind the scenes, Mockito delegates it to the `ArgumentMatcher` class. The `ArgumentMatcher` class in turn extends Hamcrest's `BaseMatcher`.

The internals of Hamcrest have been described in more depth in the *Using Hamcrest matchers for assertions* recipe.

There's more...

Remember to think twice when creating very complicated argument matchers. You want your tests to be very elegant and readable, so sometimes, it's just better to implement the `equals()` method for arguments that are passed to the mocks. Mockito matches arguments using the `equals()` method by default, so you can hide the implementation inside the matched class.

See also

▶ Refer to the Hamcrest home page at `http://hamcrest.org/`

▶ Refer to the Hamcrest creating custom matchers at `https://code.google.com/p/hamcrest/wiki/Tutorial#Writing_custom_matchers`

Using AssertJ for assertions

In this recipe, we will add AssertJ to your classpath (or check if it's already there) and take a look at a test that should show the concept that lies behind the `AssertJ` library.

Getting ready

First, let's check the differences between the different AssertJ JAR files:

▶ `assertj-core`: This file contains the vast majority of assertions (there is rarely a need to have any additional dependencies)

▶ `assertj-guava`: This file contains additional assertions for some of the `Guava` library related classes

▶ `assertj-neo4j`: This file contains additional assertions for the Neo4j graph database related classes

▶ `assertj-joda-time`: This file contains additional assertions for the `JodaTime` library related classes

▶ `assertj-assertions-generator-maven-plugin`: This is a Maven plugin for generating AssertJ assertions

In most cases, all you need is `assertj-core` since it already has plenty of useful assertions.

Regardless of the fact that you are using JUnit or TestNG, you still have to add `assertj-core` to your classpath since it isn't embedded into either of them.

The following is the dependency for AssertJ core (Maven):

```
<dependency>
    <groupId>org.assertj</groupId>
    <artifactId>assertj-core</artifactId>
    <version>1.6.0</version>
    <scope>test</scope>
</dependency>
```

The following is the dependency for AssertJ core (Gradle):

```
testCompile('org.assertj:assertj-core:1.6.0')
```

If you are not using any of the dependency managers, you have to download one of the aforementioned JAR files and add them to your classpath.

For this recipe, our system under test will be a `NewPersonGenerator` class that will call an external service, `NewIdentityCreator`, to generate a new identity for the current person, as shown in the following code:

```java
public class NewPersonGenerator {

    private final NewIdentityCreator newIdentityCreator;

    public NewPersonGenerator(NewIdentityCreator newIdentityCreator) {
        this.newIdentityCreator = newIdentityCreator;
    }

    public Person generateNewIdentity(Person person) {
        String newName = newIdentityCreator.createNewName(person);
        int newAge = newIdentityCreator.createNewAge(person);
        List<Person> newSiblings =
newIdentityCreator.createNewSiblings(person);
        return new Person(newName, newAge, newSiblings);
    }
}
```

How to do it...

In order to use the AssertJ assertions in your tests, you have to perform the following steps:

1. Add the AssertJ dependencies to your classpath.
2. Call `Assertions.assertThat(T object).someAssertionMethod(...)` to perform assertion.

The following snippet depicts the aforementioned scenario for JUnit (refer to *Chapter 1, Getting Started with Mockito* for information on the TestNG configuration):

```
@RunWith(MockitoJUnitRunner.class)
public class NewPersonGeneratorTest {

    @Mock NewIdentityCreator newIdentityCreator;

    @InjectMocks NewPersonGenerator systemUnderTest;

    @Test
    public void should_return_person_with_new_identity() {
        // given
        Person person = new Person("Robert", 25, asList
(new Person("John", 10), new Person("Maria", 12)));
        given(newIdentityCreator.createNewName(person))
.willReturn("Andrew");
        given(newIdentityCreator.createNewAge(person)).willReturn(45);
        given(newIdentityCreator.createNewSiblings(person))
.willReturn(asList(new Person("Amy", 20), new Person
("Alex", 25)));

        // when
        Person newPerson =
systemUnderTest.generateNewIdentity(person);

        // then
        assertThat(newPerson).isNotNull().isNotEqualTo(person);
        assertThat(newPerson.getName()).isNotNull()
.startsWith("And").endsWith("rew");
        assertThat(newPerson.getSiblings())
.contains(new Person("Amy", 20), new Person("Alex", 25));
        assertThat(newPerson.getAge()).isGreaterThan(25);
        assertThat(newPerson.getSiblings()).extracting
("name", "age").contains(tuple("Amy", 20), tuple("Alex", 25));
    }

}
```

How it works...

When you call `Assertions.assertThat(T object)`, you can benefit from AssertJ's overloaded `assertThat(...)` methods that can be used with different types of classes. The examples of such classes are given as follows:

- `public static BigDecimalAssert assertThat(BigDecimal actual);`
- `public static BooleanAssert assertThat(boolean actual);`
- `public static FileAssert assertThat(File actual);`
- `public static <T> ObjectAssert<T> assertThat(T actual);`

Each of the overloaded `assertThat(...)` methods delegates to the instantiation of the proper implementation of the `AbstractAssert` class that contains all of the basic assertions that come from implementing the `Assert` interface. You also have access to the actual field called `actual` that contains the object you are performing assertion against (which allows you to create your custom assertions quickly).

Due to the fact that AssertJ operates on overloaded methods that are always type-specific, your IDE will instantly help you find all of the matching assertion methods. For example, in the previous code snippet, we presented assertions for Files as assertThat(File actual). The execution of this method will return FileAssert that is file-specific and allows you to use such methods as follows (to mention only a few):

```
exists(), isDirectory(), isRelative(), hasParent(...),
  hasExtension(...)
```

Since AssertJ's main concept is to operate on fluent interfaces, and each assertion returns the assertion implementation itself, you do not have to combine several assertions into a single one as done in Hamcrest. Instead, you can just execute a chain of methods as follows:

```
assertThat(newPerson).isNotNull().isNotEqualTo(person);
```

AssertJ also proves to be extremely powerful in terms of performing assertions over iterables as follows:

```
assertThat(newPerson.getSiblings()).extracting
  ("name", "age").contains(tuple("Amy", 20), tuple("Alex", 25));
```

You can easily extract (using the extracting method) certain properties of each of the iterables and check their state in comparison to specially created objects called tuples (check AssertJ examples of asserting iterables at `https://github.com/joel-costigliola/assertj-examples/blob/master/assertions-examples/src/test/java/org/assertj/examples/IterableAssertionsExamples.java`).

Tuples allow you to create a structure matching your extracted elements. In other words, for the aforementioned siblings that are of a `Person` type, we extract two strings from the properties `name` and `age` Next, we compare them against a structure having name equal to `Amy` and age equal to `20` and then against name equal to `Alex` and age equal to `25`. Of course, this is only a small portion of AssertJ possibilities, but it should give you a clue of how powerful and readable AssertJ is.

There's more...

From AssertJ version 1.6.0, you can make your tests look even more readable and follow the BDD naming by changing the `assertThat(...)` method into the `then(...)` method. You can rewrite the test to follow that approach, as shown in the following code:

```
@Test
public void should_return_person_with_new_identity() {
    // given
    Person person = new Person("Robert", ROBERT_AGE,
newArrayList(new Person("John", 10), new Person("Maria", 12)));
    given(newIdentityCreator.createNewName(person))
.willReturn("Andrew");
    given(newIdentityCreator.createNewAge(person)).willReturn(45);
    given(newIdentityCreator.createNewSiblings(person))
.willReturn(newArrayList(new Person("Amy", 20),
 new Person("Alex", 25)));

    // when
    Person newPerson =
systemUnderTest.generateNewIdentity(person);

    // then
    then(newPerson).isNotNull().isNotEqualTo(person);
    then(newPerson.getName()).isNotNull().startsWith("And")
.endsWith("rew");
    then(newPerson.getSiblings()).contains
(new Person("Amy", 20), new Person("Alex", 25));
    then(newPerson.getAge()).isGreaterThan(25);
    then(newPerson.getSiblings()).extracting
("name", "age").contains(tuple("Amy", 20), tuple("Alex", 25));
}
```

See also

- ▶ Refer to the AssertJ home page at `http://joel-costigliola.github.io/assertj/assertj-core.html`
- ▶ Refer to the repository containing AssertJ assertions' examples at `https://github.com/joel-costigliola/assertj-examples/`
- ▶ Refer to the AssertJ features highlight at `http://joel-costigliola.github.io/assertj/assertj-core-features-highlight.html`

Creating custom AssertJ assertions

In this recipe, we will create a custom AssertJ assertion. Please refer to the previous recipe for the presented assertions in the test because in the current recipe, we will combine them into our custom assertions:

Getting ready

For this recipe, our system under test will be a `NewPersonGenerator` class that will call an external service, `NewIdentityCreator`, to generate a new identity for the current person, as shown in the following code:

```
public class NewPersonGenerator {

    private final NewIdentityCreator newIdentityCreator;

    public NewPersonGenerator(NewIdentityCreator newIdentityCreator) {
        this.newIdentityCreator = newIdentityCreator;
    }

    public Person generateNewIdentity(Person person) {
        String newName = newIdentityCreator.createNewName(person);
        int newAge = newIdentityCreator.createNewAge(person);
        List<Person> newSiblings =
newIdentityCreator.createNewSiblings(person);
        return new Person(newName, newAge, newSiblings);
    }
}
```

How to do it...

To create and use a custom AssertJ assertion in your tests, you have to perform the following steps:

1. Attach your AssertJ dependencies.

2. Create a class that extends the `AbstractAssert` class, which takes two bounds of generics: one is the assertion's class and the other is the asserted object's class.

3. Implement a constructor that has two parameters: one that passes the actual object and the other that passes the assertion's class.

4. Define custom methods that perform assertions and return the assert itself (in order to construct a fluent iterable interface).

5. Create a class that extends the `Assertions` class (in order to access core assertions). You will put your custom assertion factory method here.

6. Create an `assertThat(T object)/then(T object)` static factory method that will instantiate your custom assertion.

7. Call your custom `AssertJ` assertion in the assertion phase of your test.

The following snippet depicts the aforementioned scenario for JUnit (refer to *Chapter 1, Getting Started with Mockito*, for information on the TestNG configuration):

```
@RunWith(MockitoJUnitRunner.class)
public class NewPersonGeneratorTest {

    @Mock NewIdentityCreator newIdentityCreator;

    @InjectMocks NewPersonGenerator systemUnderTest;

    @Test
    public void should_return_person_with_new_identity() {
        // given
        Person person = new Person
("Robert", 25, asList(new Person("John"), new Person("Maria")));
        given(newIdentityCreator.createNewName(person))
.willReturn("Andrew");
        given(newIdentityCreator.createNewAge(person)).willReturn(45);
        given(newIdentityCreator.createNewSiblings(person))
.willReturn(asList(new Person("Amy"), new Person
("Alejandro Gonzales")));

        // when
        Person newPerson =
systemUnderTest.generateNewIdentity(person);
```

```
        // then
        then(newPerson).isNotEqualTo(person)
                            .hasNameEqualTo("Andrew")
                            .hasAgeGreaterThan(25)
                            .containsSiblings
(new Person("Amy"), new Person("Alejandro Gonzales"));
    }

}
```

The class shown in the following code contains all of the assertThat methods from the Assertions class and a then(...) method that instantiates our custom PersonAssert assertion:

```
public class MyBddAssertions extends BDDAssertions {

    public static PersonAssert then(Person actual) {
        return new PersonAssert(actual);
    }

}
```

The implementation of the custom assertion is shown as follows:

```
public class PersonAssert extends AbstractAssert
<PersonAssert, Person> {

  protected PersonAssert(Person actual) {
        super(actual, PersonAssert.class);
  }

  public PersonAssert hasNameEqualTo(String name) {
        String actualName = actual.getName();
        assertThat(actualName).isEqualTo(name);
        return this;
  }

  public PersonAssert hasAgeGreaterThan(int age) {
        int actualAge = actual.getAge();
        assertThat(actualAge).isGreaterThan(age);
        return this;
  }

  public PersonAssert containsSiblings(Person... siblings) {
        List<Person> actualSiblings = actual.getSiblings();
        assertThat(actualSiblings).contains(siblings);
        return this;
  }

}
```

How it works...

The flow regarding the creation of a custom AssertJ assertion is rooted deeply in the core of AssertJ that is described in greater depth in the previous recipe, so please refer to it for more information on how it exactly works.

It's beneficial to have a custom class grouping your `assertThat (...)`/`then (...)` methods that extend the `Assertions` class. You will have a single static import statement and will access all of the `Assertions` static methods.

There's more...

AssertJ allows you to easily create assertions for your classes. It comes with a command-line tool and a Maven plugin. You have to pass the fully-qualified names of classes or the entire packages of classes for which you want to create assertions. Once the generator finishes its job, you will have the assertion classes generated with all of the assertion methods for each of the fields present.

For more information on this feature, please refer to the documentation at `http://joel-costigliola.github.io/assertj/assertj-assertions-generator.html`

See also

- ▶ Refer to the AssertJ home page at `http://joel-costigliola.github.io/assertj/assertj-core.html`
- ▶ Refer to the AssertJ features highlight at `http://joel-costigliola.github.io/assertj/assertj-core-features-highlight.html`

Capturing and asserting the argument

In this recipe, we will capture an argument passed to the mock's method to perform further verification.

Getting ready

For this recipe, our system under test will be a `TaxTransferer` class that will prepare the person to be sent through the web service by marking him a Polish citizen. Only if the person is not null, the transfer of tax will take place. Let's also assume that it is absolutely crucial for us to make sure that the person that we send via the web service contains very specific data:

```
public class TaxTransferer {

    static final String POLAND = "Poland";
```

```
    private final TaxService taxService;

    public TaxTransferer(TaxService taxService) {
        this.taxService = taxService;
    }

    public void transferTaxFor(Person person) {
        if (person == null) {
            return;
        }
        taxService.transferTaxFor(makePersonPolish(person));
    }

    private Person makePersonPolish(Person person) {
        return new Person(person, POLAND);
    }

}
```

How to do it...

To create `ArgumentCaptor` that will contain the captured argument, you have to perform the following steps:

1. Annotate your test with `@RunWith(MockitoJUnitRunner.class)` for JUnit or `@Listeners(MockitoTestNGListener.class)` for TestNG (check *Chapter 1, Getting Started with Mockito*, for more details on the TestNG configuration).

2. Create a field of the `ArgumentCaptor` type and annotate it with the `@Captor` annotation.

3. To use the capturing of arguments, you have to verify a method and provide the `capture()` method of `ArgumentCaptor` as its parameter, as shown in the following code:

    ```
    verify(mock).methodToVerify(argumentCaptor.capture());
    ```

    If this procedure is followed, your captor will contain the captured arguments.

4. Now you can retrieve the last passed value with the following code:

    ```
    argumentCaptor.getValue()
    ```

5. You can get all of the captured values (if the method was executed multiple times) by calling the following method:

    ```
    argumentCaptor.getAllValues()
    ```

The following code represents the JUnit test with an example of `ArgumentCaptor` (I'm using the `BDDMockito.given(...)` static import):

```
@RunWith(MockitoJUnitRunner.class)
public class TaxTransfererTest {

    @Mock TaxService taxService;

    @InjectMocks TaxTransferer systemUnderTest;

    @Captor ArgumentCaptor<Person> personCaptor;

    @Test
    public void should_change_persons_country_before_sending_data_
through_ws() {
        // when
        systemUnderTest.transferTaxFor
( new Person("Lewandowski", "UK"));

        // then
        verify(taxService).transferTaxFor(personCaptor.capture());
        then(personCaptor.getValue()).hasName("Lewandowski")
.hasCountry("Poland");
    }

}
```

How it works...

When you call `argumentMatcher.capture()`, Mockito registers a special implementation of the Mockito `ArgumentMatcher`—the `CapturingMatcher`. This matcher stores the passed argument values for later use. When you call either `getAllValues()` or `getValue()`, Mockito retrieves the data stored in that matcher.

See also

- ▶ Refer to the Mockito documentation on argument captors at `http://docs.mockito.googlecode.com/hg/1.9.5/org/mockito/Mockito.html#15`
- ▶ Refer to the Mockito documentation on argument captors via annotations at `http://docs.mockito.googlecode.com/hg/1.9.5/org/mockito/Mockito.html#21`

8
Refactoring with Mockito

In this chapter, we will cover the following recipes:

- ▸ Removing the problems with instance creation
- ▸ Refactoring the classes that do too much
- ▸ Refactoring the classes that use the class casts
- ▸ Refactoring the classes that use static methods
- ▸ Refactoring the tests that use too many mocks

Introduction

Programmers rarely have the opportunity to work with code that they create from scratch. Often, we have to support systems that have been there for several years and were written at the time when programmers were paid for the number of typed lines of code. However, this is not always the case. Nowadays, when there are so many start-up companies emerging, people tend to sacrifice quality for money. It's all about faster delivery of new features. How you write your code is not that important until the application works fine.

This leads to maintaining legacy systems (take a look at *Working Effectively with Legacy Code*, *Martin Feathers*, available at `http://www.amazon.com/Working-Effectively-Legacy-Michael-Feathers/dp/0131177052`, for details on how to work with such systems). Such code monster-like classes are also called god classes. Most likely, their names end with a `manager` or `helper` suffix since they do everything and have access to all the possible dependencies in the system. Methods have hundreds of lines and there are no unit tests (not to mention integration or acceptance tests). Sometimes, the scenario we find once we start working on a project is not that bad, but the concept may be alike. Usually, there is no quality control and the project managers require the teams to deliver more. We have to make the code operational for now without having any broader strategic vision of how to run a project.

Working in such an environment may be frustrating and scary in terms of making any changes to the code—without the tests, how can you be sure that you didn't break anything? Well, you can't—that's why this chapter will show you how to deal with some of the most horrific coding practices I've seen in my career.

I'd like to highlight that some of the code presented in the subsequent recipes is written terribly on purpose; if you find a similar snippet in your codebase, you will already know how to refactor it. We are assuming a case in which we work in a system without tests. In this way, we'll try to first write tests for the existing functionality and then remove the bad design while already having some tests.

I'd also like to emphasize that there are whole books written about refactoring (for example, *Refactoring: Improving the Design of Existing Code*, *Martin Fowler* with *Kent Beck*, *John Brant*, *William Opdyke*, and *Don Roberts*, available at `http://martinfowler.com/books/refactoring.html`), and in this chapter, I'll only touch on the subject. The aim of these recipes is to show you how to use Mockito features and Mockito-based tools to test your code.

We'll start off by dealing with quite a common issue that has an instantiation of an object inside our method. We'll see how to mock it, and refactor it immediately after that. Then, we'll try to refactor classes that do not follow the SOLID principles (please refer to the *Introduction* section of *Chapter 2*, *Creating Mocks*, for more information) in order for them to be fully testable. Next, we will move through terrible features such as basing code on class casts—we'll use Mockito to deal with this and to change this preposterous concept into nice code. We will also test and improve code that operates using unnecessary static method execution. Finally, we will take a closer look at test classes that use too many mocks.

Removing the problems with instance creation

In this recipe, we will first test an existing class that uses `new` to instantiate an object which performs complex logic; then, we'll refactor it. The problem with the `new` operator is that it's very difficult to mock the created instance. An object's collaborators should be passed as parameters of the constructor or somehow injected via the dependency injection system.

Getting ready

Let's assume that our system under test is a system that generates a new identity for a given person who can have a name, an age, and siblings. Note that the following snippet presents a poorly designed class:

```java
public class BadlyDesignedNewPersonGenerator {

    public Person generateNewIdentity(Person person) {
        NewIdentityCreator newIdentityCreator = new
NewIdentityCreator();
        String newName = newIdentityCreator.createNewName(person);
        int newAge = newIdentityCreator.createNewAge(person);
        List<Person> newSiblings =
newIdentityCreator.createNewSiblings(person);
        return new Person(newName, newAge, newSiblings);
    }

}
```

In the preceding code, the `NewIdentityCreator` class performs the following logic (for simplicity, we only write that part of the code where we are accessing external resources):

```java
class NewIdentityCreator {

    static final String DEFAULT_NEW_NAME = "NewName";

    public String createNewName(Person person) {
        System.out.printf("Calling web service and
creating new name for person [%s]%n", person.getName());
        return DEFAULT_NEW_NAME;
    }

    public int createNewAge(Person person) {
        System.out.printf("Calling db and
creating new age for person [%s]%n", person.getName());
        return person.getAge() + 5;
    }

    public List<Person> createNewSiblings(Person person) {
        System.out.printf("Making heavy IO operations and
creating new siblings for person [%s]%n", person.getName());
        return Arrays.asList(new Person("Bob"),
new Person("Andrew"));
    }

}
```

How to do it...

In order to test the preceding implementation and then refactor it, we have to perform the following steps:

1. Write a test that verifies the behavior of the system under test (in this case, we want to be sure that the person has a new identity at the end of the day).

2. Mock out all of the collaborators, if necessary (if you know what you are doing, you can move to the next point without performing this intermediary step).

3. Refactor the code so that it follows good coding practices, including the SOLID principles.

How it works...

We start by writing a test which will verify that our application works as expected. This will give us confidence for further refactoring. Object instantiation in the method's body leads to heavy coupling between the `BadlyDesignedNewPersonGenerator` and `NewIdentityCreator` classes. What we want to achieve is component isolation, decoupling in other words. Once both the classes are decoupled, they can be tested in isolation, which makes the tests smaller and less complex.

In the following code snippet, you will find a test for your system that verifies whether the `BadlyDesignedNewPersonGenerator` class will generate a new identity for the given person. It references step 1 of the *How to do it...* section of this recipe. All the examples are presented for JUnit and AssertJ; please refer to *Chapter 1, Getting Started with Mockito*, for TestNG configuration and *Chapter 7, Verifying Behavior with Object Matchers*, for AssertJ configuration and the `BDDAssertions` static imports:

```java
public class BadlyDesignedNewPersonGeneratorTest {

    BadlyDesignedNewPersonGenerator systemUnderTest =
new BadlyDesignedNewPersonGenerator();

    @Test
    public void should_return_person_with_new_identity() {
        // given
        List<Person> siblings = asList(new Person
("John", 10), new Person("Maria", 12));
        Person person = new Person("Robert", 25, siblings);

        // when
        Person newPerson =
systemUnderTest.generateNewIdentity(person);
```

```
        // then
        then(newPerson).isNotEqualTo(person);
        then(newPerson.getAge()).isNotEqualTo(person.getAge());
        then(newPerson.getName()).isNotEqualTo(person.getName());
        then(newPerson.getSiblings())
.doesNotContainAnyElementsOf(siblings);
    }

}
```

Now that we have the test, let's move to step 2 of the *How to do it...* section of this recipe. We have to stub the method interactions that access external resources. We will try to mock out the existing object initialization and replace it with a mock by using PowerMock, as shown in the following code (remember that this should never happen in properly written code):

```
@RunWith(PowerMockRunner.class)
@PrepareForTest(BadlyDesignedNewPersonGenerator.class)
public class BadlyDesignedNewPersonGeneratorPowerMockTest {

    BadlyDesignedNewPersonGenerator systemUnderTest =
 new BadlyDesignedNewPersonGenerator();

    @Test
    public void should_return_person_with_new_identity() throws
Exception {
        // given
        List<Person> siblings = asList
(new Person("John", 10), new Person("Maria", 12));
        Person person = new Person("Robert", 25, siblings);
        NewIdentityCreator newIdentityCreator =
Mockito.mock(NewIdentityCreator.class);
        PowerMockito.whenNew(NewIdentityCreator.class)
.withAnyArguments().thenReturn(newIdentityCreator);

        // when
        Person newPerson = systemUnderTest.
generateNewIdentity(person);

        // then
        then(newPerson).isNotNull().isNotEqualTo(person);
        then(newPerson.getAge()).isNotEqualTo(person.getAge());
        then(newPerson.getName()).isNotEqualTo(person.getName());
        then(newPerson.getSiblings()).
doesNotContainAnyElementsOf(siblings);
    }
}
```

As you can see in the previous code, we do not stub methods on the `NewIdentityCreator` class so that they return any particular values. The default Mockito ones are okay for us—we just want to be sure that the input and resulting person are not the same. The YAGNI principle (the You Aren't Gonna Need it principle defined in *Extreme Programming Installed*, *Ronald E. Jeffries*, *Ann Anderson*, and *Chet Hendrickson*) makes sense here. We don't care about concrete values; we only want to be sure that the person's identity has changed.

Now that we have the test, we can refactor the code and remove any PowerMock occurrence since it only proves that our code is full of bad ideas. The following is the snippet that shows the refactored version of our `BadlyDesignedNewPersonGenerator` class. We perform step 3 of the *How to do it...* section of this recipe. This time, NewIdentityCreator is injected through the constructor as a dependency. Check the *Inversion of Control Containers and the Dependency Injection pattern* article by *Martin Fowler*, available at `http://www.martinfowler.com/articles/injection.html`, for more information on dependency injection.

```
public class RefactoredNewPersonGenerator {

    private final NewIdentityCreator newIdentityCreator;

    public RefactoredNewPersonGenerator
(NewIdentityCreator newIdentityCreator) {
        this.newIdentityCreator = newIdentityCreator;
    }

    public Person generateNewIdentity(Person person) {
        String newName = newIdentityCreator.createNewName(person);
        int newAge = newIdentityCreator.createNewAge(person);
        List<Person> newSiblings =
newIdentityCreator.createNewSiblings(person);
        return new Person(newName, newAge, newSiblings);
    }
}
```

Finally, we can refactor the test by removing all of the PowerMock dependencies and by proper injection of the `RefactoredNewPersonGenerator` collaborator, `NewIdentityCreator`. Remember that the actual logic of the test hasn't changed at all. Take a look at the following code:

```
@RunWith(MockitoJUnitRunner.class)
public class RefactoredPersonGeneratorTest {

    @Mock NewIdentityCreator newIdentityCreator;

    @InjectMocks RefactoredNewPersonGenerator systemUnderTest;
```

```java
@Test
public void should_return_person_with_new_identity() {
    // given
    List<Person> siblings = asList
(new Person("John", 10), new Person("Maria", 12));
    Person person = new Person("Robert", 25, siblings);

    // when
    Person newPerson =
systemUnderTest.generateNewIdentity(person);

    // then
    then(newPerson).isNotNull().isNotEqualTo(person);
    then(newPerson.getAge()).isNotEqualTo(person.getAge());
    then(newPerson.getName()).isNotEqualTo(person.getName());
    then(newPerson.getSiblings())
.doesNotContainAnyElementsOf(siblings);
    }
}
```

There's more...

Here's another example of the same type of refactoring. You may have had issues with mocking time in your applications. You had to see this new `Date()` instantiation passed around in your code, and you wondered how to deal with it in your test. Let's assume that we have a class which logs the time of a visit of a person and returns that time, as shown in the following code:

```java
public class BadlyDesignedVisitLogger {

    public Date logUsersVisit(){
        Date dateOfLogging = new Date();
        System.out.printf("User visited us at [%s]%n", dateOfLogging);
        return dateOfLogging;
    }

}
```

Since you already know how to extract responsibilities to separate classes, you can think of the new `Date()` instantiation as a responsibility of a certain class presented as follows (of course, at some point you will have to test that extracted class, but it will be a relatively trivial test):

```java
public class RefactoredVisitLogger {

    private final TimeSource timeSource;
```

```
        public RefactoredVisitLogger(TimeSource timeSource) {
            this.timeSource = timeSource;
        }

        public Date logUsersVisit(){
            Date dateOfLogging = timeSource.getDate();
            System.out.printf("User visited us at [%s]%n", dateOfLogging);
            return dateOfLogging;
        }

    }
```

The `TimeSource` class can be mocked, as shown in the following code:

```
public class TimeSource {

    static final String DATE_FORMAT = "dd-MM-yyyy";

    public Date getDate() {
            return new Date();
    }

    public static Date on(String date) {
        SimpleDateFormat formatter = new SimpleDateFormat(DATE_FORMAT);
        try {
          return formatter.parse(date);
        } catch (ParseException e) {
          throw new InvalidDateFormatException(e);
        }
    }

}
```

Now, the test for such a class for JUnit will look as follows (please refer to *Chapter 1, Getting Started with Mockito,* for the TestNG configuration and *Chapter 7, Verifying Behavior with Object Matchers,* for AssertJ configuration and `BDDAssertions` static imports):

```
@RunWith(MockitoJUnitRunner.class)
public class VisitLoggerTest {

    @Mock TimeSource timeSource;

    @InjectMocks RefactoredVisitLogger refactoredVisitLogger;
```

```
@Test
public void should_return_users_logging_time() {
    // given
    Date currentDate = new Date();
    given(timeSource.getDate()).willReturn(currentDate);

    // when
    Date dateOfLogging = refactoredVisitLogger.logUsersVisit();

    // then
    then(dateOfLogging).isSameAs(currentDate);
}

}
```

See also

- ► Refer to *Chapter 2, Creating Mocks*, for an introduction on the SOLID principles
- ► Refer to *Working Effectively with Legacy Code, Martin Feathers*, available at `http://www.amazon.com/Working-Effectively-Legacy-Michael-Feathers/dp/0131177052`
- ► Refer to Martin Fowler's catalog of refactoring methods at `http://refactoring.com/catalog/`

Refactoring classes that do too much

In this recipe, we will refactor a class that does not follow the S (Single responsibility) from the SOLID principles.

Getting ready

Let's assume that our system under test is a system that generates a new identity for a given person who can have a name, an age, and siblings, and who sends a JSON message over a web service. Note that the following snippet presents a poorly designed class (please refer to *Chapter 1, Getting Started with Mockito*, for the TestNG configuration and *Chapter 7, Verifying Behavior with Object Matchers*, for the AssertJ configuration and the BDDAssertions static imports):

```
public class GodClassNewPersonGenerator {

    static final String DEFAULT_NEW_NAME = "NewName";

    public Person generateNewIdentity(Person person) {
        String newName = createNewName(person);
```

```
            int newAge = createNewAge(person);
            List<Person> newSiblings = createNewSiblings(person);
            Person newPerson = new Person
    (newName, newAge, newSiblings);
            updatePersonData(newPerson);
            return newPerson;
        }


        private String createNewName(Person person) {
            System.out.printf("Calling web service and
    creating new name for person [%s]%n", person.getName());
            return DEFAULT_NEW_NAME;
        }


        private int createNewAge(Person person) {
            System.out.printf("Calling db and
    creating new age for person [%s]%n", person.getName());
            return person.getAge() + 5;
        }


        private List<Person> createNewSiblings(Person person) {
            System.out.printf("Making heavy IO operations
    and creating new siblings for person [%s]%n", person.getName());
            return asList(new Person("Bob"), new Person("Andrew"));
        }


        private void updatePersonData(Person person) {
            String json = buildJsonStringToPerformTheUpdate(person);
            System.out.printf("Calling web service to update
    new identity for person [%s] with JSON String [%s]%n",
    person.getName(), json);
        }


        private String buildJsonStringToPerformTheUpdate(Person person) {
            return "{\"name\":\""+person.getName()+"\",\"age\":\""+person
    .getAge()+"\"}";
        }
    }
```

If you are unsure about whether your class or method does too much, there is a quick solution to your problem. The best way to verify it is to check the name of the class or method name. In our case, the class name is exaggerated for you to remember not to write code this way but, in general, it turns out that this class does plenty of things; for example, it generates objects and updates data via a web service. The system under test does it all by itself, whereas it should delegate these responsibilities to its collaborators (separate classes).

How to do it...

In order to refactor a class, you have to perform the following steps:

1. Check whether the class follows common programming principles such as the SOLID principles.

2. Ensure that the functionality you are about to refactor is covered by a test (unit, integration, and so on).

3. Refactor the code by extracting the additional responsibilities to separate classes.

4. Write a test that verifies the behavior of the system under test.

 Since the class does everything (it contains the implementation of different responsibilities), we can't create a mock of any of its parts. Stubbing private methods is not an option since it violates the principles of object-oriented design and visibility of methods. It is extremely difficult to write a unit test that checks whether a new identity has been created and verifies whether a web service has been called once. In fact, it is much easier to test this system by means of an integration test. We can use an in-memory database (for example, `http://www.h2database.com/html/main.html`) and a stub of a web service (for example, `http://wiremock.org/`) to help us with this.

Assuming that we have some tests already covering the functionality that we will refactor, let's refactor the code by extracting the additional responsibilities to separate classes. We need to separate the responsibilities of the class as follows:

```
public class RefactoredNewPersonGenerator {

    private final NewIdentityCreator newIdentityCreator;

    private final PersonDataUpdater personDataUpdater;

    public RefactoredNewPersonGenerator
(NewIdentityCreator newIdentityCreator,
 PersonDataUpdater personDataUpdater) {
        this.newIdentityCreator = newIdentityCreator;
        this.personDataUpdater = personDataUpdater;
    }

    public Person generateNewIdentity(Person person) {
        String newName = newIdentityCreator.createNewName(person);
```

```
        int newAge = newIdentityCreator.createNewAge(person);
        List<Person> newSiblings = newIdentityCreator.
createNewSiblings(person);
        Person newPerson = new Person(newName, newAge, newSiblings);
        personDataUpdater.updatePersonData(newPerson);
        return newPerson;
    }
}
```

The `NewIdentityCreator` class, shown in the following code, contains the logic for generating new identity:

```
class NewIdentityCreator {

    static final String DEFAULT_NEW_NAME = "NewName";

    public String createNewName(Person person) {
        System.out.printf("Calling web service and
 creating new name for person [%s]%n", person.getName());
        return DEFAULT_NEW_NAME;
    }

    public int createNewAge(Person person) {
        System.out.printf("Calling db and
creating new age for person [%s]%n", person.getName());
        return person.getAge() + 5;
    }

    public List<Person> createNewSiblings(Person person) {
        System.out.printf("Making heavy IO operations and
creating new siblings for person [%s]%n", person.getName());
        return asList
(new Person("Bob"), new Person("Andrew"));
    }

}
```

The `PersonDataUpdater` class knows how to communicate and update data via a web service. The **JavaScript Object Notation** (**JSON**) message is created by a `UpdatePersonJsonBuilder` class as follows:

```
public class PersonDataUpdater {

  private final UpdatePersonJsonBuilder updatePersonJsonBuilder;

  public PersonDataUpdater
(UpdatePersonJsonBuilder updatePersonJsonBuilder) {
    this.updatePersonJsonBuilder = updatePersonJsonBuilder;
```

```
    }

    public void updatePersonData(Person person) {
        String json = updatePersonJsonBuilder.build(person);
        System.out.printf("Calling web service to update
new identity for person [%s] with JSON String [%s]%n",
person.getName(), json);
    }

}
```

The `UpdatePersonJsonBuilder` class is shown in the following code:

```
class UpdatePersonJsonBuilder {

    public String build(Person person) {
        return "{\"name\":\"" + person.getName() +
"\",\"age\":\"" + person.getAge() + "\"}";
    }

}
```

Now, the test looks much better. We create a mock for the collaborators and can verify them if necessary. We will be able to see the test only for `RefactoredNewPersonGenerator`, but thanks to our refactoring, we can easily write a series of tests to the newly created components, testing them in isolation as follows:

```
@RunWith(MockitoJUnitRunner.class)
public class RefactoredPersonGeneratorTest {

    @Mock NewIdentityCreator newIdentityCreator;

    @Mock PersonDataUpdater personDataUpdater;

    @InjectMocks RefactoredNewPersonGenerator systemUnderTest;

    @Test
    public void should_return_person_with_new_identity () {
        // given
        List<Person> siblings = asList
(new Person("John", 10), new Person("Maria", 12));
        Person person = new Person("Robert", 25, siblings);

        // when
        Person newPerson =
systemUnderTest.generateNewIdentity(person);

        // then
```

```
        then(newPerson).isNotNull().isNotEqualTo(person);
        then(newPerson.getAge()).isNotEqualTo(person.getAge());
        then(newPerson.getName()).isNotEqualTo(person.getName());
        then(newPerson.getSiblings())
  .doesNotContainAnyElementsOf(siblings);
      }

  }
```

See also

▶ Refer to *Refactoring: Improving the Design of Existing Code, Martin Fowler*
  (with *Kent Beck, John Brant, William Opdyke,* and *Don Roberts*), available at
  `http://martinfowler.com/books/refactoring.html`

▶ Refer to *Working Effectively with Legacy Code, Martin Feathers*, available at
  `http://www.amazon.com/Working-Effectively-Legacy-Michael-Feathers/dp/0131177052`

Refactoring the classes that use the class casts

In this recipe, we will focus on fixing the wrong design of an application that performs logic
based on the types of passed objects. The `instanceof` operator distinguishes the types,
and then class casting takes place.

Getting ready

As we did in the previous recipe, let's assume that our system under test is a system that
generates a new identity for a given person who can have a name, an age, and siblings, and
who sends a JSON message over a web service. Note that the following snippet presents a
poorly designed class (all the test examples are written for JUnit; please refer to *Chapter 1,
Getting Started with Mockito,* for the TestNG configuration and *Chapter 7, Verifying Behavior
with Object Matchers,* for the AssertJ configuration and the `BDDAssertions` static imports):

```
public class AwefullyCastingNewPersonGenerator {

    private final IdentityCreator identityCreator;

    public AwefullyCastingNewPersonGenerator
(IdentityCreator identityCreator) {
```

```
        this.identityCreator = identityCreator;
    }


    public Person generateNewIdentity(Person person) {
        String newName = identityCreator.createNewName(person);
        int newAge = identityCreator.createNewAge(person);
        List<Person> newSiblings =
identityCreator.createNewSiblings(person);
        Person newPerson = new Person(newName, newAge, newSiblings);
        if (identityCreator instanceof PersonDataUpdater) {
            ((PersonDataUpdater)
identityCreator).updatePersonData(newPerson);
        }
        return newPerson;
    }


}
```

The `IdentityCreator` interface has only three methods: `createNewName(...)`,
`createNewAge(...)`, and `createNewSiblings(...)`. There is also another interface
called `PersonDataUpdater` that has the `updatePersonData(...)` method. Let's assume
that there is a class that implements both of these interfaces, as shown in the following code:

```
public class SingleResponsibilityBreakingNewIdentityCreator
implements PersonDataUpdater, IdentityCreator {

    public static final String DEFAULT_NEW_NAME = "NewName";

    @Override
    public String createNewName(Person person) {
        System.out.printf("Calling web service
and creating new name for person [%s]%n", person.getName());
        return DEFAULT_NEW_NAME;
    }

    @Override
    public int createNewAge(Person person) {
        System.out.printf("Calling db and
creating new age for person [%s]%n", person.getName());
        return person.getAge() + 5;
    }

    @Override
    public List<Person> createNewSiblings(Person person) {
        System.out.printf("Making heavy IO operations and
creating new siblings for person [%s]%n", person.getName());
```

```
            return asList(new Person("Bob"), new Person("Andrew"));
    }

    @Override
    public void updatePersonData(Person person) {
        String json = buildJsonStringToPerformTheUpdate(person);
        System.out.printf("Calling web service to update
 new identity for person [%s] with JSON String [%s]%n",
person.getName(), json);
    }

    private String buildJsonStringToPerformTheUpdate(Person person) {
        return "{\"name\":\""+person.getName()+"\",\"age\":\""+person
.getAge()+"\"}";
    }

}
```

How to do it...

In order to test the preceding implementation and then refactor it, we have to perform the following steps:

1. Write a test that verifies the behavior of the system under test (in this case, we want to be sure that the person has a new identity at the end of the day).

2. Mock out all of the external dependencies (if you know what you are doing, you can move to the next point without performing this intermediary step).

3. Refactor the code so that it follows good coding practices, including the SOLID principles.

 Our system under test uses the `instanceof` operator and class casting. To write a test for the system, we have to tell Mockito that our mock should implement extra interfaces.

Let's first write a test for the current implementation that tests the behavior (the person's got a new identity), using the following code:

```
@RunWith(MockitoJUnitRunner.class)
public class AwfullyCastingNewPersonGeneratorTest {

    @Mock(extraInterfaces = PersonDataUpdater.class) IdentityCreator
identityCreator;

    @InjectMocks AwfullyCastingNewPersonGenerator systemUnderTest;
```

```
        @Test
    public void should_return_person_with_new_identity () {
        // given
        List<Person> siblings = asList(new Person("John", 10),
  new Person("Maria", 12));
        Person person = new Person("Robert", 25, siblings);

        // when
        Person newPerson =
  systemUnderTest.generateNewIdentity(person);

        // then
        then(newPerson).isNotNull().isNotEqualTo(person);
        then(newPerson.getAge()).isNotEqualTo(person.getAge());
        then(newPerson.getName()).isNotEqualTo(person.getName());
        then(newPerson.getSiblings())
  .doesNotContainAnyElementsOf(siblings);
    }


}
```

Now, since we wrote the missing test, we can refactor the code with a greater sense of confidence. We have to clearly split the system under test in such a way that it does not use class casts but proper injected dependencies. Take a look at the following code:

```
public class RefactoredNewPersonGenerator {

    private final IdentityCreator identityCreator;

    private final PersonDataUpdater personDataUpdater;

    public RefactoredNewPersonGenerator(IdentityCreator
  identityCreator, PersonDataUpdater personDataUpdater) {
        this.identityCreator = identityCreator;
        this.personDataUpdater = personDataUpdater;
    }

    public Person generateNewIdentity(Person person) {
        String newName = identityCreator.createNewName(person);
        int newAge = identityCreator.createNewAge(person);
        List<Person> newSiblings =
  identityCreator.createNewSiblings(person);
        Person newPerson = new Person(newName, newAge, newSiblings);
```

```
        personDataUpdater.updatePersonData(newPerson);
        return newPerson;
    }

}
```

Check the current test pass when it uses class casts, when it is possible to clean up the test. Now, the test looks simpler. Take a look at the following code:

```
@RunWith(MockitoJUnitRunner.class)
public class RefactoredPersonGeneratorTest {

    @Mock IdentityCreator identityCreator;

    @Mock PersonDataUpdater personDataUpdater;

    @InjectMocks RefactoredNewPersonGenerator systemUnderTest;

    @Test
    public void should_return_person_with_new_identity () {
        // given
        List<Person> siblings = asList
(new Person("John", 10), new Person("Maria", 12));
        Person person = new Person("Robert", 25, siblings);

        // when
        Person newPerson =
systemUnderTest.generateNewIdentity(person);

        // then
        then(newPerson).isNotNull().isNotEqualTo(person);
        then(newPerson.getAge()).isNotEqualTo(person.getAge());
        then(newPerson.getName()).isNotEqualTo(person.getName());
        then(newPerson.getSiblings()).doesNotContainAnyElementsOf
(siblings);
    }

}
```

See also

▶ Refer to *Refactoring: Improving the Design of Existing Code, Martin Fowler* (with *Kent Beck, John Brant, William Opdyke,* and *Don Roberts*), available at http://martinfowler.com/books/refactoring.html

- ▶ Refer to *Working Effectively with Legacy Code, Martin Feathers*, available at `http://www.amazon.com/Working-Effectively-Legacy-Michael-Feathers/dp/0131177052`

- ▶ Refer to Martin Fowler's catalog of refactoring methods at `http://refactoring.com/catalog/`

Refactoring the classes that use static methods

In this recipe, we will refactor classes that call static methods to execute business logic instead of having their external dependencies properly defined.

Getting ready

Similar to the previous examples, our system under test is a system that generates a new identity for a given person. Each person can have a name, an age, and siblings. Please remember that the following class is very poorly designed (all the test examples are written for JUnit; please refer to *Chapter 1, Getting Started with Mockito*, for the TestNG configuration and *Chapter 7, Verifying Behavior with Object Matchers*, for the AssertJ configuration and the `BDDAssertions` static imports):

```
public class BadlyDesignedNewPersonGenerator {

    public Person generateNewIdentity(Person person) {
        String newName = StaticIdentityCreator.createNewName(person);
        int newAge = StaticIdentityCreator.createNewAge(person);
        List<Person> newSiblings =
StaticIdentityCreator.createNewSiblings(person);
        return new Person(newName, newAge, newSiblings);
    }

}
```

The `StaticIdentityCreator` class has the following implementation:

```
class StaticIdentityCreator {

    static final String DEFAULT_NEW_NAME = "NewName";

    public static String createNewName(Person person) {
        System.out.printf("Calling web service and
creating new name for person [%s]%n", person.getName());
        return DEFAULT_NEW_NAME;
    }
```

```
    public static int createNewAge(Person person) {
        System.out.printf("Calling db and creating
new age for person [%s]%n", person.getName());
        return person.getAge() + 5;
    }

    public static List<Person> createNewSiblings(Person person) {
        System.out.printf("Making heavy IO operations and
creating new siblings for person [%s]%n", person.getName());
        return asList(new Person("Bob"), new Person("Andrew"));
    }

}
```

How to do it...

In order to test this implementation and then refactor it, we have to perform the following steps:

1. Write a test that verifies the behavior of the system under test (in this case, we want to be sure that the person has a new identity at the end of the day).

2. Stub the static method execution.

3. Refactor the code so that it follows good coding practices, including the SOLID principles.

 To feel comfortable with any refactoring, we will first try to write a test for our system. The problem is that Mockito can't stub static methods. This is why we will use PowerMock. The next step will be to refactor the code and the test.

Let's first write a test for the current implementation that tests the behavior (the person's got a new identity), using the following code:

```
@RunWith(PowerMockRunner.class)
@PrepareForTest(StaticIdentityCreator.class)
public class BadlyDesignedNewPersonGeneratorPowerMockTest {

    BadlyDesignedNewPersonGenerator systemUnderTest =
    new BadlyDesignedNewPersonGenerator();

    @Test
    public void should_return_person_with_new_identity()
    throws Exception {
        // given
        List<Person> siblings = asList(new Person("John", 10),
    new Person("Maria", 12));
```

```
        Person person = new Person("Robert", 25, siblings);
        PowerMockito.mockStatic(StaticIdentityCreator.class);

        // when
        Person newPerson =
systemUnderTest.generateNewIdentity(person);

        // then
        then(newPerson).isNotNull().isNotEqualTo(person);
        then(newPerson.getAge()).isNotEqualTo(person.getAge());
        then(newPerson.getName()).isNotEqualTo(person.getName());
        then(newPerson.getSiblings()).doesNotContainAnyElementsOf
(siblings);
    }

}
```

Now, since we wrote the missing test, we can refactor the code with a greater sense of confidence. We have to clearly split the system under test in such a way that it's not using the static method execution but using the proper injected dependency. Take a look at the following code:

```
public class RefactoredNewPersonGenerator {

    private final NewIdentityCreator newIdentityCreator;

    public RefactoredNewPersonGenerator
(NewIdentityCreator newIdentityCreator) {
        this.newIdentityCreator = newIdentityCreator;
    }

    public Person generateNewIdentity(Person person) {
        String newName = newIdentityCreator.createNewName(person);
        int newAge = newIdentityCreator.createNewAge(person);
        List<Person> newSiblings =
newIdentityCreator.createNewSiblings(person);
        return new Person(newName, newAge, newSiblings);
    }

}
```

Now, the test looks much better (we create a mock for the collaborator). Take a look at the following code:

```
@RunWith(MockitoJUnitRunner.class)
public class RefactoredPersonGeneratorTest {
```

```
        @Mock NewIdentityCreator newIdentityCreator;

        @InjectMocks RefactoredNewPersonGenerator systemUnderTest;

        @Test
        public void should_return_person_with_new_identity() {
            // given
            List<Person> siblings = asList(new Person
("John", 10), new Person("Maria", 12));
            Person person = new Person("Robert", 25, siblings);

            // when
            Person newPerson =
systemUnderTest.generateNewIdentity(person);

            // then
            then(newPerson).isNotNull().isNotEqualTo(person);
            then(newPerson.getAge()).isNotEqualTo(person.getAge());
            then(newPerson.getName()).isNotEqualTo(person.getName());
            then(newPerson.getSiblings()).doesNotContainAnyElementsOf
(siblings);
        }

}
```

See also

▶ Refer to *Chapter 2, Creating Mocks*, for an introduction to SOLID principles

▶ Refer to *Working Effectively with Legacy Code, Martin Feathers*, available at `http://www.amazon.com/Working-Effectively-Legacy-Michael-Feathers/dp/0131177052`

▶ Refer to Martin Fowler's catalog of refactoring methods at `http://refactoring.com/catalog/`

Refactoring the tests that use too many mocks

In this recipe, we will take a look at a test that uses too many Mockito mocks. In this way, the test code becomes unreadable and unmaintainable. Since your test code is your living documentation, you should always remember to put a lot of effort into refactoring it until you can read it like a book.

Getting ready

For this recipe, we will again generate a new identity for a given person. Each person has an address, and that address has a street number. Since we are performing unit testing, we will check in isolation whether `NewIdentityCreator` properly executes its logic. It is responsible for creating a new name, new street number, and new siblings for the current person, as shown in the following code:

```
class NewIdentityCreator {

    public String createNewName(Person person) {
        return person.getName() + "_new";
    }

    public int createNewStreetNumber(Person person) {
        return person.getAddress().getStreetNumber() + 5;
    }

    public List<Person> createNewSiblings(Person person) {
        List<Person> newSiblings = new ArrayList<Person>();
        for(Person sibling : person.getSiblings()) {
          Person newPerson = new Person();
          person.setName(createNewName(sibling));
          person.setAddress(sibling.getAddress());
          person.setSiblings(sibling.getSiblings());
          newSiblings.add(newPerson);
          }
        return newSiblings;
    }

}
```

Let's assume that we already have a test that verifies this functionality. We will not go through all of the test cases, but we will focus on the functionality of generating new siblings as follows:

```
public class OverMockingNewIdentityCreatorTest {

    NewIdentityCreator systemUnderTest = new NewIdentityCreator();


    @Test
    public void should_generate_new_siblings() {
      // given
      Person person = mock(Person.class);
      List<Person> oldSiblings = mock(List.class);
      given(person.getSiblings()).willReturn(oldSiblings);
```

```
        Iterator<Person> personIterator = mock(Iterator.class);
        given(oldSiblings.iterator()).willReturn(personIterator);
        given(personIterator.hasNext()).willReturn
(true, true, true, false);
        given(personIterator.next()).willReturn
(createPersonWithName("Amy"),
                          createPersonWithName("John"),
                          createPersonWithName("Andrew"));

        // when
        List<Person> newSiblings =
systemUnderTest.createNewSiblings(person);

        // then
        then(newSiblings).isNotSameAs(oldSiblings);
    }

    private Person createPersonWithName(String name) {
        Person person = new Person();
        person.setName(name);
        return person;
    }

}
```

The preceding test is badly written because it violates a few of the good practices related to Mockito and testing such as:

▸ **Don't mock a type you don't own**: There are mocks of the `Person` and `List` classes created in the code that don't concern us. Imagine a case where the library that has either of those classes changes. Since we have its classes mocked, we will not see any difference and the tests will pass. Imagine what could happen on production once the real interactions take place instead of interactions between mocks—your application could crash. Another matter is that in order to use `List` by using mocks, you have to perform plenty of stubbing. Once you look at such a test, you don't actually know what's going on any longer.

▸ **Don't mock everything**: The idea behind unit tests is to test in isolation. It does not mean that we have to mock everything out. The `NewIdentityCreator` class interacts with `Person` and performs iteration over its elements (via the iterator of the list). As you can see in the test, we've mocked all collaborating objects and stubbed all possible interactions. The question that arises now is: do we really test production code if there are no real interactions any longer? Change your viewpoint and try not to mock if possible.

▶ **Don't mock value objects**: Of course, it all depends on the context, but in the vast majority of cases, you should not mock value objects. Being structures, they don't have any logic that could be stubbed, apart from getters and setters. Why would you want to stub them? You can use the builder or factory method pattern (check out *Design Patterns: Elements of Reusable Object-Oriented Software, Erich Gamma, Richard Helm, Ralph Johnson*, and *John Vlissides*, available at `http://www.amazon.com/Design-Patterns-Elements-Reusable-Object-Oriented/dp/0201633612`), you can ask your IDE to help you, or you can use project Lombok (`http://projectlombok.org/`) to create value objects for you.

How to do it...

To properly rewrite a test that uses too many mocks, you have to perform the following steps:

1. Identify all the types that were unnecessarily mocked (in our case, these are `Person`, `List`, and `Iterator` classes)

2. Change mock creation to object creation where applicable (we will initialize the `Person` class and create an ordinary `List`)

3. If your object creation seems complex or unreadable, it's worth creating a builder or a method that will build that object for you

Let's assume that we want to extract the `Person` object creation into a separate class to make the test code more readable (see the code repository on GitHub for exact implementation details). Take a look at the following code:

```
public class PersonBuilder {
  private String name;
  private Address address;
  private List<Person> siblings;

  public PersonBuilder name(String name) {
    this.name = name;
    return this;
  }

  public PersonBuilder address(Address address) {…}

  public PersonBuilder streetNumber(int streetNumber) {…}

  public PersonBuilder siblings(List<Person> siblings) {… }

  public Person build() {
    Person person = new Person();
    person.setName(name);
    person.setAddress(address);
```

```
        person.setSiblings(siblings);
        return person;
    }

    public static PersonBuilder person() {
        return new PersonBuilder();
    }
}
```

How it works..

As you can see in the previous code, the `PersonBuilder` class has a static factory method to instantiate itself. It allows you to use less code and more ubiquitous language (check *Domain-Driven Design: Tackling Complexity in the Heart of Software, Eric Evans*, available at `http://www.amazon.com/Domain-Driven-Design-Tackling-Complexity-Software/dp/0321125215`) in your tests. It has fields that are filled up with data during the building process. The `Person` class is created upon the `build()` method execution. For the sake of readability, we will not go into the details of `AddressBuilder`, but it follows the same pattern and sets a street address on the `Address` object.

Now that we have the builder ready, we can use it to rewrite the test as follows:

```
public class NewIdentityCreatorTest {

    NewIdentityCreator systemUnderTest = new NewIdentityCreator();

    @Test
    public void should_generate_new_siblings() {
        // given
        List<Person> oldSiblings = createSiblings();
        Person person =
createPersonWithStreetNumberAndSiblingsAndName(oldSiblings);

        // when
        List<Person> siblings = systemUnderTest.createNewSiblings(person);

        // then
        then(siblings).doesNotContainAnyElementsOf(oldSiblings);
    }

    private Person
createPersonWithStreetNumberAndSiblingsAndName
(List<Person> siblings) {
        return person().streetNumber(10)
                       .siblings(siblings)
```

```
        .name("Robert")
        .build();
  }

  private List<Person> createSiblings() {
    return asList(
        person().name("Amy").build(),
        person().name("John").build(),
        person().name("Andrew").build()
    );
  }
}
```

Now, the test looks much better and it can be used as a living documentation of your application.

There's more...

When working with legacy code or third-party software, you can come across very deeply nested structures that row in hundreds of lines of code. You don't own these value objects, so you can't change it in any way. Using these objects may be tedious, so it's important to have proper factory methods/builders to create them.

Of course, context is king and there might be cases in which a more pragmatic approach will be to not build the whole object using builders but to stub a very precisely defined chain of method execution. In Mockito, such stubbing is called deep stubbing, and the `Answer` implementation that allows you to set up such stubbing behavior is called `Mockito.RETURNS_DEEP_STUBS`. The chain violates the Law of Demeter (see *Object-Oriented Programming: An Objective Sense of Style, K. Lieberherr, I. Ilolland, A. Riel,* available at `http://www.ccs.neu.edu/research/demeter/papers/law-of-demeter/oopsla88-law-of-demeter.pdf`) since we're breaking the *the friend of my friend is not my friend* rule. Remember that you really need some legitimate reasons to use deep stubbing. In a well-designed codebase, you will not need to perform such actions. For educational purposes, let's take a look at the usage of deep stubs. We test the creation of a street number, where, in order to get it, we have to pass it through the `Person.getAddress().getStreetNumber()` chain of method execution, as shown in the following code:

```
public class DeepStubbingNewIdentityCreatorTest {
  NewIdentityCreator systemUnderTest = new NewIdentityCreator();
  @Test
  public void should_generate_new_address_with_street_number() {
    // given
    Person person = mock(Person.class, RETURNS_DEEP_STUBS);
    given(person.getAddress().getStreetNumber()).willReturn(10);

    // when
```

```
        int newStreetNumber =
    systemUnderTest.createNewStreetNumber(person);

        // then
        then(newStreetNumber).isNotEqualTo
    (person.getAddress().getStreetNumber());
        }
    }
```

When calling `given(person.getAddress().getStreetNumber()).willReturn(10)` under the hood, Mockito creates all the intermediary mocks. In this case, since `Person` is already a mock, `Address` is also created as a mock. In this way `NullPointerException` is not thrown when moving down the chain of method invocations. Remember that it is not a sign of good design when you need to use this feature of Mockito.

See also

- Refer to the Mockito wiki on how to write good tests at `https://github.com/mockito/mockito/wiki/How-to-write-good-tests`

- Refer to *Working Effectively with Legacy Code, Martin Feathers*, available at `http://www.amazon.com/Working-Effectively-Legacy-Michael-Feathers/dp/0131177052`

- Refer to *Growing Object-Oriented Software, Guided by Tests, Steve Freeman and Nat Pryce*, available at `http://www.amazon.com/Growing-Object-Oriented-Software-Guided-Tests/dp/0321503627`

- Refer to the Mockito documentation on deep stubbing at `http://docs.mockito.googlecode.com/hg/1.9.5/org/mockito/Mockito.html#RETURNS_DEEP_STUBS`

9
Integration Testing with Mockito and DI Frameworks

In this chapter, we will cover the following recipes:

- ▸ Injecting test doubles instead of beans using Spring's code configuration
- ▸ Injecting test doubles instead of beans using Spring's XML configuration
- ▸ Injecting test doubles instead of beans using Springockito
- ▸ Injecting test doubles instead of beans with Guice
- ▸ Injecting test doubles instead of beans with Guice using Jukito

Introduction

Dependency Injection (**DI**) and **Inversion of Control** (**IOC**) are the terms that you have to understand to get the most out of the contents of this chapter (for more information, refer to Martin Fowler's article at `http://martinfowler.com/articles/injection.html`). We will not elaborate on the importance of those two concepts here. We will focus on using them together with Mockito and two Mockito based tools. We'll do that to inject test doubles instead of real beans in our application.

The idea behind integration tests with DI frameworks is that we want the application to have its dependencies already instantiated and injected. We may have fragments of code where we want to send or retrieve data via a web service or a system where a connection to another server is necessary. When performing integration testing, we do not want to have such connections set. Since integration tests are run from our local machines, we want to limit the need for configuring access to those external servers. You may also want to verify that a particular method was executed on a component. That is why we would have to either stub those connections or set up a test double for our external data provider (check out projects such as Moco at `https://github.com/dreamhead/moco` or WireMock at `http://wiremock.org/` for examples of HTTP server mocks). It all depends on the context, but in my opinion the latter approach gives you more reliable integration with external systems. For example, if it's a HTTP server mock, then you will send a real request and receive a real response—you will be able to test how your production code really works.

In the following recipes, we will focus on the first approach—we will create mocks of our dependencies in order to stub the call and to verify that we made that call only once (let's assume that we pay a lot of money for each call, thus we want to be sure that those method executions do not happen too often).

We will play around with two most famous and widely used DI frameworks—Spring and Guice. First, we will try to set up test doubles just by using internals of either of those frameworks and then we will check out two libraries. Springockito (`https://bitbucket.org/kubek2k/springockito/wiki/Home`) for Spring (`http://projects.spring.io/spring-framework/`) and Jukito (`https://github.com/ArcBees/Jukito`) for Guice (`https://code.google.com/p/google-guice/`). This chapter assumes that you already have either Spring or Guice on your classpath, so please consult the respective websites for more information. The whole setup (Maven and Gradle) is also present in the Mockito Cookbook's Github repository (`https://github.com/marcingrzejszczak/mockito-cookbook`).

All of the examples in this recipe will deal with transferring tax for a person via a web service. Since we don't want to send any real data, we will mock the web service, stub the method execution, and verify whether the call took place only once (because we pay plenty of money for each call). We will further check whether the message sending took place successfully.

Injecting test doubles instead of beans using Spring's code configuration

In this recipe, we will replace an existing bean with a test double using Spring's code configuration.

Getting ready

Let's assume that our system under test is the tax transferring system for a given person, as shown in the following code:

```
public class TaxTransferer {

    private final TaxService taxService;

    public TaxTransferer(TaxService taxService) {
        this.taxService = taxService;
    }

    public boolean transferTaxFor(Person person) {
        if (person == null) {
            return false;
        }
        taxService.transferTaxFor(person);
        return true;
    }

}
```

Where `TaxService` is a class that makes the web service call, as shown in the following code (for simplicity, we are only writing that we are performing such data exchange):

```
class TaxService {

    public void transferTaxFor(Person person) {
        System.out.printf("Calling external web service for person
with name [%s]%n", person.getName());
    }

}
```

Let's assume that we have an annotation-based configuration, as shown in the following code:

```
@Configuration
class TaxConfiguration {

    @Bean
    public TaxService taxService() {
        return new TaxService();
    }
```

```
    @Bean
    public TaxTransferer taxTransferer(TaxService taxService) {
        return new TaxTransferer(taxService);
    }

}
```

How to do it...

In order to perform an integration test of the system and replace the bean with a mock, you have to perform the following steps:

1. Write an integration test that sets the application context of the system under test.

2. Create an additional `@Configuration` annotated class.

3. Override the existing beans (method names have to match) that you want to mock with `@Bean` methods that return a mock or a spy.

The following snippet depicts the aforementioned scenario (the example is written for JUnit—for TestNG, consult the next information box following the snippet. Note that `BDDAssertions` static imports are used—please refer to *Chapter 7, Verifying Behavior with Object Matchers*, for AssertJ configuration).

```
@RunWith(SpringJUnit4ClassRunner.class)
@ContextConfiguration(classes = {TaxConfiguration.class,
MockTaxConfiguration.class})
public class TaxTransfererCodeConfigurationTest {

    @Autowired TaxTransferer taxTransferer;

    @Autowired TaxService taxService;

    @Test
    public void should_transfer_tax_for_person() {
        // given
        Person person = new Person();

        // when
        boolean transferSuccessful = taxTransferer.
transferTaxFor(person);

        // then
        then(transferSuccessful).isTrue();
        verify(taxService).transferTaxFor(person);
    }

}
```

For TestNG, the only thing that changes is that you do not use the `@RunWith(SpringJUnit4ClassRunner.class)` annotation but instead you make the test class extend the `AbstractTestNGSpringContextTests` class.

The additional test configuration is as follows:

```
@Configuration
class MockTaxConfiguration {

    @Bean
    public TaxService taxService() {
        return Mockito.mock(TaxService.class);
    }

}
```

There might be cases where you do want your component to perform real logic. However, you want to confirm that a particular method was executed. Let's imagine a business case where you want to ensure that a particular web service method was called. In that case, you should return a spy instead of a mock by using `return Mockito.spy(new TaxService());`.

How it works...

How Spring internally works is a subject for several books, so we will not go deep into details but what is worth mentioning is that by providing the context configuration with the production and test configuration, we are overriding the initial bean definition as follows (note that method names have to match):

```
@ContextConfiguration(classes = {TaxConfiguration.class,
MockTaxConfiguration.class})
```

In the logs, you will then see the following code:

```
INFO: Overriding bean definition for bean 'taxService': replacing [...
cropped for redability purposes...; defined in class com.blogspot.
toomuchcoding.book.chapter9.InjectingWithSpring.TaxConfiguration] with
[... cropped for redability purposes...; defined in class com.blogspot.
toomuchcoding.book.chapter9.InjectingWithSpring.MockTaxConfiguration]
```

In the integration test example, we had a single test and we didn't explicitly stub the mock's methods. If we had several tests, we most probably would like to stub the mock's behavior in a different manner in each test.

Remember that since such a created mock is a singleton bean (refer to
`http://docs.spring.io/spring/docs/4.0.5.RELEASE/`
`spring-framework-reference/html/beans.html#beans-`
`factory-scopes-singleton`), then once stubbed it will be reused
in all of your tests that use the same configuration.

To change that behavior, you would have to reset the mock by calling `Mockito.reset(mock1,`
`mock2...mockn)` and then stub the mock again.

There's more...

You may observe different behavior when having a `@Configuration` class that is annotated
with `@ComponentScan`. If you scan for components, then each `@Component` annotated class
will be treated as a singleton bean. Let's assume that our `TaxService` is annotated as
`@Component` and that it's injected through the field and not the constructor. The following is
the application context configuration:

```
@Configuration
@ComponentScan("com.blogspot.toomuchcoding.book.chapter9.
InjectingWithSpringComponentScan")
class TaxConfiguration { }
```

Next, you can find the `@Component` annotated `TaxService` class definition:

```
@Component
class TaxService {

    public void transferTaxFor(Person person) {
        System.out.printf("Calling external web service from
@Component annotated class for person with name [%s]%n", person.
getName());
    }

}
```

The Following is the `TaxTransferer` class that is the point of entry of our integration test:

```
@Component
public class TaxTransferer {

    @Autowired private TaxService taxService;

    public boolean transferTaxFor(Person person) {
        if (person == null) {
            return false;
        }
```

```
                taxService.transferTaxFor(person);
                return true;
        }

    }
```

Under the hood, Spring is instantiating beans by using `BeanPostProcessors`. Even if you create your mock configuration like the one presented in the previous snippets, it will not work and you will get the following log message:

```
INFO: Skipping bean definition for [BeanMethod:name=taxServi
ce,declaringClass=com.blogspot.toomuchcoding.book.chapter9.
InjectingWithSpringComponentScan.MockTaxConfiguration]: a definition
for bean 'taxService' already exists. This top-level bean definition
is considered as an override.
```

If possible, you should not annotate your classes with `@Component` since you will limit the possibility of configuring your application. Imagine that components are building blocks and the `@Configuration` annotated classes are blueprints of your application. In part of your applications, you will need some components that are not necessary in others. If you share the `@Component` annotated beans in jars where you have component scanning, then most likely you will have in your Spring application context plenty of beans that you don't really need. You should only use classes that you really need. Please consult Spring's source code to verify that Spring itself doesn't use `@Component` to instantiate its beans.

Let's assume that the `@Component` annotated beans are already there and before refactoring you would like to test your application. There is a possibility of using Spring's internals to manage and mock the bean. Since the `@Component` annotated class has been instantiated using `BeanPostProcessors`, you can create your own class that will create a mock of the object we are interested in (the test will look exactly the same as in the previous test—the implementation of `MockTaxConfiguration` will differ) as follows:

```
@Configuration
class MockTaxConfiguration {

    @Bean
    public BeanPostProcessor taxServiceBeanPostProcessor() {
        return new BeanPostProcessor(){

            @Override
            public Object postProcessBeforeInitialization(Object bean,
    String beanName) throws BeansException {
                    if(bean instanceof TaxService) {
                        return Mockito.mock(TaxService.class);
                    }
                    return bean;
            }
```

```
            @Override
            public Object postProcessAfterInitialization(Object bean,
    String beanName) throws BeansException {
                    return bean;
                }
            };
        }


    }
```

See also

▶ Spring Framework homepage at `http://projects.spring.io/spring-framework/`

▶ Spring Framework documentation at `http://docs.spring.io/spring/docs/4.0.5.RELEASE/spring-framework-reference/html/overview.html`

▶ Spring java based configuration at `http://docs.spring.io/spring/docs/4.0.5.RELEASE/spring-framework-reference/html/beans.html#beans-java`

▶ Spring documentation on testing at `http://docs.spring.io/spring/docs/4.0.5.RELEASE/spring-framework-reference/html/testing.html`

▶ Mockito Cookbook Github repository for more examples of Mockito and Spring integration at `https://github.com/marcingrzejszczak/mockito-cookbook`

Injecting test doubles instead of beans using Spring's XML configuration

In the following recipe, we will replace an existing bean with a test double using Spring's XML configuration.

Getting ready

Let's assume that our system under test is the tax transferring system for a given person, as shown in the following code:

```
public class TaxTransferer {

    private final TaxService taxService;

    public TaxTransferer(TaxService taxService) {
        this.taxService = taxService;
    }
```

```
public boolean transferTaxFor(Person person) {
    if (person == null) {
        return false;
    }
    taxService.transferTaxFor(person);
    return true;
}

}
```

As shown in the previous example, `TaxService` is a class that will perform a web service call. For readability purposes, we are simulating that we have such data exchanged as follows:

```
class TaxService {

    public void transferTaxFor(Person person) {
        System.out.printf("Calling external web service for person
with name [%s]%n", person.getName());
    }

}
```

Let's assume that we have an XML-based configuration of the application, as shown in the following code:

```
<beans xmlns="http://www.springframework.org/schema/beans"
        xmlns:xsi="http://www.w3.org/2001/XMLSchema-instance"
        xsi:schemaLocation="http://www.springframework.org/schema/beans
http://www.springframework.org/schema/beans/spring-beans-4.0.xsd">

    <bean id="taxService" class="com.blogspot.toomuchcoding.book.
chapter9.InjectingWithSpring.TaxService" />

    <bean id="taxTransferer" class="com.blogspot.toomuchcoding.book.
chapter9.InjectingWithSpring.TaxTransferer">
        <constructor-arg ref="taxService"/>
    </bean>

</beans>
```

How to do it...

To write an integration test for the system and replace the bean with a mock, you have to perform the following steps:

1. Write an integration test that sets the application context of the system under test.

2. Create an additional XML configuration of your application context.

3. Override existing beans (IDs have to match) with proper Mockito class factory methods (depending on mock or spy).

Let's try to test our system (the example is written for JUnit—for TestNG, refer to the next information box following the snippet. Note that the BDDAssertions static imports are used—please refer to *Chapter 7, Verifying Behavior with Object Matchers*, for AssertJ configuration):

```
@RunWith(SpringJUnit4ClassRunner.class)
@ContextConfiguration(locations =
{"/chapter9/InjectingWithSpring/application-context.xml",
"/chapter9/InjectingWithSpring/mock-application-context.xml"})
public class TaxTransfererXmlConfigurationTest {

    @Autowired TaxTransferer taxTransferer;

    @Autowired TaxService taxService;

    @Test
    public void should_transfer_tax_for_person() {
        // given
        Person person = new Person();

        // when
        boolean transferSuccessful = taxTransferer.
transferTaxFor(person);

        // then
        then(transferSuccessful).isTrue();
        verify(taxService).transferTaxFor(person);
    }

}
```

For TestNG, the only thing that changes is that you do not use the `@RunWith(SpringJUnit4ClassRunner.class)` annotation but instead, you make the test class extend the `AbstractTestNGSpringContextTests` class.

The following is the additional XML configuration that overrides the bean with a mock:

```
<beans xmlns="http://www.springframework.org/schema/beans"
       xmlns:xsi="http://www.w3.org/2001/XMLSchema-instance"
       xsi:schemaLocation="http://www.springframework.org/schema/beans
http://www.springframework.org/schema/beans/spring-beans-4.0.xsd">

    <bean id="taxService" class="org.mockito.Mockito" factory-
method="mock">
        <constructor-arg value="com.blogspot.toomuchcoding.book.
chapter9.InjectingWithSpring.TaxService"/>
    </bean>

</beans>
```

The following is the additional XML configuration that overrides the bean with a spy:

```
<beans xmlns="http://www.springframework.org/schema/beans"
       xmlns:xsi="http://www.w3.org/2001/XMLSchema-instance"
       xsi:schemaLocation="http://www.springframework.org/schema/beans
http://www.springframework.org/schema/beans/spring-beans-4.0.xsd">

    <bean id="spiedTaxService" class="com.blogspot.toomuchcoding.book.
chapter9.InjectingWithSpring.TaxService" />

    <bean id="taxService" class="org.mockito.Mockito" factory-
method="spy">
        <constructor-arg ref="spiedTaxService"/>
    </bean>

</beans>
```

If you do not want to execute the real logic of your component, you should use a mock. If however you want to execute the real logic and are only interested in verifying whether interactions took place, then you should use a spy.

How it works...

We will not go deep into details of how Spring works internally. What is worth mentioning is that by providing the context configuration with the production XML configuration and the test XML configuration, we are able to override bean definitions, as shown in the following code:

```
@ContextConfiguration(locations =
{"/chapter9/InjectingWithSpring/application-context.xml",
"/chapter9/InjectingWithSpring/mock-application-context.xml"})
```

In the logs, you will then see the following message:

```
INFO: Overriding bean definition for bean 'taxService': replacing
[Generic bean: class [com.blogspot.toomuchcoding.book.chapter9.
InjectingWithSpring.TaxService]; … cropped for readability purposes...
defined in class path resource [chapter9/InjectingWithSpring/
application-context.xml]] with [Generic bean: class [org.mockito.
Mockito]; … cropped for redability purposes... factoryMethodName=mock;
defined in class path resource [chapter9/InjectingWithSpring/mock-
application-context.xml]]
```

See also

▸ Spring Framework homepage at `http://projects.spring.io/
spring-framework/`

▸ Spring Framework documentation at `http://docs.spring.io/spring/
docs/4.0.5.RELEASE/spring-framework-reference/html/overview.html`

▸ Spring XML-based configuration at `http://docs.spring.io/spring/
docs/4.0.5.RELEASE/spring-framework-reference/html/beans.
html#beans-factory-metadata`

▸ Spring documentation on testing at `http://docs.spring.io/spring/
docs/4.0.5.RELEASE/spring-framework-reference/html/testing.html`

▸ The Mockito Cookbook Github repository for more examples of Mockito and Spring integration at `https://github.com/marcingrzejszczak/mockito-cookbook`

Injecting test doubles instead of beans using Springockito

In this recipe, we will replace an existing bean with a test double using Springockito's annotations. (refer to Springockito core at `https://bitbucket.org/kubek2k/
springockito/wiki/Home`, Springockito annotations at `https://bitbucket.org/
kubek2k/springockito/wiki/springockito-annotations`).

Getting ready

To add Springockito annotations to your classpath, refer to the following dependency configurations. The configuration for Gradle is as follows:

```
testCompile 'org.kubek2k:springockito-annotations:1.0.9'
and Maven
<dependency>
    <groupId>org.kubek2k</groupId>
    <artifactId>springockito-annotations</artifactId>
    <version>1.0.9</version>
</dependency>
```

Our system under test is the person's tax transferring system, as shown in the following code:

```
public class TaxTransferer {

    private final TaxService taxService;

    public TaxTransferer(TaxService taxService) {
        this.taxService = taxService;
    }

    public boolean transferTaxFor(Person person) {
        if (person == null) {
            return false;
        }
        taxService.transferTaxFor(person);
        return true;
    }

}
```

The `TaxService` class is responsible for making the web service call, as shown in the following code (in this example, we are only printing some information to the console instead of calling the real web service):

```
class TaxService {

    public void transferTaxFor(Person person) {
        System.out.printf("Calling external web service for person
with name [%s]%n", person.getName());
    }

}
```

Let's assume that we have an annotation-based configuration, as shown in the following code:

```
@Configuration
class TaxConfiguration {

    @Bean
    public TaxService taxService() {
        return new TaxService();
    }

    @Bean
    public TaxTransferer taxTransferer(TaxService taxService) {
        return new TaxTransferer(taxService);
    }

}
```

How to do it...

In order to integration test the system and replace the bean with a mock using Springockito, you have to perform the following steps:

1. Write an integration test that sets up the system under test's application context (annotate your class with `@RunWith(SpringJUnit4ClassRunner.class)` and provide the necessary configuration locations to `@ContextConfiguration`.

2. Add `SpringockitoAnnotatedContextLoader` as the loader of the `@ContextConfiguration` annotation.

3. Annotate those beans that you want replaced with Springockito's annotations.

The following snippet depicts the aforementioned scenario (the example is written for JUnit—for TestNG, refer to the information box following the snippet. Note that the `BDDAssertions` static imports are used—please refer to *Chapter 7, Verifying Behavior of Object Matchers*, for AssertJ configuration):

```
@RunWith(SpringJUnit4ClassRunner.class)
@ContextConfiguration(loader = SpringockitoAnnotatedContextLoader.
class, classes = TaxConfiguration.class)
public class TaxTransfererSpringockitoAnnotationsCodeConfigTest {

    @Autowired TaxTransferer taxTransferer;

    @ReplaceWithMock @Autowired TaxService taxService;

    @Test
    public void should_transfer_tax_for_person() {
        // given
```

```
        Person person = new Person();

        // when
        boolean transferSuccessful = taxTransferer.
transferTaxFor(person);

        // then
        then(transferSuccessful).isTrue();
        verify(taxService).transferTaxFor(person);
    }

}
```

> For TestNG, the only thing that changes is that you do not use
> the @RunWith(SpringJUnit4ClassRunner.class)
> annotation but instead you make the test class extend the
> AbstractTestNGSpringContextTests class.

In order to wrap the bean with a spy, you have to annotate it with a @WrapWithSpy
annotation (example for JUnit):

```
@RunWith(SpringJUnit4ClassRunner.class)
@ContextConfiguration(loader = SpringockitoAnnotatedContextLoader.
class, classes = TaxConfiguration.class)
public class TaxTransfererSpringockitoAnnotationsCodeConfigSpyTest {

    @Autowired TaxTransferer taxTransferer;

    @WrapWithSpy @Autowired TaxService taxService;

    @Test
    public void should_transfer_tax_for_person() {
        // given
        Person person = new Person();
        doNothing().when(taxService).transferTaxFor(person);

        // when
        boolean transferSuccessful = taxTransferer.
transferTaxFor(person);

        // then
        then(transferSuccessful).isTrue();
        verify(taxService).transferTaxFor(person);
    }

}
```

How it works...

As a parameter of `@ContextConfiguration`, you can provide a loader—a class that is responsible for loading `ApplicationContext` to your test. Springockito comes together with its own `SpringockitoAnnotatedContextLoader` that does the following actions in two different phases as follows:

- The Context Configuration processing phase:
  - Scans the test class to find all fields annotated with Springockito annotations
  - Maps target bean names to their corresponding SpringockitoDefinition

- The Context customization phase:
  - Registers the bean definition of the mocked beans in the Application Context

After that logic has been executed, you can see that the configuration present in the `@Configuration` annotated class in the logs gets ignored:

```
INFO: Skipping bean definition for [BeanMethod:name=taxServi
ce,declaringClass=com.blogspot.toomuchcoding.book.chapter9.
InjectingWithSpringockito.TaxConfiguration]: a definition for bean
'taxService' already exists. This top-level bean definition is
considered as an override.
```

There's more...

To use Springockito's XML configuration, you have to create an XML application context configuration file that obeys the following rules:

- Add the namespace and provide proper schema location (let's assume that we used the `mockito` namespace)
- Use `<mockito:mock>` to replace a bean with a Mockito mock
- Use `<mockito:spy>` to wrap the bean with a Mockito spy

Since in this book we are using Mockito in version 1.9.5, it's worth mentioning that Springockito (in version 1.0.9) fails to cooperate with Mockito in any version higher than 1.9.0 in terms of defining mocks in Spring's XML configuration. That's because one of Mockito's classes was removed and Springockito still references it. The following snippets from this recipe are showing a scenario that fails. In other words, having an application context configuration as the following:

```
<beans xmlns="http://www.springframework.org/schema/beans"
       xmlns:xsi="http://www.w3.org/2001/XMLSchema-instance"
       xmlns:mockito="http://www.mockito.org/spring/mockito"
       xsi:schemaLocation="http://www.springframework.org/schema/beans
                   http://www.springframework.org/schema/
beans/spring-beans-4.0.xsd
```

```
                              http://www.mockito.org/spring/mockito
                              http://www.mockito.org/spring/mockito.xsd">

    <mockito:mock id="taxService" class="com.blogspot.toomuchcoding.
book.chapter9.InjectingWithSpringockito.TaxService" />

</beans>
```

A test that uses that configuration to create a mock of `TaxService`, as shown in the following code:

```
@RunWith(SpringJUnit4ClassRunner.class)
@ContextConfiguration(locations =
{"/chapter9/InjectingWithSpringockito/application-context.xml",
"/chapter9/InjectingWithSpringockito/mock-application-context.xml"})
public class TaxTransfererSpringockitoNotCompatibleWithMockito1_9_5_
XmlConfigurationTest {

    @Autowired TaxTransferer taxTransferer;

    @Autowired TaxService taxService;

    @Test
    public void should_transfer_tax_for_person() {
        // given
        Person person = new Person();

        // when
        boolean transferSuccessful = taxTransferer.
transferTaxFor(person);

        // then
        then(transferSuccessful).isTrue();
        verify(taxService).transferTaxFor(person);
    }

}
```

This will result in the following exception:

```
java.lang.NoClassDefFoundError: org/mockito/internal/
MockitoInvocationHandler
    at java.lang.Class.getDeclaredConstructors0(Native Method)
    at java.lang.Class.privateGetDeclaredConstructors(Class.java:2493)
    at java.lang.Class.getDeclaredConstructors(Class.java:1901)
...
```

For more information, please refer to Issue#46 at `https://bitbucket.org/kubek2k/` `springockito/issue/46/springockito-fails-to-compile-with-mockito` since a ticket regarding this problem has already been created. Nonetheless, if you downgrade to Mockito 1.9.0, your test will pass successfully.

See also

▶ Spring java-based configuration at `http://docs.spring.io/spring/` `docs/4.0.5.RELEASE/spring-framework-reference/html/beans.` `html#beans-java`

▶ Spring Framework documentation at `http://docs.spring.io/spring/` `docs/4.0.5.RELEASE/spring-framework-reference/html/overview.html`

▶ Spring XML-based configuration at `http://docs.spring.io/spring/` `docs/4.0.5.RELEASE/spring-framework-reference/html/beans.` `html#beans-factory-metadata`

▶ Spring testing documentation at `http://docs.spring.io/spring/docs/` `current/spring-framework-reference/html/testing.html`

▶ Springockito homepage at `https://bitbucket.org/kubek2k/springockito/` `overview`

▶ Springockito wiki at `https://bitbucket.org/kubek2k/springockito/` `wiki/Home`

Injecting test doubles instead of beans with Guice

In this recipe, we will replace an existing bean with a test double using Guice's (`https://code.google.com/p/google-guice/`) module configuration.

Getting ready

Let's assume that our system under test is the tax transferring system for a given person, as shown in the following code:

```
public class TaxTransferer {

    private final TaxService taxService;

    public TaxTransferer(TaxService taxService) {
        this.taxService = taxService;
    }
```

```
    public boolean transferTaxFor(Person person) {
        if (person == null) {
            return false;
        }
        taxService.transferTaxFor(person);
        return true;
    }

}
```

Where the `TaxService` class is an interface that has an implementation called
`TaxWebService`, which makes the web service call, as shown in the following code
(for simplicity, we are only writing that we are performing such data exchange):

```
class TaxWebService implements TaxService {

    @Override
    public void transferTaxFor(Person person) {
        System.out.printf("Calling external web service for person
with name [%s]%n", person.getName());
    }

}
```

The following is a snippet with Guice's module configuration:

```
class TaxModule extends AbstractModule {

    @Override
    protected void configure() {
        bind(TaxService.class).to(TaxWebService.class);
    }

}
```

How to do it...

In order to integration test the system and replace the bean with a mock, you have to perform
the following steps:

1. Ensure that the component that you are going to mock is in a separate Guice module.
2. Create an additional test module (by extending the `AbstractModule` class) that will
    bind the class to be mocked with an actual mock or spy.
3. In your integration test, remember to reference all the necessary production modules.
4. Instead of providing the production module with the component to mock, pass the
    test module with the mocked version of that component.

The following snippet shows the separate Guice test module:

```
public class MockModule extends AbstractModule {

    @Override
    protected void configure() {
        bind(TaxService.class).toInstance(Mockito.mock
(TaxService.class));
    }

}
```

It is feasible to override an existing binding by calling
`Guice.createInjector(Modules.override(new`
`ProductionModule()).with(new TestModule()));`.

However, the javadoc for `Modules.overrides(..)`
recommends that you design your modules in such a way that
you don't need to override bindings. The solution to this is to
move the classes to be mocked to separate modules.

Now let's take a look at the JUnit test (note that both tests are using the `BDDAssertions`
static imports—please refer to *Chapter 7, Verifying Behavior with Object Matchers*, for the
AssertJ configuration):

```
@RunWith(MockitoJUnitRunner.class)
public class TaxTransfererTest {

    TaxTransferer taxTransferer;

    TaxService taxService;

    @Before
    public void setup() {
        Injector injector = Guice.createInjector(new MockModule());
        taxTransferer = injector.getInstance(TaxTransferer.class);
        taxService = injector.getInstance(TaxService.class);
    }

    @Test
    public void should_transfer_tax_for_person() {
        // given
        Person person = new Person();

        // when
```

```
        boolean transferSuccessful = taxTransferer.
transferTaxFor(person);

        // then
        then(transferSuccessful).isTrue();
        verify(taxService).transferTaxFor(person);
    }
}
```

 If using pure JUnit, you have to get the instances from `Injector` yourself—as we do here in the `@Before` part of your test by calling the `Guice.createInjector(...)` static method. You can also create your own `TestRunner` or use a library that will do all of the previous for you—for example Jukito.

The corresponding TestNG test is, as shown in the following code:

```
@Guice(modules = MockModule.class)
public class TaxTransfererTestNgTest {

    @Inject TaxTransferer taxTransferer;

    @Inject TaxService taxService;

    @Test
    public void should_transfer_tax_for_person() {
        // given
        Person person = new Person();

        // when
        boolean transferSuccessful = taxTransferer.
transferTaxFor(person);

        // then
        then(transferSuccessful).isTrue();
        verify(taxService).transferTaxFor(person);
    }

}
```

You can see that the test for TestNG looks much nicer in comparison to JUnit—thanks to the special @Guice TestNG annotation. It accepts as one of the parameters the modules that should be taken into consideration while setting up the context of the application.

How it works...

How Guice internally works is beyond the scope of this book, but let's take at least a high overview of what has happened in the previous snippets.

For JUnit, we have called the `Guice.createInjector(...)` static method that takes as arguments the modules from which it should build the Injector. The Injector, as the javadoc states, builds the graphs of objects that make up your application but should extremely rarely be called in the production code. It breaks the concept of DI and goes towards a Service Locator pattern (refer to `http://martinfowler.com/articles/injection.html#UsingAServiceLocator`). Anyway, we are calling it in the test environment since we want to perform integration testing, thus we want our dependencies to be initialized by Guice. Behind the scenes, Guice builds the graph of objects in such a way that when we call the `injector.getInstance(...)` method, it has all the binding information and returns the properly instantiated objects—that's why it takes into consideration our test binding of the `TaxService` interface to the mock of that interface.

For TestNG, the situation is much clearer—it produces far less boilerplate code. Guice has its own @Guice annotation that as one of the parameters accepts the modules that make up for the application. Behind the scenes, TestNG in the `ClassImpl` class instantiates or reuses the Guice injector in exactly the same way as we manually do it for JUnit—it passes the Guice modules classes to the `Guice.createInjector(...)` static method and then caches it in a map whose keys contain the aforementioned modules and the value is the injector as such. This map is present in the `TestRunner` class.

In the previous examples, we had a single test and we didn't explicitly stub any of the mock's methods. For the JUnit example, before each test we are creating a new injector so that a new mock is created. That means if you had two tests and you stubbed a mock's method in the first one, then the second one wouldn't see that stubbing. For TestNG, the situation is different.

Remember that for TestNG the modules are shared between tests. In other words, once stubbed, your mock will be reused in all of your tests!

To change that behavior, you would have to reset the mock by calling `Mockito.reset (mock1, mock2...mockn)` and then stub the mock again.

See also

- ▶ Google Guice homepage at `https://code.google.com/p/google-guice/`
- ▶ Google Guice wiki at `https://code.google.com/p/google-guice/w/list`
- ▶ Google Guice mailing list at `https://groups.google.com/forum/#!forum/google-guice`
- ▶ TestNG and Google Guice at `http://testng.org/doc/documentation-main.html#guice-dependency-injection`
- ▶ Mockito Cookbook Github repository for more examples of Mockito and Guice integration at `https://github.com/marcingrzejszczak/mockito-cookbook`

Injecting test doubles instead of beans with Guice using Jukito

In the following recipe, we will replace an existing bean with a test double using Jukito annotations (since this library has a specially defined JUnit runner, it integrates perfectly with JUnit—there is no official support for TestNG).

Getting ready

In order to profit from Jukito, you have to add it to your build. The following is the configuration for Gradle:

```
testCompile 'org.jukito:jukito:1.4'
```

A sample Maven dependency configuration is given as follows:

```
<dependency>
    <groupId>org.jukito</groupId>
    <artifactId>jukito</artifactId>
    <version>1.4</version>
</dependency>
```

We will reuse the previous example of the tax transferring system for a given person, as shown in the following code:

```
public class TaxTransferer {

    private final TaxService taxService;

    public TaxTransferer(TaxService taxService) {
        this.taxService = taxService;
    }
```

```
        public boolean transferTaxFor(Person person) {
            if (person == null) {
                return false;
            }
            taxService.transferTaxFor(person);
            return true;
        }

    }
```

Where the `TaxService` is an interface that has an implementation called `TaxWebService` that makes the web service call, as shown in the following code (for simplicity, we are only writing that we are performing such data exchange):

```
class TaxWebService implements TaxService {

    @Override
    public void transferTaxFor(Person person) {
        System.out.printf("Calling external web service for person
    with name [%s]%n", person.getName());
    }

}
```

The following is a snippet with Guice's module configuration:

```
public class TaxModule extends AbstractModule {

    @Override
    protected void configure() {
        bind(TaxService.class).to(TaxWebService.class);
    }

}
```

How to do it...

To integrate JUnit with Guice using Jukito, you have to perform the following steps:

1. Annotate your test class with `@RunWith(JukitoRunner.class)`.

2. In your integration test, if required, reference all the required production modules using the `@UseModules` Jukito annotation.

3. To mock a component, you have to either pass the interfaces to be mocked as test methods arguments or pass a test module to the `@UseModules` annotation (note that Jukito needs the module to be publicly accessible) and `@Inject` those fields to the test.

4. To create a spy of a component, you have to pass a test module to the `@UseModules` annotation.

To test our system using Jukito, you have to do the following (it's not using a separate module but passes the dependencies to be mocked as test method parameters):

```
@RunWith(JukitoRunner.class)
public class TaxTransfererTest {

    @Inject TaxTransferer taxTransferer;

    @Test
    public void should_transfer_tax_for_person(TaxService taxService)
{
        // given
        Person person = new Person();

        // when
        boolean transferSuccessful = taxTransferer.
transferTaxFor(person);

        // then
        then(transferSuccessful).isTrue();
        verify(taxService).transferTaxFor(person);
    }

}
```

If you have some more complex logic in your test module configuration, then you can provide it as a parameter of the `@UseModules` annotation, as shown in the following code:

```
@RunWith(JukitoRunner.class)
@UseModules({MockModule.class})
public class TaxTransfererUseModuleTest {

    @Inject TaxTransferer taxTransferer;

    @Inject TaxService taxService;

    @Test
    public void should_transfer_tax_for_person() {
        // given
        Person person = new Person();

        // when
```

```
        boolean transferSuccessful = taxTransferer.
transferTaxFor(person);

        // then
        then(transferSuccessful).isTrue();
        verify(taxService).transferTaxFor(person);
    }

}
```

The test module configuration may look like the following:

```
public class MockModule extends AbstractModule {

    @Override
    protected void configure() {
        bind(TaxService.class).toInstance(Mockito.mock
(TaxService.class));
    }

}
```

You can also provide the configuration in the inner static class that extends `JukitoModule`— in this way, you will access some handy helper methods such as `bindMock(...)`, `bindSpy(...)`, and so on). The following is an example depicting that and assuming that `TaxService` is a class and not an interface (to show how to deal with spies):

```
@RunWith(JukitoRunner.class)
public class TaxTransfererUseInnerJukitoModuleTest {

    @Inject TaxTransferer taxTransferer;

    @Inject TaxService taxService;

    public static class Module extends JukitoModule {

        protected void configureTest() {
            bindSpy(TaxService.class).in(TestScope.SINGLETON);
        }

    }

    @Test
    public void should_transfer_tax_for_person() {
        // given
        Person person = new Person();
        doNothing().when(taxService).transferTaxFor(person);
```

```
        // when
        boolean transferSuccessful = taxTransferer.
transferTaxFor(person);

        // then
        then(transferSuccessful).isTrue();
        verify(taxService).transferTaxFor(person);
    }

}
```

How it works...

Jukito comes along with `JukitoRunner`, which is a JUnit runner—that's why all the magic is done behind the scenes for you as follows:

- ▸ Retrieving all the passed modules to the `@UseModules` annotation. If applicable, Jukito creates `JukitoModule` with those modules.

- ▸ If there is no `@UseModules` annotation, Jukito checks if you provided a static inner class that extends `JukitoModule` and provides a test configuration for your test. If that is the case, Jukito creates `JukitoModule` with the test module.

- ▸ If there is no such `JukitoModule` extension class in your test, Jukito instantiates a default `JukitoModule` implementation (extension of Jukito's `TestModule`).

- ▸ Jukito creates an Injector using the `Guice.createInjector(...)` method and passes the instantiated `JukitoModule` (by one of the aforementioned approaches).

- ▸ Jukito then goes through test methods and checks whether there are objects passed to the test methods and verifies if either of them is `@All` annotated (more about this annotation in the *There's more* section)

- ▸ Jukito together with Guice injects all the necessary objects into the `@Inject` annotated fields and create mocks for objects passed as arguments of the test methods.

There's more...

Jukito allows you to go further with testing Guice based applications—you can perform parameterized tests. The following is a test in which we verify that regardless of the country from which the person originates, the application sends a single message via a web service:

```
@RunWith(JukitoRunner.class)
public class TaxTransfererParametrizedTest {

    @Inject TaxTransferer taxTransferer;

    public static class Module extends JukitoModule {
```

```
    protected void configureTest() {
        bindManyInstances(Person.class,
                new Person(),
                new Person("Poland"),
                new Person("France"),
                new Person("Germany"));
    }

}

@Test
public void should_transfer_tax_for_person(TaxService taxService,
@All Person person) {
    // when
    boolean transferSuccessful = taxTransferer.
transferTaxFor(person);

    // then
    then(transferSuccessful).isTrue();
    verify(taxService).transferTaxFor(person);
}
}
```

What Jukito does while executing the test is that it searches for the `@All` annotated objects and it collects all bindings matching the type of the annotated argument. In the case of the previous snippet, it will collect four bindings of the `person` instances from the static `Module` class. Next, Jukito checks if there are more `@All` annotated arguments. If that is the case, it will run the test as many as the size of the set resulting from the cartesian product. In the case of the previous test class, the `should_transfer_tax_for_person` test will be executed four times. Please check Jukito's documentation for further details on the `@All` annotation.

See also

▸ Google Guice homepage at `https://code.google.com/p/google-guice/`

▸ Jukito homepage at `https://github.com/ArcBees/Jukito`

▸ Jukito documentation at `https://github.com/ArcBees/Jukito/wiki`

▸ Jukito Google group at `https://groups.google.com/forum/#!forum/jukito`

▸ Mockito Cookbook Github repository for more examples of Mockito and Jukito integration at `https://github.com/marcingrzejszczak/mockito-cookbook`

10
Mocking Libraries Comparison

In this chapter, we will cover the following recipes:

- ► Mockito versus EasyMock
- ► Mockito versus JMockit
- ► Mockito versus jMock
- ► Mockito versus Spock

Introduction

In this chapter, we will take a look at other mocking frameworks that are quite well known in the Java world. The idea of this chapter is not to state whether one mocking framework is better than Mockito, but to point out differences in both their syntax and approach.

Remember that the examples presented in this chapter are very simple and do not show all of the possible ways of using the mocking frameworks, since you could write books about any of them.

Before moving forward, it's worth mentioning the difference between a strict mock and a non-strict one:

- ► **Strict mock**: This is a mock that will fail the moment anything differs from the expectations. In other words, if you expect your mock to call some methods and that doesn't happen, then your test will fail.
- ► **Non-strict mock**: This is a mock that will ignore any methods that were expected and were not executed. Your test won't fail even when an unexpected method is called. Mockito's mocks are non-strict.

It's important to understand the difference because EasyMock, JMockit, and JMock allow you to create either of those mocks.

Let's come back to the chapter's structure. We will start off by taking a look at EasyMock, which is Mockito's predecessor (in fact, Mockito began as the EasyMock's fork). Next, we will take a look at JMockit and JMock, which are similar to some extent. Finally, we will see how you can do things the Groovy way using Spock.

In all cases, we will use the tax transferring system which will throw an exception during the transfer of tax.

Mockito versus EasyMock

In this recipe, we will write a simple test using EasyMock that verifies the behavior of the system under test when an exception is thrown.

Getting ready

In order to profit from EasyMock, you need to add it to your classpath. This is the configuration for Gradle:

```
testCompile 'org.easymock:easymock:3.2'
```

The following is how you add the EasyMock dependency in Maven:

```
<dependency>
    <groupId>org.easymock</groupId>
    <artifactId>easymock</artifactId>
    <version>3.2</version>
    <scope>test</scope>
</dependency>
```

Let's assume that our system under test is the tax transferring system for a given person, as shown in the following code:

```
public class TaxTransferer {

  private final TaxService taxService;

  public TaxTransferer(TaxService taxService) {
    this.taxService = taxService;
  }

  public boolean transferTaxFor(Person person) {
    if (taxService.hasAlreadyTransferredTax(person)) {
      return false;
```

```
      }
      try {
        taxService.transferTaxFor(person);
      } catch (Exception exception) {
        System.out.printf("Exception [%s] caught while trying to
            transfer tax for [%s]%n", exception, person.getName());
        return false;
      }
      return true;
    }


  }
```

<h2 style="background:gray;color:white;display:inline-block">How to do it...</h2>

In order to test the system using EasyMock, you need to perform the following steps:

1. Record the mock's behavior (tell the mock how it should behave).
2. Replay the mock's behavior (stops recording).
3. Execute the logic of the system under test.
4. Verify the behavior of the system under test.

The following is an example of a JUnit test with EasyMock:

```
@RunWith(EasyMockRunner.class)
public class TaxTransfererTest {

  @Mock TaxService taxService;

  TaxTransferer systemUnderTest;

    @Test
    public void
      should_return_false_when_tax_was_not_transfered_
      and_connection_to_irs_was_refused() {
        // expect
      systemUnderTest =  new TaxTransferer(taxService);
        Person person = new Person();
      expect(taxService.hasAlreadyTransferredTax
        (anyObject(Person.class))).andReturn(false);
        taxService.transferTaxFor(same(person));
        expectLastCall().andStubThrow(new RuntimeException
("Connection refused"));
        replay(taxService);
```

```
            // act
            boolean transferSuccessful = systemUnderTest.
    transferTaxFor(person);

            // assert
            then(transferSuccessful).isFalse();
            verify(taxService);
        }

    }
```

EasyMock integrates very nicely with JUnit. You need to annotate your test class with @RunWith(EasyMockRunner.class). Only then can you profit from the @Mock annotation that will create the mock for you; @TestSubject will inject proper mocks for you. Unfortunately, as you can see in our example, our system under test wasn't annotated with @TestSubject. That's because TaxTransferer fields are final and we inject their collaborators via constructor. EasyMock doesn't support constructor injection, it only supports field injection. This is why we need to inject the collaborator manually.

The following is how you can integrate EasyMock with TestNG:

```
    public class TaxTransfererTestNgTest {

        @Mock TaxService taxService;

        TaxTransferer systemUnderTest;

        @BeforeMethod
        public void setup() {
            EasyMockSupport.injectMocks(this);
            systemUnderTest = new TaxTransferer(taxService);
        }

        @Test
        public void should_return_false_when_tax_was_not_transfered_and_
    connection_to_irs_was_refused() {
            // expect
            Person person = new Person();
            expect(taxService.hasAlreadyTransferredTax(anyObject(Person.
    class))).andReturn(false);
            taxService.transferTaxFor(same(person));
            expectLastCall().andStubThrow(new RuntimeException
    ("Connection refused"));
            replay(taxService);
```

```
        // act
        boolean transferSuccessful = systemUnderTest.
transferTaxFor(person);

        // assert
        then(transferSuccessful).isFalse();
        verify(taxService);
    }

}
```

How it works...

We will not discuss how EasyMock works internally, but focus on what happens in the test itself, and what the EasyMock approach is. EasyMock's approach towards mocks is captured in the following steps:

1. You need to record the mock's behavior, that is, teach it how it should react. By default, EasyMock creates strict mocks so their default behavior is such that if a method on a mock was called and you didn't expect it, then your test will fail.

2. Once you're done, you need to replay the mock (stop recording by calling the `replay(T mock)` static method). Afterwards, you can act and assert the results.

3. Finally, you can verify the mock's behavior. Verifying means EasyMock will check whether the methods you expected were actually called as many times as you defined in the record section.

As for stubbing, you can call the static `expect(T mock)` method to stub a method execution that returns a value. To stub void methods, you need to first execute the void method and then call the static `expectLastCall()` method. Only then can you define exactly how the mock should behave.

There's more...

Mockito's test code of the system would look like the following (example for JUnit):

```
@RunWith(MockitoJUnitRunner.class)
public class TaxTransfererTest {

    @Mock TaxService taxService;

    @InjectMocks TaxTransferer systemUnderTest;

    @Test
    public void should_return_false_when_tax_was_not_transfered_and_
connection_to_irs_was_refused() {
```

```
        // given
        Person person = new Person();
     given(taxService.hasAlreadyTransferredTax(person)).
  willReturn(false);
        willThrow(new TaxServiceConnectionException("Connection
refused")).given(taxService).transferTaxFor(person);

        // when
        boolean transferSuccessful = systemUnderTest.
transferTaxFor(person);

        // then
        then(transferSuccessful).isFalse();
        verify(taxService).hasAlreadyTransferredTax(person);
        verify(taxService).transferTaxFor(person);
    }

}
```

The primary similarities between EasyMock and Mockito are as follows:

▸ The same level of verification (in terms of unexpected, redundant invocations, and verification in order)

▸ Similar approach to argument matching (like `same(...)`, `anyObject(...)`, and so on)

The primary differences between EasyMock and Mockito are as follows:

▸ Mockito doesn't have the record replay mode since it can only stub or verify mocks. The former happens before execution and the latter after the execution.

▸ By default, Mockito creates "nice" mocks, thus if not stubbed, mocks will return a set of default values. In EasyMock, you need to create such a mock explicitly because all mocks are strict by default.

▸ Verification in Mockito is optional. In EasyMock, you would need to create a nice mock and then not call the `verify()` method.

▸ Mockito's custom argument matchers use Hamcrest matchers so you can reuse them in different parts of the application.

▸ EasyMock is a better tool for verification in order than Mockito. Let's assume that we have a method that is executed twice and mutates the input parameter like in the following pseudo code:

```
collaborator.execute(mutate(object));
collaborator.execute(mutate(object));
```

In EasyMock, since you define expectations at the beginning, you are able to verify the value of the argument of the `execute (...)` method at each step. In Mockito, you will only be able to check that at the second execution, thus having `inOrder.verify(mockedCollaborator).execute(objectAtStep1());` and `inOrder.verify(mockedCollaborator).execute(objectAtStep2());` would make only the second line pass whereas the first would fail. EasyMock's way to test it would be as follows:

```
mockedCollaborator.execute(mutate(object));
mockedCollaborator.execute(mutate(object));
replay(mockedCollaborator);
```

See also

▸ EasyMock documentation at `http://easymock.org/EasyMock3_2_Documentation.html`

▸ The Mockito versus EasyMock comparison at `https://code.google.com/p/mockito/wiki/MockitoVSEasyMock`

▸ The _Mockito Cookbook_ Github repository with test examples at `https://github.com/marcingrzejszczak/mockito-cookbook`

Mockito versus JMockit

In this recipe, we will write a simple test using JMockit that verifies the behavior of the system under test when an exception is thrown.

Getting ready

In order to profit from JMockit, you need to add it to your classpath. The following is the JMockit configuration for Gradle:

```
testCompile 'com.googlecode.jmockit:jmockit:1.7'
```

The following is how you can add JMockit to your classpath using Maven:

```
<dependency>
  <groupId>com.googlecode.jmockit</groupId>
  <artifactId>jmockit</artifactId>
  <version>1.7</version>
  <scope>test</scope>
</dependency>
```

If you do not use `@RunWith(JMockit.class)`, then you need to define the JMockit dependency before the JUnit one! Please refer to `http://jmockit.googlecode.com/svn/trunk/www/gettingStarted.html` for more information.

Let's assume that our system under test is the tax transferring system for a given person, as shown in the following code:

```
public class TaxTransferer {

    private final TaxService taxService;

    public TaxTransferer(TaxService taxService) {
        this.taxService = taxService;
    }

    public boolean transferTaxFor(Person person) {
        if (taxService.hasAlreadyTransferredTax(person)) {
            return false;
        }
        try {
            //taxService.transferTaxFor(person);
        } catch (Exception exception) {
            System.out.printf("Exception [%s] caught while trying to
                transfer tax for [%s]%n", exception, person.getName());
            return false;
        }
        return true;
    }

}
```

How to do it...

In order to test the system using JMockit, you need to perform the following steps:

1. Create mocks by passing them as the test method's parameters.
2. Stub the mock's behavior in the initialization block.
3. Stub `Expectations` instance for strict stubbing.
4. Stub `NonStrictExpectations` instance for non-strict stubbing.
5. Execute the logic of the system under test.

6. Assert the behavior of the system under test.

7. If you used `NonStrictExpectations` for stubbing, then you can define your verification logic in the initialization block of the `Verifications` instance. Otherwise, it's not needed since all verification takes place via the `Expectations` instance.

The following snippet depicts the aforementioned scenario for JUnit:

```
@RunWith(JMockit.class)
public class TaxTransfererTest {

    @Test
    public void
      should_return_false_when_tax_was_not_transfered_and_connection_
      to_irs_was_refused(@Mocked final TaxService taxService) {
        // given
        TaxTransferer systemUnderTest = new TaxTransferer(taxService);
        final Person person = new Person();
        new NonStrictExpectations() {
            {
                taxService.hasAlreadyTransferredTax(person);
                result = false;
                taxService.transferTaxFor(person);
                result = new RuntimeException("Connection refused");
            }
        };

        // when
        boolean transferSuccessful = systemUnderTest.
transferTaxFor(person);

        // then
        then(transferSuccessful).isFalse();
        new Verifications() {
        {
        taxService.hasAlreadyTransferredTax(person);
        taxService.transferTaxFor(person);
        }
        };
    }

}
```

JMockit integrates very nicely with JUnit. You need to annotate your test class with `@RunWith(JMockit.class)`. Only then can you profit from the `@Mock` annotation that you can place as an argument of the test method.

To use JMockit with TestNG, you just need to replace `@RunWith(JMockit.class)` from the JUnit example with `@Listeners(mockit.integration.testng.Initializer.class)`.

How it works...

We will not discuss how JMockit works internally, but focus on what happens in the test itself, and what JMockit's approach is.

JMockit's approach regarding mocks is such the stubbing occurs via the code block inside the implementation of the `Expectations` or `NonStrictExpectations` class. Each line executed by the mocked instance followed by the assignment to the `result` variable leads to the stubbing of the aforementioned call.

The explicit verification occurs in the code block inside the implementation of the `Verifications` class. Since we use the `NonStrictExpectations` class, we need to perform that verification through the `Verifications` instance to verify our mock's behavior. If we used the `Expectations` block, then the stubbing gets automatically verified.

There's more...

Mockito's test code of the system would look like the following (example for JUnit):

```
@RunWith(MockitoJUnitRunner.class)
public class TaxTransfererTest {

    @Mock TaxService taxService;

    @InjectMocks TaxTransferer systemUnderTest;

    @Test
    public void
      should_return_false_when_tax_was_not_transfered_and
      _connection_to_irs_was_refused() {
        // given
        Person person = new Person();
      given(taxService.hasAlreadyTransferredTax(person)).
        willReturn(false);
        willThrow(new TaxServiceConnectionException("Connection
          refused")).given(taxService).transferTaxFor(person);
```

```
        // when
        boolean transferSuccessful = systemUnderTest.
transferTaxFor(person);

        // then
        then(transferSuccessful).isFalse();
        verify(taxService).hasAlreadyTransferredTax(person);
        verify(taxService).transferTaxFor(person);
    }

}
```

The primary similarities are as follows:

- The possibility of having no explicit record or replay of the mock's methods (only possible through stubbing with `NonStrictExpectations`)
- The possibility of explicit verification (via the `Verifications` instance)

The primary differences are as follows:

- JMockit contains functionalities more similar to PowerMock than Mockito (it can stub object instantiation and final and static methods)
- JMockit supports strict mocks
- JMockit has a built-in coverage report
- Stubbing and verifying through the code block during code implementation

See also

- JMockit documentation at `https://code.google.com/p/jmockit/`
- The Mockito versus JMockit comparison at `http://stackoverflow.com/questions/4105592/comparison-between-mockito-vs-jmockit-why-is-mockito-voted-better-than-jmockit`
- The Mocking tool comparison matrix at `https://code.google.com/p/jmockit/wiki/MockingToolkitComparisonMatrix`
- The *Mockito Cookbook* Github repository with test examples using JMockit at `https://github.com/marcingrzejszczak/mockito-cookbook`

Mockito versus JMock

In this recipe, we will write a simple test using JMock that verifies the behavior of the system under test when an exception is thrown.

Getting ready

To profit from JMock, you need to add it to your classpath. There are three factors that you must take into consideration when adding JMock to your project, as follows:

- `Jmock`: This contains the core of JMock (pick it if you want to use TestNG)
- `jmock-junit4`: This is to integrate JUnit with JMock (pick this one if you want to use JUnit 4+)
- `jmock-legacy`: This allows you to create mocks of classes

The following is the JMock configuration for Gradle for a JUnit-based project:

```
testCompile "org.jmock:jmock-junit4:2.6.0"
testCompile "org.jmock:jmock-legacy:2.6.0"
testCompile "org.jmock:jmock:2.6.0"
```

The following are the JMock dependencies for Maven:

```
<dependency>
  <groupId>org.jmock</groupId>
  <artifactId>jmock</artifactId>
  <version>2.6.0</version>
<scope>test</scope>
</dependency>
<dependency>
  <groupId>org.jmock</groupId>
  <artifactId>jmock-legacy</artifactId>
  <version>2.6.0</version>
<scope>test</scope>
</dependency>
<dependency>
    <groupId>org.jmock</groupId>
    <artifactId>jmock-junit4</artifactId>
    <version>2.6.0</version>
<scope>test</scope>
</dependency>
```

Let's assume that our system under test is the tax transferring system for a given person, as shown in the following code:

```
public class TaxTransferer {

  private final TaxService taxService;

  public TaxTransferer(TaxService taxService) {
    this.taxService = taxService;
  }
```

```
public boolean transferTaxFor(Person person) {
  if (taxService.hasAlreadyTransferredTax(person)) {
    return false;
  }
  try {
    taxService.transferTaxFor(person);
  } catch (Exception exception) {
    System.out.printf("Exception [%s] caught while trying to
      transfer tax for [%s]%n", exception, person.getName());
    return false;
  }
  return true;
}

}
```

How to do it...

To test the system using JMock, you need to perform the following steps:

1. Initialize the `Mockery` context (for JUnit, you can try to use `JUnitRuleMockery`, but you will not be able to mock classes. You can either create the `Mockery` context by yourself or create a class that extends `JUnitRuleMockery` that will call `setImpost eriser(ClassImposteriser.INSTANCE)` on the `Mockery` object).

2. Stub the mock's behavior through the Mockery's checking method.

3. Execute the logic of the system under test.

4. Verify the behavior of the system under test.

The following is an example of JMock's test for either JUnit or TestNG:

```
public class TaxTransfererTest {

  /**
   * To allow creating mocks of classes
   */
  private Mockery context = new Mockery() {{
      setImposteriser(ClassImposteriser.INSTANCE);
  }};

  TaxService taxService = context.mock(TaxService.class);

  TaxTransferer systemUnderTest = new TaxTransferer(taxService);

  @Test
```

```
        public void
          should_return_false_when_tax_was_not_transfered_and
          _connection_to_irs_was_refused() {
            // given
            final Person person = new Person();
            context.checking(new Expectations(){
            {
                oneOf(taxService).hasAlreadyTransferredTax(person);
                will(returnValue(false));
                oneOf(taxService).transferTaxFor(person);
                will(throwException(new TaxServiceConnectionException
                ("Connection refused")));
                }
            });

            // when
            boolean transferSuccessful = systemUnderTest.
transferTaxFor(person);

            // then
            then(transferSuccessful).isFalse();
            context.assertIsSatisfied();
        }

}
```

 In order to use JMock to mock classes instead of interfaces, you need to provide the `setImposteriser(ClassI mposteriser.INSTANCE)` method execution for the `Mockery` implementation. That's why we are not using the `JUnitRuleMockery` JUnit rule, because you can't explicitly change that imposteriser.

How it works...

We will not discuss how JMock works internally, but focus on what happens in the test itself, and what JMock's approach is. JMock's approach regarding mocks is such that the stubbing occurs via proper method execution inside the code block of the `Expectations` class implementation. You can call methods that add syntactic sugar to your tests (such as `oneOf(...)`, `will(...)`, and so on).

The verification of the stubbed methods (whether they got executed) happens through the calling of the Mockery's `assertIsSatisfied()` method.

There's more...

Mockito's test code of the system would look like the following (example for JUnit):

```
@RunWith(MockitoJUnitRunner.class)
public class TaxTransfererTest {

    @Mock TaxService taxService;

    @InjectMocks TaxTransferer systemUnderTest;

    @Test
    public void should_return_false_when_tax_was_not_transfered_and_
connection_to_irs_was_refused() {
        // given
        Person person = new Person();
        given(taxService.hasAlreadyTransferredTax(person)).
willReturn(false);
        willThrow(new TaxServiceConnectionException("Connection
refused")).given(taxService).transferTaxFor(person);

        // when
        boolean transferSuccessful = systemUnderTest.
transferTaxFor(person);

        // then
        then(transferSuccessful).isFalse();
        verify(taxService).hasAlreadyTransferredTax(person);
        verify(taxService).transferTaxFor(person);
    }

}
```

The primary similarities between Mockito and JMock are as follows:

- Similar syntax for stubbing (not the stubbing configuration, but both stub specific methods)
- Both Mockito and JMock provide argument matchers

The primary differences between Mockito and JMock are as follows:

- JMock's mocked objects are strict by default.
- JMock uses context for creating mocks whereas Mockito has static methods.
- For JMock, you need to provide an explicit configuration in order to mock classes and not only interfaces. Mockito provides it out of the box.

- In JMock, verification happens in the Mockery's checking method when you explicitly call a mock's method. In Mockito, you need to explicitly call the `verify` method. In other words, when using JMock, remember that when verifying you check only those methods that you stubbed in the `checking` method.

See also

- The JMock homepage at `http://jmock.org/`
- The *JMock Cookbook* at `http://jmock.org/cookbook.html`
- The JMock cheetsheet at `http://jmock.org/cheat-sheet.html`
- JMock's mailing list at `http://jmock.org/mailing-lists.html`
- The Mockito versus JMock comparison (not the recent versions) at `http://zsoltfabok.com/blog/2010/08/jmock-versus-mockito/`

Mockito versus Spock

In this recipe, we will write a simple test using Spock that verifies the behavior of the system under test when an exception is thrown. Before going into details, it's worth mentioning that Spock is a Groovy-based (`http://groovy.codehaus.org/`) tool. Therefore, in order to use it, you need to know at least the basics of the Groovy language. Spock is based on JUnit and is much more than a mocking framework. It gives you a beautiful **BDD** (**Behavior Driven Development**) syntax that will convert your tests to Specifications (capital S since `Specification` is a class that you need to extend to work with Spock).

If you want to try out Spock without installing it on your machine, check out the Spock Web Console at `http://meetspock.appspot.com/`, where you can write your tests online!

Spock is a perfect tool for you if you want to introduce Groovy into your project. You can start off with writing tests and then gradually progress towards production code (if that is what you want, of course). Spock's beautiful BDD approach, combined with the power of Groovy, makes it a perfect addition to your codebase.

Getting ready

To start working with Spock, you need to add it to your classpath. Remember that you also need to have Groovy attached. The following is the Groovy and Spock configuration for Gradle:

```
apply plugin: 'groovy'
compile "org.codehaus.groovy:groovy-all:2.3.1"
testCompile "org.spockframework:spock-core:0.7-groovy-2.0"
```

The following is how you can add Groovy and Spock to your classpath using Maven (please see the *Mockito Cookbook* Github repo at `https://github.com/marcingrzejszczak/mockito-cookbook` for the exact setup for both Gradle and Maven):

```xml
<project>
<build>
    <plugins>
      <plugin>
        <groupId>org.codehaus.gmaven</groupId>
        <artifactId>gmaven-plugin</artifactId>
        <version>1.5</version>
        <executions>
          <execution>
            <goals>
              <goal>testCompile</goal>
            </goals>
          </execution>
        </executions>
        <dependencies>
          <dependency>
            <groupId>org.codehaus.gmaven.runtime</groupId>
            <artifactId>gmaven-runtime-api</artifactId>
            <version>1.5</version>
            <exclusions>
              <exclusion>
                <groupId>org.codehaus.groovy</groupId>
                <artifactId>groovy-all-minimal</artifactId>
              </exclusion>
            </exclusions>
          </dependency>
          <dependency>
            <groupId>org.codehaus.groovy</groupId>
            <artifactId>groovy-all</artifactId>
            <version>2.3.1</version>
          </dependency>
        </dependencies>
      </plugin>
    </plugins>
  </build>
  <dependencies>
    <dependency>
      <groupId>org.spockframework</groupId>
      <artifactId>spock-core</artifactId>
      <version>0.7-groovy-2.0</version>
      <scope>test</scope>
    </dependency>
  </dependencies>
</project>
```

As in previous recipes, the system under test will be the tax transferring system for a given person, as shown in the following code:

```
public class TaxTransferer {

  private final TaxService taxService;

  public TaxTransferer(TaxService taxService) {
    this.taxService = taxService;
  }

  public boolean transferTaxFor(Person person) {
    if (taxService.hasAlreadyTransferredTax(person)) {
      return false;
    }
    try {
      taxService.transferTaxFor(person);
    } catch (Exception exception) {
      System.out.printf("Exception [%s] caught while trying to
transfer tax for [%s]%n", exception, person.getName());
      return false;
    }
    return true;
  }

}
```

How to do it...

To test the system using Spock, you need to perform the following steps:

1. Make your test class extend the `Specification` class.

2. Stub the mock's behavior through the static `Stub()` or `Mock()` method. If you want to verify the mock's behavior, then use `Mock()`. If you wish to only stub the execution, then use `Stub()`.

3. Execute the logic of the system under test.

4. Verify the behavior of the system under test using the multiply operator (*) and the count of wanted executions.

The following snippet shows an example of a test with Spock (Spock as a dependency requires JUnit, and it's using a JUnit runner):

```
class TaxTransferrerSpec extends Specification {

    TaxService taxService = Mock()

    TaxTransferer systemUnderTest = new TaxTransferer(taxService);

    def 'should return false when tax was not transfered and
connection to irs was refused'() {
        given:
            Person person = new Person()
        when:
            boolean transferSuccessful = systemUnderTest.
transferTaxFor(person)
        then:
            !transferSuccessful
            1 * taxService.hasAlreadyTransferredTax(person) >> false
            1 * taxService.transferTaxFor(person) >> { throw new
RuntimeException("Connection refused") }

    }

    @Unroll
    def "should return [#transferSuccessful] when tax wasn't already
transferred and connection to irs was refused [#throwsException]"() {
        given:
            Person person = new Person()
        when:
            boolean transferSuccessfulResult = systemUnderTest.
transferTaxFor(person)
        then:
            transferSuccessfulResult == transferSuccessful
            1 * taxService.hasAlreadyTransferredTax(person) >> false
            1 * taxService.transferTaxFor(person) >> {
if(throwsException) { throw new RuntimeException("Connection refused")
} }
        where:
            throwsException  || transferSuccessful
            true             || false
            false            || true

    }

}
```

Remember that Spock is a Groovy tool and the test code is written in Groovy. That's why the syntax differs from Java-based tests.

How it works...

We will not discuss how Spock works internally, but focus on what happens in the test itself, and what Spock's approach is.

Spock forces its users to follow the **BDD** approach (with the `given`, `when`, `then`, `expect`, and `where` clauses), thus the tests become very clear and automatically separated into sections. As for the stubbing strategy, Spock has separate methods for stubbing and mocking. This is also to show explicitly the difference between the two. What is more, it's a Groovy framework (already a main testing framework for Grails), so you can profit from all of the Groovy magic, which should make your tests become really clean.

Let's take a look at the second Spock test that shows how easily you can define parameterized tests. The `@Unroll` annotation makes Spock insert values that are named according to the columns in the `where` table, for each row of the `where` part. In fact, throughout the test, you can refer to those values by the names of the columns. The `>>` operator (right-shift operator) allows you to stub values with the result of the closure (the function defined within the curly braces). As you can see, we can even provide some more complex answers (like in the case of the `transferTaxFor(...)` method stubbing). The `1 *` notation means that you want to verify that there was a single method execution.

There's more...

Mockito's test code of the system would look like the following (example for JUnit):

```
@RunWith(MockitoJUnitRunner.class)
public class TaxTransfererTest {

    @Mock TaxService taxService;

    @InjectMocks TaxTransferer systemUnderTest;

    @Test
    public void should_return_false_when_tax_was_not_transfered_and_
connection_to_irs_was_refused() {
        // given
        Person person = new Person();
        given(taxService.hasAlreadyTransferredTax(person)).
willReturn(false);
        willThrow(new TaxServiceConnectionException("Connection
refused")).given(taxService).transferTaxFor(person);
```

```
        // when
        boolean transferSuccessful = systemUnderTest.
transferTaxFor(person);

        // then
        then(transferSuccessful).isFalse();
        verify(taxService).hasAlreadyTransferredTax(person);
        verify(taxService).transferTaxFor(person);
    }

}
```

The primary similarities between Mockito and Spock are as follows:

▸ Similar BDD approach as in Mockito (for example, the methods from `BDDMockito`)

▸ When used properly, both can produce very clear and readable code

▸ You can use Hamcrest matchers in either of the frameworks

The primary differences between Mockito and Spock are as follows:

▸ Spock forces you to use BDD, whereas in Mockito it's optional.

▸ Spock is a Groovy-based tool, whereas Mockito is Java based.

▸ Since Spock operates on Groovy when stubbing, you provide the desired behavior in closures (refer to `http://groovy.codehaus.org/Closures` for more information). You don't need any additional methods, which is contrary to Mockito.

▸ You need to extend a `Specification` class to use Spock, whereas in Mockito you can use it straight away.

▸ If you want to both stub a method and verify it, in Spock, you need to do that in the verification phase (in the `then` or `expect` block), which is really unintuitive.

See also

▸ Ten reasons why you should start using Spock, at `https://code.google.com/p/spock/wiki/WhySpock`

▸ Spock interactions at `https://code.google.com/p/spock/wiki/Interactions`

▸ Incubating Spock documentation at `http://docs.spockframework.org/en/latest/`

▸ Old Spock documentation at `https://code.google.com/p/spock/w/list`

▸ Spock Google group at `https://groups.google.com/forum/#!forum/spockframework`

▸ Spock basics at `https://code.google.com/p/spock/wiki/SpockBasics`

Index

Thank you for buying
Mockito Cookbook

About Packt Publishing

Packt, pronounced 'packed', published its first book "*Mastering phpMyAdmin for Effective MySQL Management*" in April 2004 and subsequently continued to specialize in publishing highly focused books on specific technologies and solutions.

Our books and publications share the experiences of your fellow IT professionals in adapting and customizing today's systems, applications, and frameworks. Our solution based books give you the knowledge and power to customize the software and technologies you're using to get the job done. Packt books are more specific and less general than the IT books you have seen in the past. Our unique business model allows us to bring you more focused information, giving you more of what you need to know, and less of what you don't.

Packt is a modern, yet unique publishing company, which focuses on producing quality, cutting-edge books for communities of developers, administrators, and newbies alike. For more information, please visit our website: www.packtpub.com.

About Packt Open Source

In 2010, Packt launched two new brands, Packt Open Source and Packt Enterprise, in order to continue its focus on specialization. This book is part of the Packt Open Source brand, home to books published on software built around Open Source licenses, and offering information to anybody from advanced developers to budding web designers. The Open Source brand also runs Packt's Open Source Royalty Scheme, by which Packt gives a royalty to each Open Source project about whose software a book is sold.

Writing for Packt

We welcome all inquiries from people who are interested in authoring. Book proposals should be sent to author@packtpub.com. If your book idea is still at an early stage and you would like to discuss it first before writing a formal book proposal, contact us; one of our commissioning editors will get in touch with you.

We're not just looking for published authors; if you have strong technical skills but no writing experience, our experienced editors can help you develop a writing career, or simply get some additional reward for your expertise.

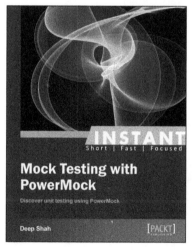

www.ingramcontent.com/pod-product-compliance
Lightning Source LLC
Chambersburg PA
CBHW060525060326
40690CB00017B/3388